A LIBRARY MANAGER'S GUIDE TO THE PHYSICAL PROCESSING OF NONPRINT MATERIAL

Editorial Consultants

A Library Manager's Guide to the Physical Processing of Nonprint Materials

Karen C. Driessen and Sheila A. Smyth

Sponsored by
Online Audiovisual Catalogers, Inc. (OLAC)

THE GREENWOOD LIBRARY MANAGEMENT COLLECTION
Gerard B. McCabe, *Series Advisor*

Greenwood Press
WESTPORT, CONNECTICUT • LONDON

Library of Congress Cataloging-in-Publication Data

Driessen, Karen C.
    A library manager's guide to the physical processing of nonprint
materials / Karen C. Driessen and Sheila A. Smyth.
        p.   cm. — (The Greenwood library management collection, ISSN
0894–2986)
        "Sponsored by Online Audiovisual Catalogers, Inc. (OLAC)."
        Includes bibliographical references and index.
        ISBN 0–313–27930–6 (alk. paper)
        1. Physical processing of nonbook materials (Libraries)—United
States.   I. Smyth, Sheila A.   II. On-Line Audiovisual Catalogers,
Inc.   III. Title.   IV. Series.
    Z688.N6D75   1995
    025.3'4—dc20   94–17983

British Library Cataloguing in Publication Data is available.

Library of Congress Catalog Card Number: 94–17983
ISBN: 0–313–27930–6
ISSN: 0894–2986

First published in 1995

Greenwood Press, 88 Post Road West, Westport, CT 06881
An imprint of Greenwood Publishing Group, Inc.

Printed in the United States of America

The paper used in this book complies with the
Permanent Paper Standard issued by the National
Information Standards Organization (Z39.48–1984).

10 9 8 7 6 5 4 3 2 1

Copyright Acknowledgments

The editor and publisher are grateful for permission to reprint from the following sources:

Nancy B. Olson, *Audiovisual Material Glossary*. Dublin, OH: OCLC Online Computer Library
Center, 1988. Used by permission of OCLC.

Michael Gorman and Paul W. Winkler, Anglo-American Cataloguing Rules, Second Edition, 1988
revision. Reprinted with permission of the American Library Association (50 E. Huron St., Chicago,
IL 60611). Copyright © 1988.

Kent Dunlap, Letter to Eric Childress, Special Materials Cataloger, Elon College, North Carolina,
January 6, 1992.

Illustrations were provided by Nick Baker, Richard Johnson, and Sheila Smyth with the assistance
of Sue Atkins, Michael Naud, and Colleene Abair. Several drawings have been reproduced by
permission of Peter J. Jacobs of Professional Media Service Corp. Figures 6.12 and 6.14 have been
reproduced by permission of and copyrighted by Minnesota Mining and Mfg. Co. © copyright 1965
by Minnesota Mining and Mfg. Co.

Contents

Figures

Preface

The impetus for this book originated with Online Audiovisual Catalogers, Inc. (OLAC). Its development has been in direct response to catalogers' requests voiced at physical processing workshops during the 1988 and 1990 OLAC conferences. OLAC's Cataloging Policy Committee recognized that processing was not a cataloging issue. However, catalogers often are the ones who make the decisions on the processing of nonprint materials for the shelf. Following the OLAC Executive Board's approval, the authors began working on this physical processing manual under the sponsorship of Online Audiovisual Catalogers, Inc.

This book is intended for use by the library manager, the technical services librarian, the cataloging librarian, the paraprofessional, or the one and only person in the library who is responsible for making decisions about the physical processing of nonprint library materials. It also may serve as an introductory source book for library and information science students who are concerned with the physical processing of library materials.

The authors have two purposes in mind. The first is to provide the reader with a foundation for decision making as it relates to the physical processing of nonprint materials. This foundation is intended to serve as a basis for planning and to provide a common language of topics to be considered when one is approaching physical processing decisions. The second purpose is to demonstrate how these decisions move from the theoretical to the practical physical processing issues of packaging/repackaging, treating accompanying materials, labeling, preparing circulation pockets and date due notices, using and placing barcodes and security strips, etc. In addition, this book may serve as a basis from which to build local processing manuals in individual libraries that address the special needs and considerations unique to each situation.

Nonprint materials are used in a variety of settings—public libraries, school libraries, academic libraries, and special libraries—with a variety of purposes and patrons. Therefore, this manual cannot be the final authority on processing nonprint materials. The authors have attempted to include a variety of current practices, but by no means is this an exhaustive summary of all practices. New technologies as well as new products will require new procedures. Unique situations will dictate other considerations.

Because this book is intended to be used as both a guidebook for making processing decisions and as a generic manual for the physical processing of nonprint materials, it is divided into two parts. Part I provides the background and interpretations for making sound processing decisions; Part II presents a manual of guidelines and options which are relevant for specific kinds of nonprint material.

Choosing the proper terminology for this subject was a complicated decision. The terms *media, audiovisual (AV), nonbook,* and *nonprint* all have been used at different times by different people either to mean the same or different things. For the purposes of this book, the authors have chosen the term *nonprint* to represent the materials that are being discussed. In this definition nonprint materials include items that are other than printed matter, often known as either nonbook, media, or audiovisual materials. However, not all nonbook materials will be covered; serials, microforms, printed music, pamphlets, broadsides, and manuscripts are excluded. Materials which traditionally focus on both hearing and sight are included in addition to map materials, computer files, art originals, realia, and various instructional media (for example, games, models, and kits).

Another terminology issue throughout the manual is the use of the terms *disc* and *disk.* The term *disc* with a *c* has been applied to sound discs, both analog and digital. Until recently the term *disk* with a *k* had been used for computer disks in any of several media both magnetic and optical. However, it is now recognized that the computer industry itself has standardized the spelling of computer optical storage devices as discs and the spelling of magnetic computer storage devices as disks. The authors have tried, therefore, to adhere to computer industry distinctions when discussing various computer formats. Chapters 7 and 9 will provide more detailed information.

The scope of these nonprint materials follows the breakdown of media groups as used in *Anglo-American Cataloguing Rules, Second Edition, 1988 Revision (AACR 2, 1988 rev.).* The chapter arrangement thus consists of cartographic materials, sound recordings, motion pictures and videorecordings, graphic materials, computer files, and three-dimensional artifacts and realia. A final chapter has been included which covers multimedia materials. Some of these materials fit the traditional *AACR 2* definition of kit or multimedia, and others belong to a new and evolving technology not yet defined as a media group in *AACR 2,*

1988 rev. but variously known as interactive multimedia, interactive media, or optical disc media. For the purposes of this manual, the term *interactive multimedia* will be used for this new technology. Each chapter looks at the effects of organization and storage upon processing decisions for that particular media type and provides alternatives and options for the physical processing of each format.

In preparing this book for publication, the authors have drawn on a wide range of librarians, museum specialists, special collection experts, and preservationists for their expertise on processing. Visits to various types of libraries, institutions, retail outlets, and conferences have also provided primary resource information. The authors have led and participated in workshops, sought advice and input from commercial library supply vendors, and have carried out an extensive literature search. In addition, more than thirty physical processing manuals have been examined from libraries of all types and sizes throughout the United States and Canada.

Acknowledgments

The authors are grateful to many people and institutions for their assistance during the writing of this book.

Those individuals who generously shared their institution's local processing manuals include: Arlington Heights Memorial Library, Arlington Heights, Illinois (Ellen Hines); Ball State University, Bracken Library, Muncie, Indiana (Diane E. Hill); Boston College, Thomas P. O'Neill, Jr. Library, Boston, Massachusetts (Anne Campbell Moore); California State University, Stanislaus, Turlock, California (Agnes L. Bennett); Columbia Bible College & Seminary, Columbia, South Carolina (Cleta E. Dunaway); Duval County Schools, Educational Media Center, Jacksonville, Florida (Charlotte B. Miller); Elon College, Elon, North Carolina (Eric Childress); Erie Community College, Buffalo, New York (Margaret Giles); Fort Wayne Community Schools, Fort Wayne, Indiana (Kevin S. Roe); Hamilton Public Library, Hamilton, Ontario, Canada (Pamela Haley); Houston Community College System, Houston, Texas (Helen Chang); Louisiana State University Law Center, Baton Rouge, Louisiana (Ajaye Bloomstone); Mankato State University, Memorial Library, Mankato, Minnesota (Rosie Mock); Missoula County High Schools Library Central Processing, Missoula, Montana (Dorothy Fauver); National Library of Medicine, Dept. of Health & Human Services, Bethesda, Maryland (Alice E. Jacobs and Meredith Horan); Nazareth College, Lorette Wilmot Library, Rochester, New York (Sheila Smyth); Ohio State University Libraries, Columbus, Ohio (Marilyn L. Kercher);

Plymouth State College, Plymouth, New Hampshire (Allison Howard); Rochester Institute of Technology, Wallace Memorial Library, Rochester, New York (Marcia Trauernecht); Stark County District Library, Canton, Ohio (Brenda Callahan); State University of New York at Brockport, Drake Memorial Library, Brockport, New York (Joyce Ogden); University of Akron, Bierce Library, Akron, Ohio (Virginia M. Berringer); University of California, The University Library, Irvine, California (D. Kathryn Weintraub); University of Montana, Instructional Media Services, Missoula, Montana (Karen C. Driessen); University of Rochester, Carlson Library, Rochester, New York (Diane Reiman); University of North Texas, Media Library, Denton, Texas (Sharon Almquist); University of Washington, Seattle, Washington (Catherine Gerhart); Virginia Polytechnic Institute and State University, University Libraries, Blacksburg, Virginia (Lowell Ashley); and Western Iowa Tech, Sioux City, Iowa (Barbara Glackin).

Those organizations that generously allowed us to visit their institution's libraries and who willingly demonstrated their procedures and shared their experiences with us include: East High School, Rochester, New York (Bonnie Cestra); Erie Community College/North, Williamsville, New York (Margaret Giles); Hellgate High School, Missoula, Montana (Bill Haffey); Hobart & William Smith Colleges, Warren Hunting Smith Library, Geneva, New York (Amy Ugent); Margaret Woodbury Strong Museum, Rochester, New York (Jan Guldbeck); Missoula County High Schools Library Central Processing, Missoula, Montana (Dorothy Fauver); Rochester Institute of Technology, Wallace Memorial Library, Rochester, New York, and Rochester Museum and Science Center, Museum Library, Rochester, New York (Lea Kemp, Adelle Daresay, and Parti Ford); Rochester Toy Library, Rochester, New York (Joan Westerman); State University College of New York at Brockport, Drake Memorial Library, Brockport, New York (Joyce Ogden); State University College of New York at Buffalo, University Libraries, Buffalo, New York (Barbara Vaughan and Lori Widzinski); Texas Women's University, Mary Ellen Blagg-Huey Library, Denton, Texas (Connie Maxwell); University at Buffalo, State University of New York, Lockwood Library, Buffalo, New York (Sue Neumeister); University of North Texas, Media Library, Music Library, Denton, Texas (Sharon Almquist); University of Rochester, Carlson Library, Rochester, New York (Isabelle Kaplan); University of Rochester, Map Center, Asia Library, Rush Rhees Library, Rochester, New York (Datha Karbas); and University of Texas Health Science Center at San Antonio, Briscoe Library, San Antonio, Texas (Claudia Kaufman).

Special acknowledgment must be given to Online Audiovisual Catalogers, Inc. (OLAC) for their moral and financial support of this project. Their sponsorship has been an integral part of the manual's evolution.

Three outstanding members of OLAC agreed to serve as editorial consultants for the manual. They are Bobby Ferguson, Director of Technical Services, Louisiana State Library, Baton Rouge, Louisiana; Nancy B. Olson, Professor, Memorial Library, Mankato State University, Mankato, Minnesota; and Jean Weihs, consultant and owner of Technical Services Group, Toronto, Ontario. The authors especially thank them for their contributions. Their advice, expertise, insights, and suggestions have been invaluable throughout the writing and rewriting process.

Illustrations for the text were provided by Nick Baker, Richard Johnson, and Sheila Smyth with the assistance of Sue Atkins, Michael Naud, and Colleene Abair. Together they have translated the authors' thoughts and ideas into many fine images. In addition, Peter J. Jacobs (Professional Media Service Corp.) and Virginia Johnson (Minnesota Mining and Manufacturing Co.) gave the authors permission to use or adapt one or more of their drawings.

Particular thanks are extended to Nazareth College of Rochester and to the University of Montana for their support. Thanks to Dr. Rosemarie Beston (President of Nazareth) and Dr. Dennis Silva of Nazareth's (Vice President for Academic Affairs), and thanks to the Sabbatical Committee and Administration at the University of Montana for the sabbatical leaves granted the authors.

Colleagues at Nazareth College were especially supportive, kind, and encouraging to Sheila over the past three years. At the Lorette Wilmot Library, particular thanks go to Dick Matzek (Library Director), Janet Smith, and Marion Simplicio for their editorial assistance and support and to the Technical Services staff for their patience, kindness, and encouragement. Special thanks are also due to Sue Atkins (Media Center Director) and her staff, who answered many questions, and to Mary Bartolotta and her academic computing staff for teaching Sheila how to use the computer to create illustrations.

Colleagues at the University of Montana were equally supportive and encouraging to Karen. Special gratitude goes to Ruth Patrick and Karen Hatcher, former and present deans of the Mansfield Library, and to Devon Chandler, the former Instructional Media Services (IMS) Director, for their collective encouragement and support. Additional appreciation goes to Harriet Ranney for taking on new responsibilities during Karen's sabbatical; to Polly Haffey, who endured the transition with grace and patience; and to the entire IMS staff for their moral and real support. Thanks also to other Mansfield Library colleagues and the Interlibrary Loan staff for their extra efforts in satisfying many requests.

Finally, distinct recognition and unfailing gratitude are owed to two extraordinary individuals for their constant caring and encouragement throughout the past three years: Jon J. Driessen and Christine M. Bochen.

Introduction

Libraries are rapidly accepting the doctrine for which we have contended for many years, that what we call books have no exclusive rights in a library. The "library" has lost its etymologic meaning and means not a collection of books, but the central agency for disseminating information, innocent recreation, or, best of all, inspiration among the people. Whenever this can be done better, more quickly, or cheaply by a picture than a book, the picture is entitled to a place on the shelves and in the catalog.

—Melville Dewey, 1906

When Marshall McLuhan coined the phrase "the medium is the message" (1964), he was talking about the impact of various media apart from their content. Just as McLuhan saw each type of media as an extension of humankind and each media as constituting its own importance as well as its own interaction with other media, today's library user has come to see each type of new technology as an extension of information and each carrier of information as constituting its own importance as well as its own interaction with other media.

In libraries today there is a desire and need for knowledge that goes beyond the physical carrier in which it is found. User demand for information contained in evolving technologies has expanded dramatically. Thus diverse formats of nonprint information are commonplace and expected by users of all types of libraries. As demand for these new and varied informational formats expanded and libraries began to incorporate them into their collections, librarians found themselves making many decisions regarding the integration of these different formats into their existing collections.

One of the first questions addressed was how to describe these materials in such a way that they could be found by users in the same catalog as the one used for print materials. Language and rules for cataloging the various formats of nonprint material needed to be developed and standardized, just as they had been in earlier years for books. This task actually began in the 1950s, and nonprint cataloging rules were fully integrated with those for books and serials in the second edition of the *Anglo-American Cataloguing Rules* published in 1978 (*AACR 2*) and revised in 1988 (*AACR 2, 1988 rev.*).

Standardization for other phases of the integration of print and nonprint material within the same collection has not been achieved so easily. Many questions continue to be raised which involve decisions for managing librarians and working catalogers who wish to enhance the accessibility of nonprint material for the user and at the same time ensure the security and physical protection of the material within their libraries.

Such questions include the following:

- Should nonprint materials be housed in the same facility as print materials?
- Should nonprint materials be classified like print materials, and, if so, should they be intershelved with print materials on the same topic?
- Should nonprint materials be shelved by format and then by classification number, or should they be shelved by format in accession number arrangement?
- Should nonprint materials be put in open stacks or kept in closed stacks?
- Should nonprint materials be circulated under the same guidelines as print materials?
- How important are the issues of security and preservation?

The answers to many of these questions will determine other processing decisions, such as whether nonprint materials should be repackaged, whether multiple parts are housed together or separately, how items are to be labeled and identified, and how barcodes and security strips are to be placed and used. This manual discusses these questions and poses various options and solutions for the physical processing of nonprint material based on specific situations.

Too often decisions relating to physical processing are not what the authors call *informed* decisions. Instead they are made in isolation without regard to related policies and procedures, such as those just mentioned. Although nonprint physical processing decisions may not be the most important decisions of the library manager, they can be some of the most time consuming and expensive. They can also have a significant impact on the user's ability to utilize the collection.

Informed processing decisions are made when library managers keep in mind the need for accessibility to the collection by the library user, the specific type of nonprint material in question, and the unique management policies and practices of a particular library setting. Libraries of today, whether they be academic, public, school, or special, are dealing with information in all kinds of carriers—

books, periodicals, CD-ROMs, videotapes, videodiscs, computer files, sound tapes and sound discs, films, pictures, models, charts, realia, etc. Each of these formats requires different considerations for processing treatment, and each should be equally accessible by the library user. The following chapters are offered as both a practical model for physical processing decisions and a guide to processing practices for nonprint materials.

REFERENCES

Dewey, Melville. 1906. Library pictures. *Public Libraries* 11: 10–11.
McLuhan, Marshall. 1964. *Understanding Media: The Extensions of Man.* New York: McGraw-Hill.

PART I

A Guide to Making Informed Processing Decisions

1

The Foundation for Decision Making

The problem is that our thinking, our attitudes and consequently our decision making have not caught up with the reality of things . . . the level of change involved is so fundamental yet so subtle that we tend not to see it, or if we see it, we dismiss it as overly simplistic, and then we ignore it.
—John Naisbitt, *Megatrends*

Decision making is usually defined as a process in which one decides or makes a judgment, selecting from two or more choices. The purpose of this book is to look at decision making in libraries as it relates to judgments that will extend traditional access expected for print materials to nonprint materials. In so doing, specific issues will be examined that will affect nonprint material physical processing decisions.

The foundation for good decision making is good library management. Although there are many popular theories of library management, every manager's goal is to have an environment which reflects the library patron's needs and makes an efficient use of the library collection, the facilities, the equipment, and the staff. The question is, How is this goal accomplished? If there were a pat prescription that would work in every library, there would be only one book on library management. What we have instead is a combination of management factors that must be examined within the context of each library setting. The results of such an examination will allow the library manager to begin making policies on specific library issues that will have a bearing on final physical processing decisions.

MANAGEMENT FACTORS

The handling of print and nonprint materials varies in every library according to its particular combination of management factors. These factors generally include the users, the library philosophy, the budget, the facilities, the physical environment, the equipment, the available staff and/or time, and the various formats of the collection. Decision making depends on the unique mix of these factors in each library.

The Users

Who uses the library? Students, members of the community, a specialized staff, a network, or some combination of these? Every library is different depending on the type of library, the size of its collection, the size of its staff, and the needs of its users. In academic libraries the users' information needs are likely to come from formal scholarly research, instructional assignments, informal general education, and perhaps even recreation. The needs of school library users may be similar to those in academic libraries but at different scholarly levels. In public libraries the users' information needs are apt to be more varied but usually will focus on general interest information, informal education, recreational topics, and children's interests. Special library users may require narrowly focused but in-depth types of information on such fields as law, medicine, and business, or the users may be interested only in specific formats of information such as maps, slides, pictures, or archival materials.

The Library Philosophy

For whom and why (i.e., patrons and their needs) the library exists should determine the library's goals and objectives. Goals are usually philosophical in nature and provide a general direction in which the library wishes to move. An overall goal of the library may be to create an atmosphere which stimulates learning, reading, listening, viewing, research, and exploration in an interactive environment. Objectives are more operational in nature. They are statements which relate to goals and describe what is to be done with specific resources. Objectives are measurable within time frames, and the outcomes can be specified. Specific goals might be either of the following:

Goal 1. To provide easy access to the collection.

Goal 2. To preserve the collection.

If we examine the foregoing two goals, we can see how each could provide different objectives, policies, and procedures. If the first goal means that the library would provide unlimited access to the user, several objectives could follow.

Objective 1. The circulation period would be generous and all material types would circulate out of the building.

Objective 2. If certain formats require specialized equipment not readily available to most users at home, the library would provide equipment to use the media conveniently near the materials within the library, or it would make such equipment available to the user for checkout.

Objective 3. The stacks would be open to the user and all formats interfiled in a single classified subject arrangement. To accommodate such an arrangement, a processing decision might be that all materials would be packaged in uniform-sized packaging to accommodate shelving, and all formats would have complete identification labels on the packaging to provide the maximum information possible to the user when the item is taken from the shelf. Security would be a significant factor.

Objective 4. For the convenience of the user, accompanying information would always be kept packaged together with its primary parts.

If the second goal means that preservation of the collection is the primary goal of the library, several objectives could follow.

Objective 1. Circulation would be restricted to specialized clientele or to building use only. If items do not circulate outside of the library, the processing decision might be that uniform or extra protective packaging could be eliminated.

Objective 2. To reduce wear and tear from browsing and open access, materials would be housed in closed stacks and arranged by format in accession number order. If housed by format, repackaging might not be necessary because sizes within formats are often uniform.

Objective 3. Users would not be allowed to use original materials if some other arrangement could be made:

A. Sound and moving image materials would be handled by staff only and played from a central location for use in listening or viewing booths. Thus, the processing decision might be that sturdy packaging and detailed labeling would not be necessary.

B. Where copyright permits, copies of material would be available for use rather than the originals. Users might have to pay the library to make copies of pictures, slides, maps, etc.

If materials were to be used only in the library or if only copies were to be circulated, a security system might not be needed.

Objective 4. Accompanying information could be housed separately as long as labels on the item indicated to the staff where it was available and as long as there was staff time for retrieval.

These two examples demonstrate how goals and objectives, as well as information about the type of library and its collections and patrons, are used to determine library policies.

The Budget

Budgetary considerations may be the overriding factor in all library decisions. Money is necessary to purchase a collection of print and nonprint materials and to process them. Money is also necessary to provide adequate space, staffing, shelving, equipment, materials, preservation, replacement, and supplies. The wise use of money must be examined continually. Every decision should consider these questions: How much will it cost? Is it worth it? What are the alternatives? Is there a balance between monies for salaries, cost of materials, and effective services?

The Facilities

The physical space and its layout can affect many of the decisions the library manager must make. Every library will probably have space problems at one time or another. The organization of space is often critical to making decisions regarding open or closed shelving, compact shelving, physical arrangement of material on the shelves, security, and staffing levels.

The dilemma for many libraries is that nonprint materials were added to print collections almost as an afterthought. Space was unavailable for required equipment and staff. Therefore, nonprint materials often were not housed with the print materials, and more often they were not intershelved with one another. That is, the printed version of *Hamlet* might not be housed in the same room or maybe not even in the same building as the film and video versions of *Hamlet*. Further, the videotape version would not be shelved with the videodisc version, and the sound cassette version would not be shelved with either of the sound disc versions (analog or digital). The design of existing physical space, whether traditional or flexible, will affect the potential for change and growth in a library.

The Physical Environment

Other physical concerns include climate control and acoustics. The ability to maintain proper temperature and humidity levels is crucial to the preservation of library materials (especially to nonprint materials). If nonprint material is housed separately from print material, the media facility should have its own controls for heating, ventilation, and air conditioning. Acoustical considerations are important when using nonprint materials that have audio components. The ability to control lighting in certain areas of the library may also be critical in using certain print, film, video, and computer-based materials.

The Equipment

Special types of equipment are necessary for the utilization of many nonprint materials. If circulation policies require materials to be used only in the library, readily accessible equipment must be provided for the patron in the library. This decision requires sensitivity to the noise generated by equipment, users, and staff. Quiet areas, such as special or archival collections, should be avoided. At the least, sound-absorbing partitions should be placed around equipment to preserve a noise-free atmosphere. When the library allows items to be checked out of the library for use elsewhere, the library may or may not want to provide the necessary equipment. For any library equipment, maintenance must be performed on a regular basis. If trained library personnel are not available to take care of such tasks, equipment should be serviced on a regular basis by outside maintenance contracts.

An additional set of concerns related to equipment arises when a library can no longer repair or maintain a particular type of equipment for a specific format. Should the library retain nonprint materials for which it no longer has the equipment? Does a library have a responsibility to retain such material when it is not available elsewhere in the state or region? Answers to these questions are essential when establishing processing decisions.

The Staffing Level

Adequate staffing levels are a key to every library's success. The amount of staff time allotted for providing service to patrons, for circulation activities, and for the technical service areas of acquisitions, cataloging, and processing will influence decisions and procedures throughout the library. It is important to remember that whatever decisions are made, staff should be consulted and involved in the process. When decisions are imposed from above without staff input, they are bound to fail.

The Available Time

Time considerations are extremely important when it comes to making processing decisions. One must weigh how important the time element is in terms of processing and in preparing items for the shelf once they have been received. The following questions should be considered:

- How much extra time do processing decisions add?
- Does the time spent processing material add sufficient value to the item?
- Does the extra time make the item more usable for the patron or less likely to be stolen or damaged?

- Does the time spent processing the item preserve its useful life?
- Are there some types of items that always require rush processing?

The Collection

The variety of formats included in a collection is another key factor in making processing decisions. Generally, there are special handling and storage considerations for each type of material. Not only does the packaging differ from format to format, but often similar formats come in different sizes and shapes. The determination of the physical processing needs for each particular format is a task in itself.

When one considers all of the management factors discussed so far, one begins to understand that processing decisions can be complicated. Taken together, all of these management factors should influence the kinds of decisions and policies that are established in any given library.

LIBRARY DECISIONS AND POLICIES

> In today's Baskin-Robbins society, everything comes in at least 31 flavors.
> —John Naisbitt, *Megatrends*

Information today comes in all formats—CD-ROM discs, videotapes and videodiscs, computer disks, sound tapes and sound discs, film formats, interactive multimedia, pictures, models, charts, maps, realia, and printed forms. Each of these formats requires different considerations for physical processing, yet each must be integrated into a library collection with all of the other formats for easy access by the library user. What are some of the specific library decisions and policies that will have a bearing on the physical processing of all nonprint formats? The main ones include circulation, storage, preservation, and security.

Circulation

How could circulation policies have an effect on physical processing decisions? All library materials must be prepared for circulation either in house or out of the building. The main consideration, of course, is whether certain kinds of nonprint materials are restricted to in-house use or whether all materials circulate beyond the library building or media center. If all materials circulate out of the building, processing decisions generally will be more uniform (i.e., all materials will need sturdy packaging, security strips or labels, date due slips, etc.).

On the other hand, if certain nonprint materials do not circulate, special provisions must be made to accommodate their use in the library building. Those that are machine dependent will have to have conveniently located equipment available for users in dedicated library space. Examples of such machine-dependent material include computer software, interactive media, sound recordings, videorecordings, motion pictures, films, filmstrips, and slides. Each format requires special equipment for its use, and in some cases various combinations of media and equipment may be necessary for use at the same time.

Some nonprint items which are not machine dependent may require other kinds of special library assistance. Large tables may be needed to examine original art, realia, flat pictures, and maps. The library may be expected to provide copies of some of these materials for which the user is asked to pay. If certain sound or moving image formats do not circulate, the library also may be asked to make copies of these materials when copyright provisions allow.

Instructing the user on the proper use of nonprint materials is often a function of circulation personnel. Staff must be instructed on the proper care and handling of nonprint materials and the proper operation of any required equipment. They also need to know how to troubleshoot simple equipment and software problems. Because circulation people are often responsible for the handling and shelving of materials, they are in a useful position to identify preservation needs of the materials as well. It is a good idea to maintain an open line of communication between circulation personnel and those who are responsible for the physical processing of library materials.

The kind of physical packaging required for nonprint materials depends to some extent on whether the material will circulate. Circulating materials require sturdy packaging that will withstand being shoved into backpacks and that will protect the contents when the materials are returned in bookdrop-type receptacles. Various informational labeling may also be required. When nonprint material is handled only by library staff, special packaging and labeling often are not necessary. If the library has an automated circulation system, each circulating item may require that some type of barcode be attached.

Storage

Every library must plan its storage options based on the needs of its users and the library's space constraints. Many questions must be considered to arrive at the right decisions for each library. If the size of the facility allows users to browse the shelves, the collection may lend itself to intershelving formats and to classification in a single subject arrangement. On the other hand, if the size of the facility forces the collection to be closed to browsing, there may be no need to assign subject classification call numbers or to intershelve formats. In cramped quarters shelving by format and then by accession number (e.g., CD 100, CD 101) may be the answer because it uses less space than filing by classification number (which requires expansion space for each number).

Some librarians believe that a library which puts the needs of the user first would choose to intershelve all of the library's formats (including print materials) in a single classified arrangement on open shelves. The advantage of this type of complete integration is that all materials on the same subject are together. The collection thus lends itself to browsing, and users may find materials in formats they never imagined were available. For a more comprehensive discussion of the advantages of intershelving the entire library collection, see Jean Weihs's book, *The Integrated Library: Encouraging Access to Multimedia Materials* (Phoenix: Oryx Press, 1991).

Conversely, some librarians believe that the user would rather have formats separated because the user generally wants only one or two formats and is not interested in having to sort through everything in the library to find what is wanted. The advantage of dividing the collection by format is that it allows the user who only wants videorecordings to go directly to that material type. Once there, the materials can be arranged by classification numbers or broad subject areas for easy browsing. Closed storage of materials arranged by format will require the patrons to go to a staff person for access.

Still other librarians choose to integrate some materials such as books, periodicals, videorecordings, and sound cassettes on open shelves and separate other formats in closed storage. Another arrangement is to have dummy containers located on the open shelves or in browsing bins and racks near the checkout area. A user can peruse the packaging, but the media is stored behind the circulation desk or in some other protected area where the item itself is retrieved at the time of checkout.

Finally, some librarians assign format-type accession numbers to nonprint materials for arrangement on the shelves but add classification numbers to the cataloging record for purposes of classification-based retrieval in an automated catalog. This procedure is especially useful when carrying out collection assessments for nonprint materials that are physically arranged by format and accession number. In this case librarians rely on the computer to provide various complex and sophisticated approaches to retrieving items (e.g., subject, producer, format, date, language, and physical details such as VHS, Beta, 12 inches, 4¾ inches).

Questions include the following:

- Should nonprint materials be intershelved with books on the same subject?
- Should similar formats be housed together?
- How large are the nonprint collections and how much growth is expected?
- Could commercial compact shelving be part of the solution?

Many librarians are reporting that nonprint collections are growing proportionately faster than traditional print collections. Although librarians want to make all types of materials equally accessible, they must face the realities of finite storage space. Intershelving a large number of nonprint materials with each other as well as with books and periodicals presents an additional space problem in many libraries because of the added variations in size and shape of materials. Twelve-inch sound discs and videodiscs require shelves to be at least 15 inches apart and 13 inches deep. Compact discs and sound cassettes require only 6-inch shelves. Intershelving all formats may prompt consideration of uniform packaging because small items may come in big boxes, bags, or no container at all. Special shelf supports such as clip-on shelf holders, shelf supports that hang from the shelf above, pamphlet boxes, and various kinds of stacking units are other storage considerations. Shelving inserts are also available to assist in storing various media formats together; they help prevent small items from getting pushed behind larger ones or larger ones from falling over when something is removed from the shelf. Dummies for unusually shaped items or for flat materials such as maps and art reproductions are another alternative.

If space is a consideration, shelving formats separately may be much more practical (e.g., folded maps in drawers or vertical files, or wall maps in bins). Shelving by format also lends itself to having the appropriate equipment nearby if users are allowed to use the nonprint materials in the library.

When libraries decide to arrange materials by classification number, space will still be a consideration. Initially each shelf should be left at least one-half to one-third empty to allow for expansion within that range of numbers. If materials are arranged by format and accession number, every shelf can be filled completely except the last shelves for expansion. Oversize shelving will probably be necessary in either case.

In some cases, a librarian or library manager may have to make decisions he or she would rather not make. Lack of physical space in a nonintegrated shelving environment might dictate the decision to have nonprint materials housed in closed shelves by format or even in separate facilities. In other cases, such a decision may not be based so much on space or format but more on the subject matter and convenience of the user (e.g., a separate music library which houses music books, scores, and sound recordings).

Storage questions may be the most critical decisions in organizing library materials (i.e., whether all materials should be integrated on the shelves by subject classification, or divided by format, or partially integrated). The answers to these questions will directly affect the physical processing decisions. For more detailed descriptions of the storage, handling, and care of nonprint materials, refer to Jean Weihs's book, *The Integrated Library.*

Preservation

The preservation problem in libraries is only partly about books, but must also include films and prints and maps and all the broad range of media that are part of our stock in trade. We are entering a new era where we need not only to be more aware of that stock and its place in history, but [to be] active in our own position as knowledgeable preservers. (Sullivan 1990, *School Library Journal:* 19)

Although this manual does not concentrate on archival methods of preservation, it does present some practical methods of preserving materials that both the library and the patron should utilize to protect circulating nonprint materials. One way is to educate the library user about the proper care and handling of library materials and the equipment required for their use. This can be accomplished through personal, one-on-one instructions as well as by providing written instructions in the containers of nonprint materials.

There are other things the library itself can do to preserve materials for long-lasting circulation. Such activities include special replacement packaging; reinforcement of existing packaging; protective binders or folders for loose sheets of accompanying information; lamination, encapsulation, or mounting of maps and graphic materials; photocopying of printed materials while filing originals in noncirculating library files; and duplicating of sound recordings, slides, and videorecordings for backups where copyright permits. It is also important to remember that some things will deteriorate no matter what we do—color will fade on some types of film because of the film base, machines will jam and cause damage to film and magnetic tape, and magnetic tape particles will eventually flake off of tape.

If the library is engaged in preservation efforts for its books and periodicals, efforts of this nature can be undertaken for nonprint materials as well. To become more knowledgeable about appropriate preservation materials for processing, a good reference source is the "Glossary of Selected Preservation Terms" published by the Association for Library Collections and Technical Services in the *ALCTS Newsletter,* vol. 1, no. 2 (1990): 14–15. This glossary was developed by the Library/Vendors Task Force of the ALCTS Preservation of Library Materials Section (PLMS) and is sanctioned for distribution by the Association for Library Collections and Technical Services, a division of the American Library Association.

Acid-free containers are available to house a variety of different types of media and their accompanying printed materials. Acid-free containers also may be preferred for certain kinds of old or rare materials that are stored separately in special files. It is a good idea to ask a library supplier for specifications sheets on its products (i.e., labels, containers, etc.). This will tell you about the chemicals in the adhesives and the paper and the amount of acidity in the containers. The only disadvantage in using acid-free containers is that certain types of containers may be two to three times more expensive than ordinary containers. Cost, of course, must be weighed against the preservation advantages.

As we begin to consider preservation issues, we should ask the following questions:

- What is the purpose of a particular library item?

- What is the item's value, both in terms of dollars and in terms of whether it can be replaced?

- How vulnerable to damage is this item? How long will it be before it wears out?
- Is the item readily available for purchase, or is it a one-of-a-kind type of item that could not be replaced?
- Will the item become obsolete before the package wears out?
- Are the packages reusable?

A good example is whether a picture or photograph is used for research purposes only, or whether it is collected primarily for instructional and/or recreational purposes. Usually such items are of a paper medium and can easily be damaged or destroyed. Basic care should always be given to these kinds of materials to prevent them from being stained, torn, bent, or stolen.

From the foregoing example one can see that answers to various questions will determine in part how extensive preservation efforts should be. The particular circumstances of each library will dictate which items should receive special preservation considerations and which items will not. Sound disc jackets and boxes, inner sleeves and album covers, compact disc albums, filmstrip cans, and sound and video albums are all examples of packaging that can preserve non-print items and extend their normal circulation life. The type of material chosen for each of these containers can further affect the preservation outcomes.

Repair activities are another way of providing protection. Film and tape leader and tail can be trimmed or replaced on 16-mm films, filmstrips, videotapes, sound cassettes, and sound reels. Other types of repairs include reinforcement of original packaging and accompanying materials as well as replacement of labels, date due slips, circulation pockets, security strips or labels, and barcodes. Some items will be beyond repair and should be weeded from the collection.

Security

Every library engages in some type of security provisions, even if they are as simple as placing ownership marks on the library materials and requiring the user to sign for the materials that are borrowed from the library. More sophisticated methods of securing library materials include installing some type of commercial security system that requires sensitizing each item of library material and/or placing the most vulnerable materials closest to supervised areas in the library and storing certain kinds of materials in closed stack areas.

The first method, placing vulnerable library materials close to a checkout area or near a reference desk, works best in small libraries in which there are not many of these kinds of materials and in which the traffic is not so heavy that it would be difficult to keep an eye on the materials.

Storage in closed stack areas has already been discussed to some extent, but not as a security issue. There are a variety of security cabinets, files, and display racks that are lockable storage alternatives if particular formats require such segregated and separate treatment. The advantage in terms of security is that such materials will be retrieved for the user by a library staff person and the material can be checked out directly. This kind of one-on-one service virtually eliminates any chance of theft in the library. However, this type of arrangement is obviously labor intensive and is not as user friendly as other methods of control. It also eliminates the possibility of the user being able to browse collections for "unknown treasures."

Commercial security systems offer the most user-friendly environment, but they are initially labor intensive for the library. At the point of installation, all such security systems require that some type of sensitive material be attached to each item in the collection or to its packaging. As new items are added to the collection, they too must have security devices attached to them.

Security systems are of two types. They are either based on radio frequency technology or electromagnetic technology. The radio frequency system uses a radio signal that is concealed in a pressure-sensitive label or in a circulation pocket that is attached to the library item or its packaging. A book card placed in the pocket detunes the pocket's radio signal, or a special detuning label placed over a targeted label will block its radio signal when the item is checked out. Removing the date due card or the detuning label when material is returned reactivates the security signal.

The electromagnetic system uses a thin metallic thread or strip that is placed in an inconspicuous place on the library item or its packaging (e.g., the inside of book spines or CD container spines) or is covered by a label or tape to camouflage and protect it. Some systems may even combine the security strip with the barcode. A newer microprocessor technology is also available which utilizes magnetic labels instead of strips. These labels have a thin magnetic configuration embedded in the underside of the label. Top surfaces may be blank for some type of informational labeling, or they can be preprinted with ownership marks or other important designations. During checkout, both types of magnetic devices are deactivated by passing items through a desensitizing machine.

For both radio and magnetic security systems, if the library item has not been detuned or desensitized during the checkout procedure, the system will sound an alarm, activate voice instructions to return to the circulation area, and/or close a gate as the library material passes through the detection exit.

There are advantages and disadvantages of both types of systems. With the radio frequency system, a sophisticated user might be able to block the signal and prevent detection. With the magnetic system, an equally determined user could remove the magnetic strip or label. Another major concern with magnetic systems is the need to protect magnetic nonprint materials from erasure or distortion at the time of desensitization. Susceptible materials include sound tapes, videotapes, and computer disks. Exit gates do not seem to cause any erasure problems, but some types of desensitizing equipment used at the time of checkout can damage such materials.

Although newer desensitizing equipment may emit a low enough magnetic field to eliminate accidental erasure, libraries with older equipment must take precautionary measures to protect their magnetic materials. Special storage and/ or labeling arrangements may have to be employed for magnetic materials. Closed storage is one option so circulation personnel will be alerted to treat these materials differently during circulation. Another option is to house magnetic materials on open shelves but in brightly colored containers (e.g., red boxes or bags) that alert circulation personnel not to pass them through normal desensitizing equipment. One other option is to cover the barcode with a colored transparent label or place a large fluorescent label in a conspicuous place on the item with the following warning: DO NOT DESENSITIZE. For books that have accompanying computer disks or cassettes in an inside pocket, libraries often resort to housing the disks or cassettes behind the circulation desk and placing an information label on the book explaining that the accompanying material is housed in another location or at the circulation desk.

Magnetic materials raise other concerns for security in the library beyond that of commercial security systems. There is always the potential of accidental erasure or distortion caused from contact with other magnetic fields. Any piece of electrical equipment can create a magnetic field strong enough to erase a disk or cassette. Libraries must exercise extreme caution not to house magnetic materials near any such equipment. For example, videocassettes should not be put on top of VCRs or monitors, and computer disks should be kept away from printers and other electrical computer devices. Accidental erasure can also occur with cassettes when the recording tabs have not been removed after a recording has been completed. All physical processing procedures for cassettes should include a routine check for tab removal.

Security for nonmagnetic materials is also important. All library materials should be provided as much security as is reasonable and yet allow the materials to be conveniently available to the user.

Once decisions and policies have been made regarding circulation, storage, preservation, and security, the library manager is ready to move on to considering basic physical processing options. In the next chapter, we will explore various aspects of physical processing that apply to all formats of nonprint materials. In Part II, the same topics will be covered as they apply to specific formats of material and to various processing options.

REFERENCES

Association for Library Collections & Technical Services, Preservation of Library Materials Section, Library/Vendors Task Force. 1990. ''Glossary of Selected Preservation Terms.'' *ALCTS Newsletter* 1, no. 1: 14–15.

Naisbitt, John. 1982. *Megatrends: Ten New Directions Transforming Our Lives.* New York: Warner Books.

Sullivan, Peggy. 1990. ''Preservation and Judgment.'' *School Library Journal* 36, no. 1:
    16–19.
Weihs, Jean. 1991. *The Integrated Library: Encouraging Access to Multimedia Materials.*
    2nd ed. Phoenix: Oryx Press.

2

Options for Physical Processing

Uncontrolled and unorganized information is no longer a resource in an information society.
                                    —John Naisbitt, *Megatrends*

Once the selection and acquisition of nonprint library materials has taken place, the library's task is to organize and control those materials in such a way as to make them available to the library user. This task is accomplished in three basic ways. The first is to make the collection accessible to the user through an index and description of the materials. Generally this is accomplished by cataloging each item and adding it to a card or online catalog as well as by including it in special listings and bibliographies. The development of nonprint cataloging rules and their importance to the integration of nonprint materials with traditional print collections were discussed in the introduction to this work.

The second way the collection is made available to the user is by assigning each item a location designation in the library. For nonprint materials this location device or call number usually consists of a classification designation and/or a format designation. In some libraries format designations are composed of alphabetic symbols for format plus accession numbers rather than classification numbers. The section on storage in Chapter 1 discussed whether nonprint items should be classified and interfiled with print materials or whether they should be given format-type call numbers and be stored separately from print materials.

Libraries must find answers to these questions based on their own local assessment of the issues.

The third and final way materials are made available to the user is through physical processing. This group of tasks involves physical preparation of items for the shelf to ensure that they are properly located, identified, coded for circulation, and protected from theft, damage, and loss of parts and are thus used easily by patrons.

COMMERCIAL PROCESSING

Although commercial physical processing is beyond the scope of this book, it is an available option. Commercial vendor preprocessing began with shared cataloging. Such services usually include cataloging, classification, and processing for a fee. The processing portion generally includes preparing labels that include call numbers, authors, and titles for placement on library items, packaging, and circulation pockets. Special library packaging and security strips are sometimes an additional option. Most commercial vendors provide all or some of these services depending on the client's wishes. Items most often receiving commercial treatment are sound discs (both CD and 33⅓), sound cassettes, videocassettes, and videodiscs. Processing for filmstrip packages and kits is also available from some sources.

When deciding if commercial processing is an option, the following questions should be considered:

- What is the extent of services offered?
- Will the services help alleviate the backlog?
- Are the types of available materials comprehensive enough for the library's needs?
- Would all of the library's materials have to be processed through the same vendor?
- How important is consistency of treatment from one material type to the other?
- What custom features does the library require and can they be accommodated by the vendor?
- How much time is needed for vendor processing?
- How does the service compare to the price?

The answers to these questions will determine whether commercial processing is a viable option for your library.

> All aspects of processing have a potential impact on the life and maintenance of library materials.
> —Dean A. Larsen, "Preservation and Materials Processing,"
> *Library Technical Services*

This chapter explores a variety of nonprint processing practices and possibilities that can be used in individual libraries or local processing centers. There are some key concepts to keep in mind. Processing should provide maximum protection and information about the item with the least amount of staff time possible. It should be obvious when looking at the item or its container just what the item is and whether any special equipment is required for its use. Additionally, the item should be stored in such a way that it is protected from unnecessary damage or deterioration.

COST FACTORS FOR PHYSICAL PROCESSING

Space, maintenance, utilities, equipment, repairs, processing supplies, salaries, and fringe benefits are cost factors for nonprint physical processing. These components enter into the overall determination of the cost effectiveness of various physical processing decisions. It is the responsibility of the library manager to analyze and plan how each of these factors enters into the overall processing picture. Most of these elements are discussed in Chapter 1, but the cost factor of processing supplies requires further examination.

Processing Supplies

The cost of processing supplies is part of the actual costs associated with preparing an item for the shelf. Although expenditures for nonprint processing supplies are small compared to monies spent on the library collection, they can take up a significant portion of the overall supplies and equipment budget. Processing supplies should have their own budget category. This situation is analogous to having a separate binding and preparations budget for monographs and serials.

Planning for a nonprint supplies budget presents problems because nonprint materials come in a variety of formats with correspondingly diverse supply needs. Many items require special packaging and special labeling. If costs for various supplies are monitored over time, however, the planning process becomes easier. It is a good idea to begin keeping a record of expenditures to establish future budget projections. One method of analysis is to determine an individual cost basis for each type of special processing supply. Once these amounts are established, it is possible to keep track of specific processing costs for each nonprint category over a given period of time. The results of such an analysis will provide a basis for developing a nonprint processing budget. Figure 2.1 illustrates the type of analysis that can be helpful. It shows the costs of preparing a set of two sound cassettes for the shelf.

This analysis does not take into consideration labor costs of securing copyright permission to make the backup cassettes or the copies. If processing costs appear to be excessive, an evaluation can be done to determine which processing supplies are cost effective when compared to the original cost of the item, its predicted shelf life, and its projected usefulness or value to the collection. For example, by analyzing the example shown in Figure 2.1, it might be determined that backup cassettes are an unnecessary processing cost or that some type of alternative packaging might be more suitable and less expensive.

Figure 2.1
Sample Cost Analysis for Preparing Two Sound Cassettes for the Shelf

```
One vinyl album with pocket   = $1.85
One backup cassette for each
    tape @ $1.70 ea.          = $3.40
One circulation pocket        = $ .01
One photocopy of 1 page
    guide                     = $ .08
TOTAL                         = $5.34
```

The volume of supplies used over a six-month period should provide a good beginning budget estimate, although ordering patterns of various media may vary from year to year. In general, it is more efficient and less expensive to order processing supplies for all formats of media in quantities to last at least one year in advance. These should include repackaging containers, protective materials such as lamination and encapsulation film, magnetic tape and film leaders, warning and special instruction labels, etc. Because several nonprint formats will utilize many of the same supplies (i.e., blank labels, circulation pockets with preprinted ownership marks, barcode labels, security strips or labels, and preprinted ownership labels), such supplies can be ordered in even larger quantities and less frequently. It is most efficient to have supplies on hand to be used as needed, but if certain items are used infrequently and are expensive, the decision may be to order them only when actually needed. Having adequate secured storage space is another important consideration. With all supplies it is important for processing personnel to keep a running inventory of items used to ensure that necessary supplies do not run out.

> All the steps in processing materials are necessary, but they are merely a
> means to an end.
>
> —Mildred L. Nickel, *Steps to Service*

That end, of course, is to make a variety of materials available to library patrons. The steps in processing nonprint materials will vary according to the kind of material being processed and the nature of the library for which they are being prepared. In arriving at solutions for specific media types, it is necessary to have a general understanding of typical physical processing issues. The discussions that follow focus on packaging/repackaging, accompanying materials, ownership marks, labels, circulation pockets, date due notices, and barcodes.

PACKAGING/REPACKAGING

For clarification, it seems appropriate to define a few terms that will be used throughout this manual. The terms *packaging* and *container* are used interchangeably. *Packaging* means any generic kind of container which holds the nonprint material being discussed (i.e., album, bag, binder, box, case, envelope, etc.). Similarly, a *container* is "any housing for an item, a group of items, or part of an item that is physically separable from the material being housed" (*AACR 2, 1988 rev.*). *Repackaging* refers to modifying or reinforcing original packaging to make it more suitable for circulation or to replacing original packaging with a container that is different in style, design, or size.

In this manual the term *album* is used in one of two ways. An album is the original jacket or slipcase container for analog sound discs and videodiscs or it is used to describe a container or package that is available from commercial supply vendors that has been designed to hold two or more sound cassettes, compact discs, CD jewel boxes, analog sound discs, videocassettes, videodiscs, filmstrip canisters, or computer disks. When the term *album* is used in this way, it refers to the vinyl albums that often have preformed compartments for holding specific types of material and clear, wrap-around sleeves or pockets on the outside of the container to hold printed information. Frequently these albums have snap-tight closures and provide protection against dirt and moisture. In addition, they provide uniformity of packaging for the shelves, house multiple-part items, and usually provide a space to store accompanying information. Disadvantages of such albums are that they are expensive and may be made from petroleum-based products that crack and split after heavy use. Some do not have secure closures, the interior hubs can loosen, and they usually can be used for only one type of media.

A binder is a container or package that is designed to fasten or secure loose items together. Binding covers are made from pressboard, photomount, vinyl- or cloth-covered fiberboard, rigid plastic, clear vinyl, or bonded polyethylene fibers. Many binders have pockets or envelopes attached to the inside covers. Some binders include inside rings to hold printed materials, polypropylene photo and slide pages, antistatic plastic pages with pockets for computer disks, or premolded trays that hold sound and videocassettes. Another type of binder has cloth strips or clamps inside and is designed to hold printed material or plastic photo pages. Advantages of binders include the following: (1) A variety of different nonprint materials can be housed in them; (2) they are generally uniform in size (e.g., 8½ inches by 11 inches); (3) most are rigid enough to stand on the shelf; (4) they usually provide a pocket for accompanying information; and (5) they are relatively inexpensive. Disadvantages are that they often do not have secure closures and thus do not protect the contents from dust and/or light.

Packaging/repackaging is generally the first decision in physical processing. Packaging choices depend on whether the material will circulate out of the building, if the item will be damaged because of the way it is currently housed, if the item has accompanying materials (e.g., guides, CDs, or computer disks), how expensive the material is, how hard it will be to replace, the amount of money available for processing, and how the material is to be arranged on the shelves. Whether formats are being intershelved or housed by themselves, some type of uniform packaging may be necessary. It has been suggested that when trying to determine which packaging will serve your library's needs, drop a sample on the floor to see what happens to it. If it breaks or pops open, the choice may be obvious.

It is important to remember that from the librarian's point of view the purpose of packaging is to protect the library material and to make the material accessible for users. Producers and distributors, on the other hand, are not thinking of how their packaging will meet a library's needs but of how their product can best be marketed. Consequently, the quality of packaging varies enormously. A 1973 study showed the lack of research in the area of packaging and distribution of multimedia materials (Hart 1973). More than twenty years later, there still appears to be a need for research and professional recommendations about appropriate packaging for various types of media.

To illustrate the complexity of decisions, one can look at the possible choices for the library collecting sound cassettes. At the time of purchase, there may be an option to choose packaging alternatives at varying prices. If the library does not choose one of these alternatives, the original packaging may consist of no more than a shrink-wrap covering or the original mailing container. In that case the library will probably choose to repackage the sound cassette in one of the various containers available commercially. Such choices include a plastic box with a clear, hinged cover and built-in hub locks (often referred to as a Norelco box); a soft polypropylene box with a hinged or separate lid; a polyethylene hanging bag or a vinyl hanging pouch; a vinyl album with a premolded inner compartment to hold the cassette; a clear vinyl album with or without hubs to hold the cassette; a three-ring binder with a rigid premolded page to hold the cassette; a clamp binder with a vinyl page that includes a pocket for the cassette; a clear pouch with stiff backing for use in a browse bin; or a variety of corrugated fiberboard boxes with or without inserts or premolded interiors to hold the cassette. Further alternatives include the range of sizes in which these packaging materials come—from a 2⅝-inch by 4¼-inch cassette box to an 8½-inch by 11-inch binder to a 10-inch by 12½-inch album, and anything in between. Packaging options are almost endless.

Particular problems can arise when it has been determined that the library should use the original packaging because it contains attractive and/or important information about the contents. Flimsy cardboard video cases are a good example of material needing reinforcement. These can be reinforced by applying a delayed action laminate to the surface of the cardboard similar to that used to reinforce the covers of a paperback book. Alternatively, an original flimsy package can be retained by cutting it apart and slipping it into the outer sleeve or pocket of a commercial vinyl video case or sound cassette storage album. Heat lamination or encapsulation are other examples of reinforcement for single-sheet items such as maps, charts, and posters. These kinds of reinforcements allow materials to be housed in drawers without additional packaging. Different kinds of reinforcement include those available for analog sound discs. Paper sleeves with protective antistatic polylined inner sleeves are available to replace paper disc sleeves, and clear vinyl album covers are made to protect original sound disc or videodisc jackets. Without dwelling on the preservation aspects of packaging, it should be stated that materials that are sensitive to light or to chemicals in ordinary paper or polyvinyl chloride (PVC) should be housed in acid-free containers.

Many types of replacement containers are available commercially—boxes of plastic, vinyl, corrugated fiberboard, and corrugated polypropylene; albums and cases of vinyl, polypropylene, and pressboard; bags of nylon mesh, vinyl, cloth, and spunbound olefin; binders of vinyl and pressboard, etc. Some of the containers have special molded or corrugated inserts to hold individual items securely. Others, such as the corrugated storage boxes, are designed to be assembled on demand. They have the advantage of taking up less storage space but the disadvantage of requiring staff time to assemble them. Numerous types of noncommercial package options are also available. Jean Weihs suggests using gift boxes, shoe boxes, or any other type of sturdy box. "Local druggists or camera stores may be willing to donate used boxes, many of which will be acid free" (Weihs 1991: 26). The obvious advantage of these containers is that they are cost free. The disadvantage is that staff time is required to collect them.

One additional container is the security package. Reusable security boxes or packages are available for cassettes, compact discs, and videocassettes and are designed to house these materials in their original containers. After the nonprint item is labeled, it is placed in the security box and locked. It then can be put into a browse bin or on the shelf. When the item is brought to the circulation area, a key is used to unlock the contents for the patron, and the security box is available to be reused for another item in the bin or on the shelf. The security box is somewhat larger than the original item and prevents use of the item until the box is unlocked. Security boxes also can be sensitized with barcode strips or labels to accommodate various security systems. Having adequate storage space for these boxes can be a problem.

A final type of packaging to consider is the mailer. For libraries that participate in interlibrary loan or rental of nonprint materials, a number of distinct types are available. There are heavy fiberboard envelopes which prevent bending of computer software, vinyl discs, pictures, and transparencies. Usually they provide preprinted statements on the outside which give special instructions such as DO NOT FOLD OR BEND or MAGNETIC MATERIALS ARE ENCLOSED. Diskette boxes are another option. These have a foam inner cushion and are made of stiff board with a water-repellent coating. They are ideal for shipping computer discs as well as compact discs. Bubble and foam cushion envelopes are another alternative and come in a variety of sizes. They can be used to mail CDs, cassettes, sound discs, small sets of filmstrips, slides, and single videocassettes. Art and study prints, charts, and maps can be transported in mailing tubes of various sizes. For mailing films, slide sets in carousel trays, and videocassettes, there are impact-resistant polyethylene or plastic cases with special locking mechanisms to prevent items from falling out during transit. Additionally, corrugated mailers in different sizes and shapes are usable for several purposes.

ACCOMPANYING MATERIAL

Definitions

Accompanying material is material issued with, and intended to be used with, the item being catalogued. (*AACR 2, 1988 rev.:* 615)

It is a complementary part of a work, physically separate from the predominant part of the work and frequently in a different medium, such as a sound disc in a pocket inside a book cover, . . . a libretto accompanying a sound disc, or a teacher's guide and script accompanying a videorecording. (Olson 1988: 1)

Issues related to accompanying materials are probably the most troublesome ones to deal with in processing. More and more materials are issued with accompanying material. Books come with computer software and sound cassettes; computer software comes with manuals and videodiscs; sound cassettes come with study guides; filmstrips come with sound cassettes, etc. The first question to be asked is, What should we do with this stuff? The answer, of course, is that whenever possible, accompanying material should be housed with its predominant companion because this will be most convenient for both the user and the library staff. Users will not risk missing important materials, and staff will not have to retrieve materials from other locations.

Unfortunately, many producers sell nonprint materials without packaging that accommodates the accompanying material. Prime examples are the single sound cassette in a clear plastic box accompanied by a 10-inch booklet or a small box of loose slides accompanied by an 8½-inch by 12-inch manual. Fortunately, as described earlier in the section on packaging/repackaging, there are several commercial options that can help in such situations. Albums, binders, boxes, and hanging bags are just a few of the choices that are available to keep multisize materials together.

Sometimes, however, because accompanying material comes in such a variety of forms and sizes, it is not possible or practical to provide common storage. If, for example, a videodisc is accompanied by a wall map, such a huge container would be required to accommodate the two items together that the option becomes impractical. If a library has a magnetic security system, a decision to keep a book and its accompanying computer disk or sound cassette together on the shelf raises the risk of the accompanying magnetic material being erased during the checkout process. In other words, there may be times when there are valid and practical reasons not to house accompanying materials together with their predominant counterparts.

Let us consider the processing issues of housing all items together as well as housing them separately. In either case, all significant pieces should be labeled with the same identification numbers and an ownership mark. When common packaging can accommodate both the predominant item and its accompanying

Figure 2.2
Physical Contents Label To Be Placed on the Outside of a Common Container

```
Contents: 50 slides
           1 sound cassette
           1 guide
```

part(s), it is advisable to create an informational contents label that enumerates what is contained in the package. It should be placed on the outside of the packaging in a prominent place. Figure 2.2 illustrates a typical physical contents label.

When the library determines that common packaging is not a viable option, a number of other procedures should occur to prevent accompanying material from being lost and damaged. If barcodes are used, a unique barcode should be placed on the accompanying material. This allows the library to track the circulation of separately housed materials. Obviously, it is important to alert both patron and staff that accompanying material exists. In an open stack library, it is a good idea to use a special informational label which explains that accompanying material exists and where it is located (see Figure 2.3).

In a closed stack environment, an abbreviated label may be used alerting the library staff that accompanying materials exist. In this case it is the staff's responsibility to alert the patron to the materials' availability and to retrieve them if they are wanted. In such cases an abbreviated label can be used because the staff knows the location of the accompanying guides, computer disks, cassettes. etc. Figure 2.4 shows examples of abbreviated labeling that may be combined with the call number for alerting staff that accompanying material is available. In the first example, *w/guide* indicates ''With guide'' and could be modified to indicate ''w/cassette,'' ''w/disk.'' The second example abbreviates *accompanying* to *acc.* and can be used to indicate ''various accompanying materials.''

Protective treatment is also an important consideration for safeguarding accompanying materials. Making backup photocopies of important instruction sheets and manuals is a good idea if copyright permits. Originals can be filed in a safe place to assure that replacements will always be available. If the instruction sheet or guide is a single sheet, it may be mounted on fiberboard or laminated and put into a binder of some kind. If archival preservation is a concern, an acid-free folder, envelope, or binder might be chosen. When multiple pages are involved without protective covering, a binder, envelope, or folder can be a good choice for protection. All protective devices should be identified with the call number designation of the predominant material to which they belong as well as by an ownership mark. Once the accompanying material has been protected appropriately, it should be filed by call number in accessible file drawers or oversize storage.

Figure 2.3
Informational Label for Locating Accompanying Material

> *ACCOMPANYING MATERIAL IS AVAILABLE FOR*
> *THIS ITEM.   ASK AT CIRCULATION DESK.*

OWNERSHIP MARKS

An ownership mark is a visible means of identifying the legal proprietorship of an object by affixing or impressing a symbol or inscription on the item. A library uses ownership marks to identify every item in its collection as belonging to that library. Thus, when a library patron borrows an item from the library, it is apparent to the patron just who owns the borrowed item and where it should be returned.

When using ownership marks, care should always be taken to avoid damaging the library item. Except in archival collections, marks should be long lasting and, when possible, placed on a surface that will not have other items rubbing against it. Usually ownership marks should be placed on the container and on all important nonprint items, including accompanying materials. Factors to be considered when deciding on the method and location of ownership marks are rareness of the bibliographic item, condition of the material, the physical format, and the type of surface to be marked.

Various methods are available for creating ownership marks, and the choice of more than one may be necessary depending on the types of nonprint material that the library collects. Methods include hand lettering, stamping, embossing, engraving, typing or embossing blank labels, labeling with preprinted labels or tape, choosing barcodes that are preprinted with the library's name, and using preprinted circulation pockets, date due slips, or identification tags.

Hand lettering with some type of permanent ink is recommended for odd-shaped items and surfaces to which adhesive labels might cause damage or not adhere well. Artist's oils and acrylic paints are also effective for some types of hard objects. Medium lead pencils are recommended for paper items that are rare or fragile and therefore should not receive permanent marks. If using any type of hand-lettering method, it is advisable to develop a simple and clear ownership designation.

If ownership stamps are used, care should be taken to make the stamp neat, straight, and legible. Both permanent and nonpermanent inks are available for lettering and stamp pads. If plastic surfaces such as slide mounts or cassettes are to be lettered or stamped, permanent ink should be used because nonpermanent inks can be removed easily. When archival materials are to be marked permanently, inks need to be chemically stable and resistant to light, heat, and water.

Embossing is a method frequently used for print materials that transfers an

Figure 2.4
Abbreviated Informational Labels for Showing Availability of Accompanying Materials

impression of the ownership mark in relief to a paper surface. A similar embossing method has been developed for applying a property identification name or number to the clear plastic inner portion of an optical compact disc. However, because of the fragile nature of the optical disc, extreme caution should be exercised when considering the use of any device that might cause a strain on its protective lacquer coating. Another embossing device is the portable label maker that embosses impressions of letters and numbers onto tape that can be attached to irregular or contoured surfaces.

Engraving an ownership mark is another option for identifying large, expensive nonprint materials made of steel, plastic, wood, glass, and ceramic. Engraving is often used for marking audiovisual equipment and computers. Neither the engraving nor the embossing technique should be used on any portion of the coated metallic surface of optical discs, on any magnetic mediums (e.g., computer disks and sound or videotapes), or on any rare or archival material because both techniques cause permanent altering of the medium.

One more option for ownership markings is to create identification markings on blank labels, which can then be attached to nonprint materials. Such markings can be typed, stamped, or printed with a computer printer or a portable electronic label maker. However, if many items are to be processed, it may be more cost effective to order preprinted ownership labels or rolls of preprinted tape. The minimal cost of preprinting will be outweighed by the neatness of appearance and the standardized method of identification. This type of ownership marking can be used on a variety of formats and comes in many sizes. Specialized styles of property labels are also available (i.e., round labels for the clear center gripping ring of CDs, curved labels for analog sound discs, cut-out labels for sound cassettes). However, it is a good idea to investigate the kind of adhesives that are used on all blank and preprinted labels and tapes to be sure that they will not cause an adverse reaction with the surfaces to which they will be attached. In addition, some librarians may be concerned that adding any type of label to the CD will affect the balance of the disc when it is spinning.

The last ownership designations to consider are the preprinted barcodes, circulation cards and pockets, multiform circulation slips, and identification tags that are available. Barcodes may be preprinted with an institution's or library's name, which appears directly above the barcode itself. Pockets come in a variety of sizes and may be preprinted with the name and/or address of the library. If circulation cards or date due slips are used, they also may be preprinted with the library's name. A final preprinted option for ownership designation is to use preprinted identification tags. They may be tied to objects that otherwise do not lend themselves to ownership marking.

Location of ownership marks on library materials will vary from format to format, but the mark should always be easily readable and conveniently accessible on each item. Consistency and prominence of identification markings serve multiple purposes. From the library's point of view, the prominence and permanence of ownership marks may deter the potential theft of items and make it easier to identify lost materials. Consistency of placement on each format, when possible, serves both the library staff and patrons well if they know where to look for ownership identification. Circulation staff benefit by having consistent places to check for ownership marks in order to verify that returned materials belong to the library. Processing staff are able to speed up routines when there is consistency of placement for ownership marks, even if it is only within each particular format. The library patron who borrows materials from more than one library is able to determine easily which items are to be returned to which library.

LABELING

Labeling refers to a library's local practice of adding markings to its library materials to identify and give information about the nature of its materials. Identification labeling and informational labeling are the two types of labeling to be discussed in this manual.

For either type of labeling, the extent and completeness of the labels will depend on local needs and practices (i.e., open or closed shelving), circulation policies (including whether items are available for interlibrary loan), the importance of labeling to the use and purpose of the item, and the purpose of the collection (e.g., consumable or preservation). These factors are weighed against the time and expense needed for the labeling process.

In the process of gathering data from many libraries about processing nonprint materials, we discovered that accession numbers are still being used in various instances. We had been aware of the practice of making call numbers out of format designations (such as AT for audiotape) and adding an accession number. This type of call number and storage arrangement is discussed in Chapter 1 and needs no further discussion here.

However, the continued use of accession numbers and classification numbers deserves additional explanation because library literature would lead one to believe that such a practice is no longer followed. We discovered that some libraries that do not have unique call numbers (e.g., a Dewey number without a Cutter number) use accession numbers to identify individual items and copies, and some libraries include these accession numbers on their identification labels.

This practice is apparently helpful for tracking withdrawn and lost copies and/ or volumes. Accession numbers also link items to bibliographic records when barcodes are missing. They are used when a library does not assign barcodes to items until they are checked out. In that instance the accession number is used to match the item to the bibliographic record. Circulation staff have to check only one field instead of having to match author, title, date, and edition. One librarian said, "I realize that item record numbers do the same thing, but a six-digit accession number is much easier to use than a fourteen-digit barcode."

Identification Labeling

Identification labeling consists of ownership marks (discussed earlier in this chapter) and bibliographic marks that distinguish the unique aspects of library materials (i.e., call number; part, copy, or volume number; accession number, if used; title; author and series, when applicable).

The essential question, of course, is how much labeling should be done for nonprint material and how extensive the labeling should be. Using a videocassette with an accompanying guide as an example, consider the possibilities. The least amount of bibliographic identification for both the videocassette and the guide would be to place a call number of some kind on each so that both staff and patrons will know where to locate the items and so they are related to one another. The next most desirable piece of information (if it has not been provided by the commercial publisher) is the title. It should be applied to the spine of the cassette and to the spine of the container which houses the cassette and the guide. It is recommended that the title be added to the front of the cassette and the container as well. Other labeling information that may be considered essential (if not commercially provided) would be enough physical description of the item to know what type of equipment is required (e.g., VHS, Beta, super VHS) and, if applicable, a volume or part number, edition information, publisher/distributor/releasing agent, date, physical description (color or black and white, running time, stereo or mono), and series information.

Depending on the type of library and the nature of both the collection and user, other types of labeling information may also be desirable. If applicable, these would include a statement of responsibility such as author, director, or performer's name; parallel title; language (if not English); ISBN number; and a summary of the intellectual contents. In the final analysis, each library must decide how much material is to be labeled and how extensive the labeling is to be.

Many of the same methods described in the previous section on ownership marks also apply to identifying the unique aspects of library items. They include hand lettering on the item or container and typing or printing on blank labels. Selin labeling is another option, but it requires a special typewriter attachment. This process calls for typing labels on a strip of plastic tape, which is covered by another strip of tape to protect the label from smudging. Labels are cut apart,

Figure 2.5
Marking the Cataloged Title when More Than One Title Appears on an Item

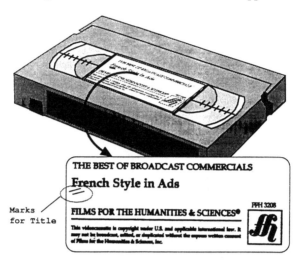

the backing is peeled away from the strips, and the labels are attached to the library materials. A heating element such as a tacking iron is used to seal the label onto the item. The use of a teflon shield will provide protection for plastic and vinyl containers.

Other methods of labeling include a variety of label-printing software programs that are available for installation on local computers. Through bibliographic utilities, local integrated library systems, and various library supply vendors, software programs can generate spine labels, pocket labels, and author/title labels from electronic cataloging records.

Identification labeling should be placed in consistent locations on each format as much as is workable to assure that items can be identified easily. If possible, labels should be placed on surfaces where no objects will be sliding or rubbing against them. The location selected should be visible when the item is stored on the shelf. If nonprint items have a spine, it is the prime location for a call number and a title. When a nonprint item lacks a visible commercially printed title and/or author designation, such a label can be added as appropriate.

The local processing manual should record all labeling routines that a library chooses. For example, when more than one title appears on an item, some libraries may choose to mark the title under which the item is cataloged. Figure 2.5 illustrates a marked label that distinguishes the cataloged title from the series title.

When cataloging nonprint materials, audiovisual (AV) catalogers often find that the container title differs from the cataloged title that comes from the chief source of information (e.g., the title screen from a videocassette). In such instances many librarians believe that the cataloged title should be added to the

Figure 2.6
Example of Punctuation Policy Decisions To Be Recorded in the Local Manual

```
                                    Use only last
                                    name of author
                                    and follow it
    ┌─────────────────────────┐     with a period.
    │   Mozart.               │
    │   [Nozze di Figaro]     │     Place brackets
    │   Figaro.               │     around uniform
    │                         │     titles.
    └─────────────────────────┘
```

item during processing for positive identification. Thus a label with the main entry author, uniform title (if applicable), and title as it appears in the cataloging record may be prepared for placement in a prominent location on the item.

If a library uses punctuation marks on labels such as a period after the author's name, this practice should be recorded in the library's processing manual. If a library chooses to use only the last name of an author on labels, or to include uniform titles in brackets to distinguish them from the title appearing on the item, these decisions should also be recorded in the manual (see Figure 2.6).

Alternatively, a library that is a member of a bibliographic network or local automated cataloging system may generate a copy of the cataloging record which can be attached to the nonprint container. In both cases, care should be taken *not* to cover the container title, because the container title may be the title the patron recognizes from a catalog or some other bibliographic source.

Should every item in a multiple-piece package be labeled? Nancy B. Olson gives practical advice on this subject in the introduction to her book, *Cataloging of Audiovisual Materials:*

A workable guideline is to label everything necessary for use of the item. If loose-leaf pages have a running title that matches the item title, they can be matched up with little difficulty. If five beads of the 1,000 in a set are missing, little harm is done. (Olson 1992: 8)

This is sound advice with any type of multiple-part material. In other words, all significant parts of an item should be labeled with the same identification number to ensure that if the parts are separated, they can easily be traced back to their original container. Accompanying information should always be labeled with the call number of its corresponding media, whether it is housed in the same container or kept in a separate location.

An additional issue to consider is whether the librarian will want to add individual part designations to each component in a set and whether each component is to receive an ownership mark. There are several methods of indicating parts (e.g., v. 1; no. 1; pt. 1; v. 1, pt. 1; no. 1, pt. 1; pt. A, no. 1; series, 1, pt. A; etc.). Often the order and type of numbering system to be used may be dictated by the actual bibliographic item or a producer's guide or catalog listing. Some libraries may try to maintain a type of consistency, such as always using the term *volume* (v. or vol.) or *number* (no.) on their labels in case there are parts (pt. or pts.) that follow. It is a good idea for every library to establish its own guidelines for handling multiple-part materials and to record these decisions and abbreviations in the local manual. (For a further discussion of multiple-part items, see Chapter 9, "Kits and Interactive Multimedia.")

Another use for identification labels is the labeling of dummies. A dummy is an empty box or board that files on the shelf in its proper place and replaces the real item, which is shelved elsewhere (e.g., oversize materials). Dummies should be labeled with the call number and title and/or author of the actual item for which they are substituting. It is also helpful to provide an informational label giving a detailed description of the real item as well as its actual location. For libraries with computerized cataloging, a copy of the cataloging record may be especially appropriate in this case to give the patron as much information as possible about the record before the patron goes to the trouble of seeking out the other location.

Informational Labeling

Informational labels are especially important for nonprint materials because they can furnish critical information which otherwise might not be evident from looking at the item on the shelf. Such information may include a description of the intellectual contents and the physical contents and special instructions and/ or warning notices.

Because special equipment is often required to scan the intellectual content of nonprint items, the use of an intellectual contents label on the container may provide a convenient substitute that, in effect, allows the patron to peruse the item. Information can be made complete enough for the user to decide whether he or she wants the item without having to open the package. Figure 2.7 illustrates an intellectual contents label for a sound cassette.

When cataloging nonprint material, part of the process is to describe the physical characteristics of the material. When material consists of more than one component, it can also be helpful during processing to describe the physical contents of the item. A physical contents label can take several forms. A listing for a game can be specific (e.g., "1 set of dice, 1 board, 1 set of cards, 1 rule sheet") or may be as general as "1 game (various pieces)." This kind of label is also helpful when common packaging holds a predominant item and its accompanying parts, as was shown in Figure 2.2. Contents labels not only alert patrons to the physical contents of the material and the type of equipment that is needed, but they also provide valuable information to circulation personnel at the time of charging and discharging materials.

Special instructions and warning statements are the final type of informational labels to be considered. If an item is known to have missing parts, a note on

Figure 2.7
Intellectual Contents Label for a Sound Cassette

```
Side 1: The very thought of you.
        Paper moon.
        Route 66
        Mona Lisa
        L-O-V-E
        This can't be love
        Smile
        Lush life
        That Sunday that summer
        Orange colored sky
```

the physical contents label can alert both the user and the circulation staff when the rest of the item is still being circulated. Figure 2.8 illustrates such a label used on a box of filmstrips titled *South America.*

Other informational labels can be used to provide special information, as shown in the examples in Figure 2.9, or to give instructions to the user (e.g., RESTRICTED USE, TURN TAPE AND CONTINUE, REWIND, etc.).

When specialized equipment is required for the use of a specific type of media, a label that indicates such is a good idea. For example, if a videorecording has been recorded in an extended play mode, a variable speed VCR would be required to play back the video. Because some VCRs are standard play only, it might be helpful to make a label (as shown in Figure 2.10) for the videocassette container to alert potential users about the required equipment.

Warning labels such as copyright restriction labels are another valuable information label and, in some cases, are required for use by libraries. Preprinted labels can be obtained from various library supply vendors, or a library can create its own. Since March 28, 1991, federal law requires that nonprofit libraries that lend computer programs for nonprofit purposes without the permission of the copyright holder must affix a warning of copyright to the package containing the computer program that details the specifications of the copyright restriction. For more detailed information regarding this requirement, refer to Chapter 7, "Computer Files."

Labels come in a variety of sizes, and each library must determine the sizes it will use. Library supply vendors also provide custom rolls of labeling material that can be cut to accommodate unusual sizes. In this manual, sizes for labels and label placements are given as guidelines only. Each library must decide on its own desired placement for labels, record the decisions in the local manual, and carry out the decisions as consistently as possible.

It is important to choose labels which will not come loose in the required equipment. One must be particularly careful with labels on slides (which can

Figure 2.8
Physical Contents Label with Inventory Notes

```
Filmstrip no. 3: Peru    (missing (2/10/90))
```

get caught in carousel trays or slide projectors) and with those used on sound and videocassettes (which might jam in playback equipment).

Labels are frequently made of paper, plastic, tape, cloth, or metal and are designed to be affixed in some way to the library item. Paper labels and tags come in regular or acid-free paper, can be typed or hand lettered, and can be attached by adhesives, sewn, or tied to certain types of library objects. Commercially supplied adhesive labels vary from removable to permanent and come as pressure-sensitive, foil-backed, acid-free, colored, or some combination of these. Cloth labels can be hand lettered and sewn or tied to a variety of library objects. Hand-stamped metal labels might be attached to large, heavy objects such as globes and various types of realia. Each library will want to investigate the specifications of these various options and determine which labels will best meet its needs.

Paper labels can be protected by covering them with clear plastic tape or clear adhesive labels. One should check the specifications of the chemicals in the adhesives, however, to see what reactions they have on labels placed on vinyl and cardboard surfaces. Some adhesives will cause labels and containers to turn yellow. Chemicals inherent in some containers may also cause labels to change color. Special kinds of library objects may require the use of lacquers or acrylics as protective coverings. One should refer to museum and archival manuals for detailed marking instructions on special library collections.

CIRCULATION POCKETS, CARDS, AND DATE DUE NOTICES

As Nancy Olson has observed correctly, "In an online system, book cards and pockets may no longer be used" (1992: 8). However, for the purposes of this manual, discussions will assume the presence of some type of physical pocket or date due notice devised to alert the patron when the item is due to be returned to the library. Circulation cards, pockets, and date due notices traditionally have been physical manifestations of the library's desire to keep track of who has borrowed a library item and when it is due to be returned. Library pockets are envelope-type receptacles made of either heavy opaque paper or clear vinyl designed to be attached inside or outside a library item. They are open on one end and are used for storing circulation cards or slips which describe the item checked out and the name of the borrower. The advantage of the clear vinyl variety is that one can read information below the pocket when

Figure 2.9
Informational Label: Availability of Accompanying Material

```
VIDEO IS PART OF SPECIAL ASIAN
    MATERIALS COLLECTION
         ----
ASK AT CIRCULATION DESK FOR
    RELATED ITEMS
```

it is placed over printed material. The disadvantages may be that the composition of the plastic vinyl or its self-adhesive backing may not be environmentally sound. In addition, small print underneath the pocket may be difficult to read. Paper pockets have the advantage of coming in various sizes, and they can be custom preprinted. However, unless they are made of acid-free paper, they too can be chemically unstable, as can the adhesive used to attach them.

Pockets may be attached to nonprint materials in several ways. Self-adhesive varieties are available in both paper and clear vinyl. A number of double-stick tapes are also on the market. Another method of attaching paper pockets is with rubber cement. If this method is used to create a permanent bond, care must be given to apply the cement to both the surface to which it will adhere and to the back of the pocket. Both surfaces should be left to dry partially (ten to fifteen minutes) before cementing them together. If done correctly, this will form a secure bond. Another method of attachment is to hinge a pocket so that it can be raised on one side to view what lies below. For this process, run a piece of tape with half of the tape attached to the front side of the pocket and the remaining tape attached to the surface of the library item. Flip the pocket over and repeat the process on the back of the pocket. This method will be more secure and less likely to pull away. This process works well when all surfaces have printed information that should not be covered (e.g., backs of sound disc album jackets, inside lids of boxes, etc.).

Proper placement of pockets is always a question. As Olson has stated eloquently, "Placement of card and pocket, date due slip, ownership information, etc., requires a good deal of common sense. There is no one place on any type of audiovisual material where processing staff can expect to put these things" (1992: 8). What can be expected, however, is that there will be a consistency of location for similar formats with similar types of packaging. The least protected location for pockets is the exterior of the container, but there are many containers which leave no alternative. The clear, hinged plastic cassette boxes lack room inside for anything other than the cassette and perhaps a paper liner. Vinyl albums with preformed trays on both sides lack a flat interior surface for pocket placement. Therefore, if pockets are to be used, decisions are often between the front or the back of containers. Some libraries prefer placement on the front so that the pocket can be placed adjacent to the identification label for the item. Other libraries will choose the back of the container because, in many

Figure 2.10
Required Equipment Information Label

VARIABLE SPEED PLAYBACK EQUIPMENT REQUIRED

---

cases, that location is less likely to contain important information. Once the location has been decided, the important thing is to be as consistent as possible when processing that type of material. However, covering important information may require another location.

Libraries using automated circulation systems may not need to use circulation pockets. With the use of barcodes, libraries already have a link between the patron and the item being checked out. The only problem remaining is to provide information to the patron regarding the date the item is to be returned. Permanent and pressure-sensitive date due labels are available. Such labels are imprinted DATE DUE and have space below for application of a small date label or stamp as a date due reminder. The small date label has a removable adhesive which allows it to be placed over old labels or to be removed when needed.

Date due labelers, which generate a small date due label that can be placed onto any designated surface, are also available. These are hand-held labelers similar to those used in grocery and variety stores. Either single- or double-line printing bands can be chosen. With any of these systems, one must be sure that there will not be problems because of the label adhesives. Check with label suppliers for the type of adhesives used on their products.

BARCODES

Barcodes or OCR (optical character recognition) labels are used to link physical item records with corresponding database records in automated library systems. Once a library item has been so linked to its database record, it can be used to keep track of the item's circulation status in the local automated system. For each library item, a unique barcode number label is attached to the physical item or to its container, and that same number is assigned to the corresponding database record. The label includes both the Arabic version of the number and a digital zebra version of the number in light and dark bars and spaces that can be scanned by a laser from either direction.

Barcode labels come in various sizes and configurations depending on a library's specific needs. Although standard-size barcodes of approximately 2 inches may be used for most library items, smaller barcodes (e.g., ¼ inch by ¾ inch) may be used for such items as individual slides or sound cassettes. Often the library's name and/or address may be printed above the coded portion of barcode labels. Some libraries use "one-and-a-half" or "half-up" barcodes, which consist of the full barcode label with another "half" label or "stub" that has the eye-readable Arabic number printed on it. These can be used as matching devices for materials that have more than one part to them, such as a videocassette and its packaging container or a kit box and its manual. The full barcode may be placed on the videocassette and the eye-readable half on the container, or vice versa depending on a library's preference. For kits the full barcode may be placed on the container and the half on the verso of the title page of the manual or on some other important part of the kit (in case they are separated or one is lost).

Placement of barcodes will vary according to individual library policies. The important concept to keep in mind is that once placement policies have been agreed on by staff, those policies should be followed consistently. Although consistency with each format and container is an important consideration, it may be necessary to allow some variation to avoid covering up important information (such as the only occurrence of a music publisher number or a series statement and number).

Where to place barcodes on library materials is probably the first question asked when implementing an automated library system. As with other aspects of processing nonprint materials, there is no single correct answer. The characteristics of each local system, the library's circulation policies, and the available level of staffing should all be considered when making this decision. Many libraries choose to place barcodes on the container, whereas others believe the barcode should be placed on the item itself. Reasons for placement of barcodes on the container and adjacent to the circulation pocket are to expedite the circulation process at checkout and to make inventory easier. Other reasons may be to coordinate the placement of barcodes with the outside placement of security labels. (With the radio frequency type of security system, stickers may need to be placed over the security label to deactivate the system.) Even though label and tape barcode protectors are available, it is important to choose a location that will have as little friction and rubbing of the surface as possible. It is also a good idea to place a contents label on the outside of the container if it houses more than one item. When items are returned, circulation staff can easily check the contents to be sure they are all there. Many automated circulation systems can be programmed to beep, to remind circulation staff to check the contents of the container for the right parts.

Libraries that choose to put the barcode on the inside of the container or on the media item itself are assured that the container will be opened and checked for the presence or absence of the actual item when the barcode is scanned out or cleared. This may be especially important, for example, in a film or video library, where items are rented or loaned to other institutions and there may be an added risk of materials being mixed up with another library's materials. When barcodes are placed on the items themselves, it is still helpful to place a contents label on the outside of the container if it houses more than one component. The circulation staff will know exactly what to look for, and so will the user.

Another important aspect of the question of where to put barcodes is whether barcodes should be put on individual parts of a nonprint item or whether one barcode is sufficient for a set. One of the factors to consider is whether the parts can be checked out individually. A set of videocassettes, for example, may be treated as a multiple-volume set with each cassette barcoded separately and circulated separately. Conversely, the set may be packaged together and only circulated as a unit. In the latter case, there may be no need to barcode each cassette unless the library has some other reason to do so, such as to keep item number statistics rather than title statistics. Similarly, individual items within a kit do not need individual barcodes if the kit always circulates as a unit, unless the library policy is to track each individual item. A contents label on the box will provide both the circulation staff and the user with sufficient information about what belongs in the kit.

One more factor to consider is whether the local online system allows more than one barcode per title. Some systems do not, whereas others allow one barcode per item record so that individual items, parts, and copies can all have their own barcodes. In such a system, an accompanying manual or guide that does not fit into a container may also be tracked with its own barcode. If the system allows multiple-item records, one option may be to barcode each part in a container and have the system alert the check-in staff if each barcode is not cleared. If any part is missing at the time of return of the unit, it would be immediately evident. Remember that the placement of individual barcodes on each piece requires more staff time during processing and circulation. When each piece is recorded in the system, each piece must be cleared. Thus, there are increased costs due to additional staff time and the costs of the additional barcodes. For some libraries, however, the accountability for lost items may outweigh any disadvantage of added costs.

A LOCAL PROCESSING MANUAL

A local processing manual has many purposes. It documents the development of the library's processing policies and ensures continuity of treatment until a valid reason for changing that treatment occurs. It helps maintain consistent and efficient levels of processing library materials, which translates into early use by the library patron. It ensures a smooth transition for changing library personnel. It provides explanations for how to handle the various formats of material that the library collects. It allows for fiscal responsibility in planning and spending processing funds.

In the chapters that follow in Part II, a number of topics will recur that have been discussed already. Because of the various formats to be covered, however, these topics will be viewed in many different ways.

REFERENCES

Anglo-American Cataloguing Rules, Second Edition, 1988 Revision, ed. by Michael Gorman and Paul W. Winkler for the Joint Steering Committee for Revision of AACR. Chicago: American Library Association.

Hart, Thomas L. 1973. *Conceptualizing a Model for Access to Multi-media Materials in Elementary and Secondary Schools: A Study of Cataloging and Processing by Commercial, Centralized and Local Processing Units,* Ph.D. dissertation, Case Western Reserve University.

Larsen, Dean A. 1984. "Preservation and Materials Processing." In *Library Technical Services: Operations and Management,* ed. by Irene P. Godden. Orlando, FL: Academic Press.

Naisbitt, John. 1982. *Megatrends: Ten New Directions Transforming Our Lives.* New York: Warner Books.

Nickel, Mildred L. 1984. *Steps to Service: A Handbook of Procedures for the School Library Media Center.* Rev. ed. Chicago: American Library Association.

Olson, Nancy B. 1988. *Audiovisual Material Glossary.* Dublin, OH: OCLC Online Computer Library Center.

————. 1992. *Cataloging of Audiovisual Materials: A Manual Based on AACR 2.* 3rd ed. DeKalb, IL: Minnesota Scholarly Press.

Weihs, Jean. 1991. *The Integrated Library: Encouraging Access to Multimedia Materials.* Phoenix: Oryx Press.

PART II

A Guide to Physical Processing Practices

3

Cartographic Materials

Cartographic material. Any material representing the whole or part of the earth or any celestial body at any scale. Cartographic materials include two- and three-dimensional maps and plans (including maps of imaginary places); aeronautical, navigational and celestial charts, atlases; globes, block diagrams; sections; aerial photographs with a cartographic purpose; bird's-eye views (map views), etc.

(AACR 2, 1988 rev.: 616)

Cartographic materials present their own set of problems in the library because they come in so many different forms—earth and celestial representations on globes and three-dimensional models, wall maps on rods and sticks, large sheet maps with and without overlays, rolled maps, folded maps, and relief maps that cannot be folded. This nonstandard form and variations in durableness present storage and processing dilemmas. One must compare the features of each type of storage and their implications for processing in relation to the size of the collection, the amount of available storage space, the desired accessibility for the collection, and the relative costs of each method.

GLOBE

Definition: A model of the earth or other celestial body, depicted on the surface of a sphere. (*AACR2, 1988 rev.:* 618)

General Information

Globes vary in size and in type, including political, physical-political, raised relief, slated outline, or celestial. Various mountings or stands are available in wood, metal, and plastic and include cradle, gyro-disc, semimeridian, plain, geosphere, and hinged horizon. The surfaces of globes may be protected by painting or spraying polyurethene varnish on them.

Considerations for Globe and Geographic Model Storage

- Globes and relief models may be displayed as decorative items rather than on special shelves.
- Globes and models may be stored on the tops of library shelving or in oversize areas and covered with cloth dust covers or clear plastic material.
- Globes and models may be stored on regular library shelving in their original containers, which help keep them dust free and protect them from physical damage.
- Globes lacking storage boxes may be stored in standard supply cabinets, where they will stay clean and are less likely to receive physical damage.
- Plastic relief models can have one or two holes punched in one of their sides and may be suspended from hooks or wires. Some relief models come framed and ready to hang.
- Clips may be attached to one edge of plastic models, and they may be hung from rods, racks, or clothesline.

Globe Labeling

Option a: Processing without Labels

1. Markings on globe. Using a pen with permanent ink, write the call number and the copy and/or accession number (if used) on the globe in an area lacking important information (see Figure 3.1). This method is useful for beach-ball globes, plastic globes, or globes lacking a base. When dealing with nonporous substances, a designated marking area might be brushed with a naphtha-based varnish that later could be removed with acetone. Paint or write the call number, title, and the copy and/or accession number (if used) in acrylic paint on the naphtha-brushed strip. Seal with another coat of varnish. This process cannot be used on plastics.

2. Markings on base. Choose a space on the base and, using a pen with permanent ink, print the title, call number, and the copy and/or accession number (if used). These numbers may be printed to the left and/or the right of the center support as space permits. Print the title under these numbers or where space is available.

Figure 3.1
Processing a Globe without Labels

Ownership marks. Ownership marks may be printed using a pen with permanent ink in an area lacking other important information.

Option b: Processing with Labels

On an identification label, type the call number, the copy and/or accession number (if used), the title, and the number of parts or accompanying material (see Figure 3.2). Place the label on the base or stand so that it is visible. If the base is ornate and it is difficult to attach a label, place the label on the wood encircling the globe. Trim to fit as necessary. If preferred, the label may be placed on the bottom of the base.

Ownership marks. Labels commercially imprinted with the library's ownership mark may be attached to the globe in an area that lacks information. Small labels stamped or embossed with the library's name may also be used. A preferred location for the ownership label is the bottom edge of the base.

Container Labeling

On an identification label, type the call number, the part number (if the globe is part of a set), the copy and/or accession number (if used), the author's name (if appropriate), the title, and the accompanying material contents (see Figure 3.3). Placement of this label in the upper left corner of the container's side is a good location so both patrons and shelvers can read the contents.

Ownership marks. The ownership marks should be placed visibly on the top

Figure 3.2
Processing a Globe with Labels

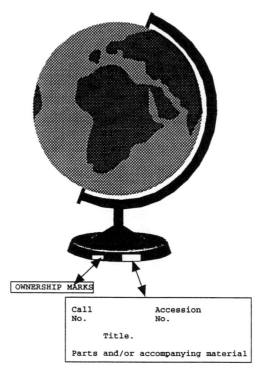

and/or sides of the container using either a label, a stamp, or a marker to print the library's name.

Informational labels. Informational labels, such as STORE AWAY FROM LIGHT, may be placed on the top cover.

Pockets for Circulation

Option a: Globes Stored in Boxes

Consistency of placement in accordance with library policy and avoidance of covering important information are essential. Circulation pockets may be attached to the side of the box that is visible when the box sits on the shelf, or the circulation pocket may be placed on the top of the box. Another placement option is inside the top of the lid, where the pocket will be free from surface friction (see Figure 3.3).

Option b: Globes Not Stored in Boxes

For globes not stored in boxes, other methods are available for attaching pockets. For example, using a hole-punch device, make a hole in the circulation

Figure 3.3
Globe Container Labeling

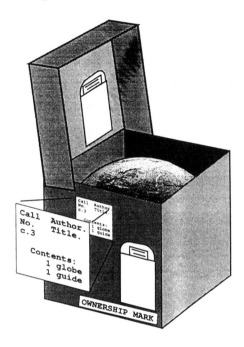

pocket. Insert floral wire, cord, or nylon fishing line through the punched hole in the pocket and tie or glue the ends (see Figure 3.4).

Barcodes

Barcodes may be placed on the globe base or on the wood encircling the globe.

Security Devices

Libraries may decide not to include security devices on globes because they are usually housed in special cases or in locations which may require staff assistance. Globes are difficult to remove from a library because they can be detected visually. If security devices are used, they may be placed on the base of the globe or the container and be covered with a label or piece of opaque tape. Security devices may also be attached to the back of circulation pockets and wired or taped to the globe.

Figure 3.4
Circulation Pocket for Globe Not Stored in Box

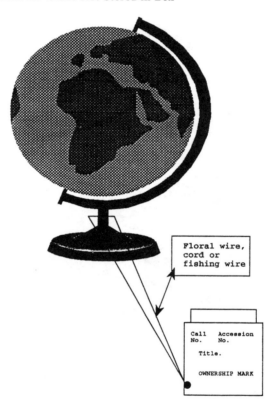

Accompanying Material

Accompanying material for globes should follow the guidelines discussed in Chapter 2. If possible, accompanying material should remain in the box or container with the globe. Accompanying material may be protected by placing it in a large envelope with an identification label. If the globe lacks a container, the accompanying material may be placed in an envelope with a hole punched in it. The envelope may be attached to the globe base using the floral wire method. Larger pieces of accompanying material should receive more permanent covering. Accompanying material should always be labeled. A label with an identification number should be placed on the cover of the accompanying material so that it is linked to its globe. It is advisable to place ownership designations (stamps or labels) in a position consistent with library policy. When accompanying material is stored separately and barcodes are in general use for the rest of the collection, a unique barcode should be placed on each piece of accompanying material. This practice will help the library keep track of each separate circulation.

Gift Plates

Gift plates may be attached to the base or to the wood circling the globe. They also may be attached to a piece of cardboard that is cut to the size of the plate and attached to the globe using the floral wire method. Valuable globes or special donation globes may have a metal donor's plate attached to the wooden frame or cradle on which the globe rests. Another option is to attach such plates to the storage box that houses the globe. Additionally, plates may be attached to the reverse side of a floral-wired pocket, or they may be attached to a stringed shipping tag and tied to the globe stand.

MAPS

Definition: A representation, normally to scale and on a flat medium, of a selection of material or abstract features on, or in relation to, the surface of the earth or other celestial body. (*AACR 2, 1988 rev.:* 619)

General Information

When maps arrive in a map cylinder and are to be stored in map cases or on a flat surface, flatten by rolling them in the reverse direction in which they were stored and place them on a flat surface curled side down. Place weighted material on top. Check periodically to see if flattening has occurred. For maps that have been laminated or encased in clear plastic, holes should be punched in the covering to allow for air circulation. Older and more fragile maps may be lined with deacidified paper and encased in polyester film for preservation. This is usually done commercially and can be expensive but worth the investment. Some libraries prefer to use acid-free cloth tape to reinforce the edges, folds, and cracks of maps. There is no single correct way of storing maps. Both size and format should be considered when making storage decisions. It also is necessary to compare the features of each type of map storage and their implications for processing in relation to the size of the collection, the amount of available storage space, the desired accessibility for the collection, and the relative costs of each method. Because of the bulkiness, size, and awkward nature of maps, storage near the physical processing area of the library may be desirable.

Handling even small numbers of awkward, flapping, large maps requires much maneuvering room, ample consultation space, and copious storage spots. . . . Maps demand ample consultation space also because often the only map available on the studied topic is in a foreign language which must therefore be used with the help of foreign language glossaries, special indexes, or translation manuals. (Alonso 1975: 361–362)

Considerations for Horizontal Map Storage

- Multidrawer storage units are available in either steel or wood. Steel drawers may cost more but have the advantage of safety stops and run-on ball bearings, which guarantee ease of opening and closing. Wooden cases might be more attractive, but their bottoms can sag when heavily loaded.

- Cases stacked over eye level are less accessible than lower ones. If storage space is critical, more than one case may be stacked upon the other. For cases lower than eye level, the tops can be used for work space.

- Shallow drawers approximately 43 inches by 32 inches and no more than 2 or 2½ inches high are recommended (Ristow 1980: 64). These allow for easy removal and return of maps from the bottom as well as the top drawers. The unnecessary moving of sheet maps increases the danger of wear and tear as maps are filed in drawers.

- Some cases are equipped with fabric dust covers that hook at the back and front of the drawer and protect maps from dust as well as from catching or rubbing on the underside of the drawer above. Others have metal hoods at the back to keep maps in the drawer and flaps in the front to keep them from curling.

- Methods of protecting maps within drawers include placing them in transparent plastic open pockets, folders of pressboard, acid-free pliable material, or acid-free paper jackets. Maps can be grouped by geographic area, topic, or some other scheme and labeled with their contents. If entire folders are removed, the wear and tear on individual maps will be diminished.

- Large buckram-covered boxes similar to large pamphlet boxes are another option. They are made of plywood or heavy fiberboard and provide access through the front of the box with a double-hinged opening. The outer part of the box folds back on the top of the box, and the inner part folds down when opened. This allows for easy access to maps or folders without having to handle them all.

Considerations for Vertical Map Storage

- Vertical storage lends itself to quick browsing and easy accessibility. It also offers a minimum of wear and tear to items as they are handled. If this type of case has a lid, it protects the maps from dust.

- Most vertical or suspension cases require that a self-adhesive strip of material punched with holes be added to one edge of the map (top or side), and the strip is fitted over prongs in the case. Top access cases cannot be stacked one upon the other.

- Office file cabinets may serve for vertical storage of desk maps, but they are detrimental to larger formats, which would have to be folded to fit.

- Panel-style vertical storage is a type of hanging file often found in commercial stores that can be used in libraries as well. It uses hanging, framed clear panels in which maps may be placed.

Other Considerations for Map Storage

• Folded maps may be stored in drawers, boxes, and vertical files. Acid-free cloth strips can be used to reinforce folds. If folded maps are to be stored for any length of time, consideration should be given to flattening them, especially if they are to be retained permanently. As Nichols points out, "The folding and unfolding of the paper, even if always done correctly, creates a breaking strain on the paper at the folds and holes soon appear initially at the intersections of folds at right angles to one another" (Nichols 1982: 96).

• Maps mounted on rollers and stick mounts are two methods of storing large maps. Maps may be ordered commercially on sticks and roller mounts, or they may be mounted locally. When single-sided maps are to be placed on sticks locally, it is a good idea to mount them first on some type of linen or cloth backing. Double-sided maps may be protected by lamination or encapsulation before attaching sticks.

• Heavily used flat maps may be protected with lamination, encapsulation, or mounting cloth before they are stored in drawers or cylinders or are tied in rolls.

• There are three ways to store rolled maps: (1) upright in specially built bins or in large round containers (e.g., metal cans) that have been divided into partitions to help keep maps separated; (2) horizontal in pigeon-hole shelves built lengthwise to go under other shelving or on top of other shelving; or (3) horizontal on free-standing or wall-mounted map racks.

Map Labeling

Labels should be placed so that they are visible to the shelver, do not cover any essential information, and are located in a position consistent with library policy. Placement of identification labeling will depend on how maps are housed. For those stored in drawers or boxes, a label in the lower right or left corner of the map will be visible to the user and the shelver without having to remove the item from the drawer. Labeling the top of maps is handy for those hung from prongs or rods. For maps mounted on rollers or sticks, placing the identification label on the stick or roller allows easy identification without unrolling the map.

Single-Sided Map Labels

Option a: Processing without labels

Using a pen with permanent ink, write the call number, the map or part number (if there are multiple maps in a set), the copy and/or accession number (if used), the title, and the accompanying material designation on the front of the map in a location consistent with library policy. For example, some libraries may choose the lower left corner of the map for this type of information, or they may choose to place such marks near the title or copyright designation of the map, exercising caution not to cover important information (see Figure 3.5).

Figure 3.5
Processing a Single-sided Map without Labels

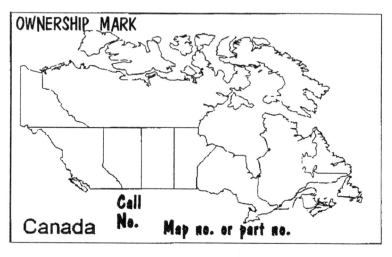

Option b: Processing with minimal labels

Brief call number labels may also be placed in the lower left corner of the map or in another location readily visible to staff and patrons and not covering essential information. Placement of the label should be in a position consistent with library policy.

Option c: Processing with labels

On an identification label, type or print the call number, the map or part number (if there are multiple maps in a set), the copy and/or accession number (if used), the author entry (if appropriate), the title, and the accompanying material designation (see Figure 3.6). By attaching this label on the reverse side of the map in either the upper or lower left corner, significant information is not covered.

Double-Sided Maps and Maps Mounted on Rollers

Option a: Processing without labels

In the lower left corner of side one, define a space which will hold approximately six lines of hand printing. Using a pen with permanent ink, write the call number, the map or part number (if there are multiple maps in a set), the copy and/or accession number (if used), the title, and the accompanying material designation on the map in a position consistent with library policy (see Figure 3.7).

Figure 3.6
Processing a Single-sided Map with Labels

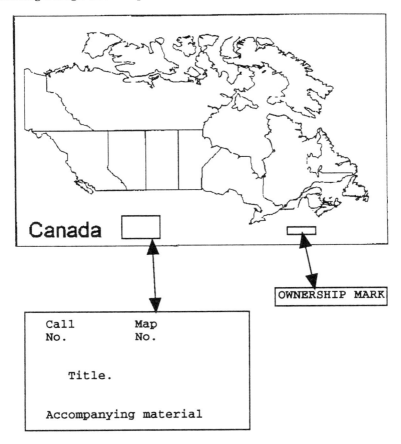

Option b: Processing with minimal labels

Relying on the commercially supplied information for the title, type or print the call number, the map or part number, and the copy and/or accession number (if used) on a label or on separate labels. Placement of the label should avoid covering any important information and be in a position consistent with library policy.

Option c: Processing with full labels

Attach an identification label with the call number, the map or part number, the copy and/or accession number, the author (if appropriate), the title, and the accompanying material designation to any area where significant information will not be covered (see identification label in Figure 3.8). Trim to fit if necessary.

Figure 3.7
Processing a Map Mounted on a Roller without Labels

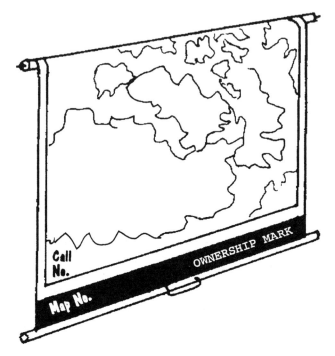

Ownership marks. Ownership stamps or labels should not cover vital information. Placement and consideration should depend on the type of storage and the method of preservation that is chosen. The library's ownership mark may be stamped along the blank borders or where space is available if there is printing in the borders. Preprinted or stamped labels with the library's ownership mark may be placed similarly.

Container Labeling

Option a: Maps stored in cylinders

On an identification label, type the call number, the map or part number, the copy and/or accession number (if used), the author (if appropriate), and the title (see the identification label in Figure 3.6). The label may be attached near the top of the cylinder opening.

Figure 3.8
Processing a Map Mounted on a Roller with Labels

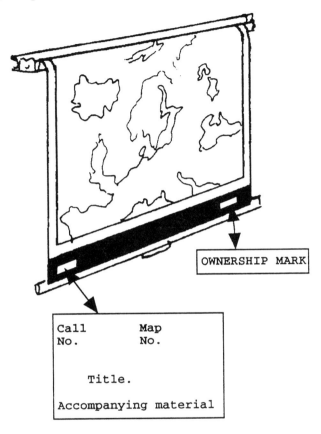

Option b: Folded map sets in boxes

If the container lacks a title, create a title label for one edge by typing the title on a label. Place an identification label (see the identification label in Figure 3.6) in a consistent place so it will be readable on the shelf. Placement of the label near the top will guarantee its life and protect it from smudging and tearing. Place a call number label on the lower part of the spine in a position consistent with library policy. If the spine is not wide enough, place the title label on the box top. It may be necessary to tie the box with archival string to ensure that it will stay shut. Be sure to use enough string so that someone with big fingers can still tie it.

Ownership marks. Using an ownership stamp, stamp three of the outside edges of the container, or place an ownership label on a conspicuous outside location.

Figure 3.9
Pockets for Circulation Spaced at Intervals for Flat Storage

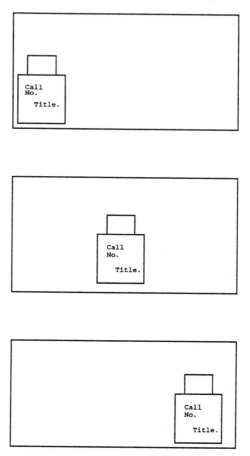

Pockets for Circulation

Option a: Single-sided maps

Pockets may be spaced at intervals on the reverse side of single-sided maps to prevent bulges from pocket buildup when maps are stored flat one upon the other. Attach pockets to the lower left corner on the first map, in the center lower edge for the next, and on the lower right edge for the next map (see Figure 3.9).

Option b: Double-sided maps

Pockets can be hinged using clear tape so that information may be read when the pocket is lifted. Attach these pockets along the lower edge as described in

"Option a: Single-sided maps." An alternative would be to attach a clear adhesive-backed pocket to map surfaces. This method is more secure and allows viewing beneath the pocket.

Option c: Maps stored in containers

Attach the pocket to the cylinder below the identification label.

Option d: Stick or roller maps

Circulation cards for roller maps may be stored at the circulation desk. Alternatively, a clear adhesive pocket may be affixed to the back of the map itself, near the attached stick or roller.

Option e: Folded map sets in boxes

Place circulation pockets on the inside top of the box lid.

Barcodes

Barcodes may be attached to the maps on areas lacking information, such as on borders or adjacent to circulation pockets. Barcodes may be placed on the boxes, either on the inside lid or on the outside edge of the lid in a position consistent with library policy.

Security Devices

Libraries may decide not to include security devices on maps because they usually are housed in special cases or in locations which require staff assistance. Large maps, due to their size, are difficult to remove from a library because they can be detected visually. If security devices are used, they may be placed on the bottom of containers used for storing maps. For individual maps, security devices may be placed on the map in a location lacking important information. These devices may be covered with a piece of opaque tape, which may or may not be stamped with an ownership mark. Security devices may also be located beneath opaque circulation pockets.

Accompanying Material

Accompanying material should follow the guidelines discussed in Chapter 2. If possible, such material should remain in the original container. Larger pieces of accompanying material should receive more permanent covering and should always be labeled. A call number should be placed on the cover of the accompanying material so that it is linked to its map. It is advisable to be consistent in placing ownership designations (stamps or labels) in a position consistent with library policy. When accompanying material is stored separately and barcodes are in general use for the rest of the collection, a unique barcode should be placed on each piece of accompanying material. This practice will help the library keep track of each separate circulation.

Gift Plates

Traditional gift plates may be attached adjacent to circulation pockets on single-sided maps and maps stored in cylinders. This placement will avoid bulges when the maps are laid on top of each other in map cases. Another choice includes typing GIFT OF and the donor's name on a small rectangular label and attaching it to a corner of the map or to an area lacking information.

REFERENCES

Alonso, Patricia Greechie. 1975. "Conservation and Circulation in Map Libraries." In *Map Librarianship: Readings,* compiled by Roman Drazniowsky. Metuchen, NJ: Scarecrow Press.

Anglo-American Cataloguing Rules, Second Edition, 1988 Revision, ed. by Michael Gorman and Paul W. Winkler for the Joint Steering Committee for Revision of AACR. Chicago: American Library Association.

Nichols, Harold. 1982. *Map Librarianship.* 2nd ed. London: Clive Bingley.

Olson, Nancy B. 1988. *Audiovisual Material Glossary.* Dublin, OH: OCLC Online Computer Library Center.

Ristow, Walter W. 1980. *The Emergence of Maps in Libraries.* Hamden, CT: Linnet Books.

4

Sound Recordings

Sound Recording. A recording on which sound vibrations have been registered by mechanical or electrical means so that the sound can be reproduced.

(AACR 2, 1988 rev.: 623)

Sound recordings include such diverse formats as discs, tapes, cartridges, cylinders, wires, and piano rolls. Each of these formats presents unique processing considerations. Although it is recognized that archival libraries and museums still may be dealing with some of the older sound formats (e.g., the wire recorder, the wax cylinder, and the piano roll), the emphasis of this chapter is on the sound formats commonly available from commercial suppliers and circulating in most libraries today. Included formats are the standard analog sound cassette (3⅞ inches by 2½ inches), the digital sound disc or CD (4¾ inches), the analog sound disc (33⅓ rpm, 78 rpm, or 45 rpm), and the analog sound tape reel (¼ inch). Some libraries may be adding new sound formats to their collections, but the processing specifications for the included formats can easily be extended to these new formats (e.g., analog cassette specifications may be applied to the digital compact cassette (DCC); and the 4¾-inch compact disc (CD) specifications may be applied to the MiniDisc, which measures 2½ inches).

Figure 4.1
Cassette with Knockout Tabs and Barcode

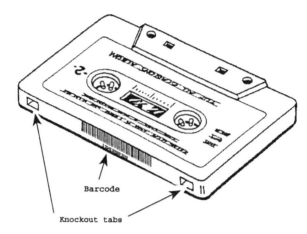

Barcode

Knockout tabs

SOUND CASSETTE

Definition: A permanently encased sound tape system incorporating both supply and take up reels. The term generally refers to the compact cassette system standardized by the North American Phillips Co. in 1963, the characteristics including a case measuring 3⅞ by 2½ in.; ⅛ in. tape; a playing speed of 1⅞ ips; four tracks with either one-channel sound (mono.) and two programs, one on each side, or two-channel sound (stereo.) and two programs, one on each side. (Olson 1988: 30)

General Information

Remove the erase protect tabs from the cassette (see Figure 4.1) if they have not been removed previously. This prevents the user from accidentally recording new information over the material or erasing the material from the tape.

Considerations for Cassette Storage

- Cassettes may be stored upright in their original plastic boxes with the tape rewound to the original supply reel.
- Cassettes may be stored in vinyl albums and binders with preformed trays to hold the cassettes.
- Cassettes may be stored in fiber and pressboard binders and boxes.
- Cassettes may be stored in cabinet drawers or catalog tray files.

(See also sections on storage in Chapter 1 and packaging/repackaging in Chapter 2.)

Cassette Containers

A variety of cassette containers are on the market. Price and user needs will determine what type of packaging to consider. For example, tapes cataloged individually may be stored in individual containers or in tape binders or albums that hold multiple cassettes. More than one user may want simultaneous access to individual tapes cataloged as a set. A decision must be made regarding whether they will be housed individually or together in multiple-cassette containers.

Option a: Cassette boxes

Cassette boxes are the small, hard plastic containers in which cassettes are usually sold. Depending on institutional policy, they may be used by themselves to house and circulate cassettes, or they may be placed into larger cassette albums or binders. When replacement packaging such as cassette albums or binders are used, often the original cassette boxes are not needed.

Option b: Vinyl containers

Vinyl sound cassette containers allow for storage of single and multiple cassettes. These containers come in two varieties. One is a three-ring binder which also allows for securing cassette storage pages and accompanying materials. The other type is the vinyl album with molded plastic storage trays and outer clear protective sleeves in which accompanying material may be stored. Such albums snap-lock shut, thus preventing loss and keeping material dust free. They also can be stored free standing on the shelf. Cassette boxes are generally eliminated when using these albums. The number of pages in accompanying material and other library preferences will determine which type of container will be more useful. Vinyl containers may be made from oil-based products and, therefore, may not be an environmentally sound product.

Option c: Pressboard binders

Pressboard cassette binders are more economical than the vinyl containers, but they do not lock shut and they lack storage space for accompanying material. Original cassette boxes may or may not be used in pressboard containers.

Option d: Corrugated boxes

Cassettes also may be stored in corrugated boxes made of fiberboard or heavy cardboard. Boxes come with or without inserts to hold the materials in place. These boxes require assembly. Corrugated boxes are simple to repair, and labels adhere well to their surfaces. The glue on labels does not break down because it is readily absorbed by the corrugated boxes.

Figure 4.2
Processing a Cassette without Labels

Cassette Labeling

Option a: Processing without labels

Using a pen with permanent ink, write the call number, the tape or part number (if there are multiple tapes in a set), and the copy and/or accession number (if used) directly on the cassette label above the knockout (see Figure 4.2). The knockout is the cutout portion of the cassette where the sprocket reels are located.

Ownership marks. The library's ownership mark may be printed on the 2⅞-inch by ⁵⁄₁₆-inch raised plastic section below the knockout if space is available and it will not cover any important information (see Figure 4.2).

Option b: Processing with minimal labels

Print with a pen using permanent ink or type the call number, tape or part number, copy number, and accession number (if used) on a label (see Figure 4.3). Apply to the cassette and avoid covering any important information on the cassette. Small labels may be used, thereby eliminating the need to cut or trim. Attach labels in preferred positions, as shown in Figure 4.3.

Ownership marks. The library's ownership mark may be stamped on a label or imprinted commercially on a label and applied in the raised section below the knockout, if space is available.

Option c: Processing with full labels

Full cassette labels, also called cutout or face labels, may be purchased as blank labels or commercially imprinted with the library's logo or ownership mark. (*Caution:* Over a period of time, the adhesive on some types of cassette labels may dry up and cause the labels to come off. If this happens, the label could become lodged in a cassette player, causing it to jam.) On a label, print

Figure 4.3
Processing a Cassette with Minimal Labels

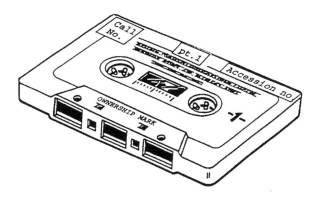

with a pen using permanent ink, or type the call number, the tape or part number, the copy number or accession number (if used), the author's name, and the title. Type "side A" or "side 1" to the right of the knockout. Libraries may choose to use the space below the knockout to type additional information, such as the individual pieces included on each side of the tape (see Figure 4.4).

Ownership marks. If using preprinted face labels, the ownership mark may be located below the knockout portion of the label, or this space may be used for in-house ownership stamps (see Figure 4.4).

Informational labels. A library may apply a small copyright protection label to the right of the knockout or below it on other available space on the cassette or its various packages. Such labels must be specially ordered by size and imprint. Preprinted or locally typed or printed REWIND or CONTINUED ON OTHER SIDE labels also may be applied where space is available (see Figure 4.4).

Cassette Box Labeling

Labels or other identification marks may be placed directly on the cassette box or on the paper liner inside the cassette box if the box is transparent. A cassette liner, sometimes called an inlay card or insert, is the heavy-weight paper inside the box that is supplied by the commercial producer. It lists the title, performer(s), specific titles of songs, and/or general program notes.

Option a: Cassettes in boxes with commercially prepared liners

The author and/or title information is usually part of the supplied data on cassette liners, so often it does not have to be repeated. However, title labels may be appropriate for both the front of the cassette box and its spine if they are otherwise lacking.

Spine labels. Create a call number spine label and attach it approximately ¼ inch from the bottom (see Figure 4.5). Call numbers may be placed on the front

Figure 4.4
Processing a Cassette with Full Labels

of the box in the upper left corner and on the bottom edge of the box spine or next to the hinged spine on the lower left bottom edge of the front of the box. Libraries may choose this latter position if they place call number labels in a position consistent with library policy on both print and nonprint materials (see Figure 4.5). If the box is transparent, the label may be placed on the liner spine rather than on the box itself (see Figure 4.5).

Ownership marks. A small label stamped, embossed, or imprinted with the library's name or logo (see Figure 4.5) may be placed on the front and/or back cover of the box in a position consistent with library policy. Another option includes using a permanent ink marker to write the ownership mark on the cassette box. It is advisable to develop a simple clear ownership mark if using this method.

Informational labels. Informational labels (e.g., copyright or loan period) may be placed on the front and/or back cover of the cassette box.

Option b: Locally produced cassettes or cassettes without commercial box liners

1. Create a box liner. If one is lacking, it may be desirable to create a liner by cutting a 4-inch by 6-inch index card or paper of equal weight into a 4-inch by 4⅛-inch rectangle. Create a fold at 2⁹⁄₁₆ inches and a second fold at 3¹⁄₁₆ inches on the 4⅛-inch width. The following is a suggested format for information to be included on the liner. Institutional guidelines will determine what is needed for each library. On the larger portion (4 inches long by 2⁹⁄₁₆ inches wide), type the call number, the tape or part number, the copy number, the accession number (if used), the author's name (if applicable), and the title. Type "side A" or "side 1" and its contents followed by "side B" or "side 2" and its contents. On the 1-inch section, type the author's name (if applicable) and the title. This is typed perpendicular to side A's typing. On the 1¼-inch portion, type or stamp the library's name and/or ownership mark (see Figure 4.6).

Figure 4.5
Commercially Produced Cassette Box Labeling

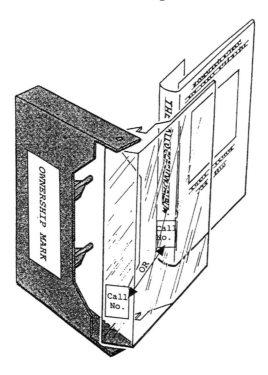

2. Create a brief box label. Using a label not larger than 2 inches by 3¾ inches, type or print the call number, the tape and/or copy number, the accession number (if used), the author's name (if applicable), and the title. Contents may be added if space is available. Attach to the front cover of the box (see Figure 4.7).

Labeling for Cassettes Stored in Cabinet Drawers or Catalog Trays

A small call number label may be placed on the left top edge of the cassette itself if the tray or drawer prohibits the use of cassette boxes. If cassette boxes are used in the drawers, follow the instructions for labeling cassette boxes; bypass the next section on cassette package labeling and proceed to the section on pockets for circulation.

Cassette Container Labeling

Labels or other identification marks may be placed directly on cassette albums, binders, and corrugated boxes. If the author and/or title information is

Figure 4.6
Locally Produced Cassette Box Liner

not already on the front cover, attach a label to the front of the container with the author's name (if applicable), the title, and possibly the contents of the set (see Figure 4.8). To create a title spine label, type the title on a label and apply it to the spine at least ¼ inch from the top. Call numbers may be placed on the front of the cassette package in the upper left corner and on the bottom edge of the package spine or next to the hinged spine on the lower left bottom edge of the front of the package. Libraries may choose this latter position if they consistently place call numbers in the same location on both print and nonprint materials.

Ownership marks. Ownership marks, whether commercially printed or stamped in house on a label, may be placed on the front and/or back cover of the package, being careful not to cover important information. However, labels are difficult to remove once they are in place for an extended period of time.

Informational labels. Copyright restrictions and rewind labels may be attached on the front cover of the container. Permanent pressure-sensitive date due labels also may be placed on the front cover.

Pockets for Circulation

The least protected place for the pocket is on the exterior of the container. Consistency of placement is important, but it will be affected by the availability

Figure 4.7
Locally Produced Brief Cassette Box Labeling

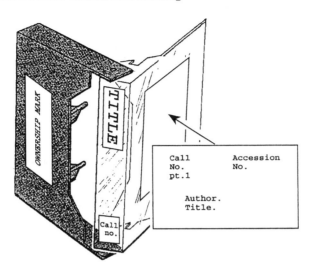

of a flat surface absent of critically important printed information. Circulation pockets may be affixed to the inside front cover of the binder or album if the surface is flat. It is also possible to place the pocket on the inside of the front or rear protective sleeve. Two strips of double-stick tape will secure the pocket to the inside of sleeves. Self-sticking vinyl pockets are also available. When no other option is available, pockets may be located along the center edge of the cover on the outside of the container.

Barcodes

If the library's policy is to place barcodes directly on items themselves rather than on their containers, a couple of options may be considered. Either the front or back of the cassette (where space is available) is a possibility, although side 2 may provide the most likely location that will not conflict with other information (see Figure 4.9). Another option is to place a small barcode along the top edge of the cassette between the protect tabs (see Figure 4.9).

If the container is the preferred location for barcodes, several locations are possible. The upper center edge of the front or back of the container is a convenient location, or the barcode can be placed adjacent to the circulation pocket as long as it does not cover important information. If the library's policy is to use duplicate barcodes or one-and-a-half barcodes, one may be placed on the cassette and another on the container, thus matching the cassette to the container. Another possibility is on the back of the container, parallel to the spine in the

Figure 4.8
Cassette Container Labeling

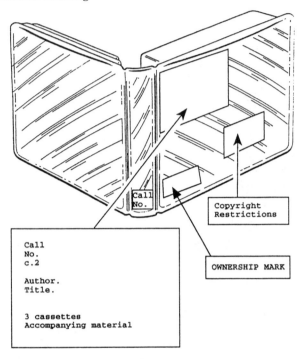

upper right-hand corner (see Figure 4.9). This location is easily accessible during shelf inventory.

Security Devices

Security strips or labels may be attached to the container without affecting the stability of the information on the cassette. Because such devices are magnetic, caution must be exercised to ensure that erasures will not happen during the desensitization process. Special equipment for desensitizing materials may be needed. It is advisable to make sure that existing security systems are compatible with new security devices. For a more complete discussion of security issues, refer to the section on security in Chapter 1.

Option a: Securing the cassette

A security device (i.e., label or strip) which is applied to the cassette itself is available. Small cassette-sized security strips or blank security labels may be placed under the full cassette face label, as described earlier in "Cassette La-

Figure 4.9
Barcode on Cassette

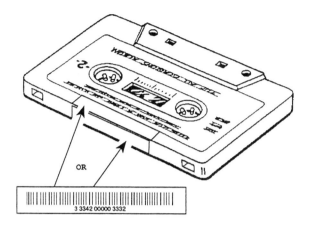

beling,'' options b and c. If the device is short, it also may be placed under the barcode.

Option b: Securing the container

Security devices that are embedded in labels (such as date due labels) may be placed on the front cover of the cassette container. Security strips may be placed under container labels or any other labels large enough to cover them.

Option c: Security boxes

Locked security boxes eliminate the need to secure the cassette itself or its box. They are available for the storage of the cassette and its container. Security strips similar to those used on print materials may be applied to the inside edge of the security box. The cassette container is then locked in the box. It is removed at the time of circulation. It is advisable to store security boxes at the circulation desk, where they are readily available for use when the cassette is returned. This process requires storage space but is a good theft deterrent.

Accompanying Material

Accompanying material for sound cassettes, including program notes, texts for plays, biographical or historical notes, and program guides, should be handled according to the guidelines discussed in Chapter 2. If possible, the accompanying material should remain in the case with the cassette. For example, vinyl cassette albums with clear plastic sleeves provide an ideal location for accompanying material. When folding is required to fit the accompanying material into the sleeve, it will be necessary to weigh the damage factor resulting from folding against the possibility of loss of the item. When using three-ring cassette binders, it usually is necessary to punch holes in accompanying material and place it in the binder. Larger pieces of accompanying material should receive more permanent covering. Accompanying material should always be labeled. A label with an identification or call number should be placed on the cover of the accompanying material so that it is linked to its cassette. It is advisable to be consistent in placing ownership designations (stamps or labels) according to individual library guidelines yet allow for flexibility if the choice is to cover essential information. When accompanying material is stored separately and barcodes are in general use for the rest of the collection, a unique barcode should be placed on each piece of accompanying material. This practice will help the library keep track of each separate circulation.

Gift Plates

A gift plate may be applied to the case which stores the cassette and/or its plastic box. It may be glued or cemented to the outside back cover or inside of the front cover, if room is available. When cassettes are stored in catalog trays or in their plastic boxes, some innovation is required in determining a location for gift plates. The plates may be cut to size and applied to an available area. In addition, plates may be inserted into the circulation pocket or hinged to the container if important information would otherwise be covered. Another option is to use a small pressure-sensitive label and type GIFT OF followed by the donor's name, if used. This may be applied to the container, the tape box, or the circulation pocket depending on the availability of space.

SOUND DISC: ANALOG

Definition: A flat circular platter or disc of plastic or other material on which sound vibrations are registered, and which is designed to be played back on a machine that reproduces the sound. The term includes . . . the conventional grooved Analog disc that is played with a stylus. . . . Also called Gramophone disc, Gramophone record, Phonograph record, Phonodisc, Record, etc. (Olson 1988: 30)

Considerations for Analog Disc Storage

- Sound discs may be stored in their original album jackets and boxes or in replacement albums and boxes.
- Sound discs should be stored vertically. Horizontal storage or off-vertical storage, as found in browse bins, can cause disc warpage.

(See also sections on storage in Chapter 1 and packaging/repackaging in Chapter 2.)

Analog Disc Containers

Inner sleeves. Inner sleeves are available commercially with and without poly lining. To ensure quality of sound, discs should be stored in inner sleeves to protect them from scratches, dust, and static electricity. Inner sleeves also protect the disc from hand oils when the disc is removed from the jacket.

Protective album covers. Clear vinyl album or jacket covers are an excellent choice for protecting the long life of commercial disc jackets and the recording itself. The covers are available for both single and multiple recordings. Some album covers come with heat-sealed circulation pockets, thus making them more attractive for processing. If pockets are not provided, follow the directions for pockets given in the section "Pockets for Circulation," which appears later in this chapter. To avoid theft of clear covers, it is a good idea to attach ownership marks to them. Some libraries staple the upper left corner through the plastic cover and the cardboard album cover. Thus the cardboard album cover cannot be easily removed from the protective cover.

Replacement disc holders. Pressboard disc holders, boxes, and replacement jackets are available commercially and are especially useful when the album cover is no longer serviceable.

Boxed set reinforcement. To increase shelf life, a library may want to reinforce the corners of original or replacement boxes which house disc sets. Measure the depth of the container and cut a piece of 3-inch-wide clear tape to the same width as the depth of the case. Cut it in half and apply to the corner. Repeat for the remaining corners. Repair tape wings for books could also be used in some cases.

Sound Disc Labeling

Each library's processing policies will determine whether commercially supplied information will be covered by labels that are created in house. Any of the following options may be used on single or multiple discs. It is important to maintain consistency in method whenever possible.

Option a: Processing without labels

Using a pen with permanent ink, write the call number, the disc or part number, and the copy number and/or accession number (if used) directly on the sound disc label (see Figure 4.10).

Ownership marks. Ownership marks may be written on the commercially produced label where space is available (see Figure 4.10).

Option b: Processing with minimal labels

If the commercially supplied label contains the author/composer and title, this information does not need to be repeated. If it is not supplied, print with a pen

Figure 4.10
Processing Disc without Labels

using permanent ink, or type the call number, disc or part number, and copy number and/or accession number (if used) on a label. Another alternative is to print or type the desired information on several small labels. Place label(s) on the commercially supplied label, making sure not to cover any important information (see Figure 4.11).

Ownership marks. The library's ownership mark may be typed or stamped on a label. Curved preprinted labels with the library name or ownership mark also can be obtained commercially. Either may be used when processing with minimal labels (see Figure 4.11).

Option c: Processing with full labels

On a curved disc label or rectangular label, type the call number, the disc or part number, the copy number and/or the accession number (if used), the author's name (if applicable), and the title. These labels are placed over the disc's commercially supplied label (see Figure 4.12).

Ownership marks. The library's ownership mark may be printed or stamped on the commercial sound disc label or on the curved label. When using the half-moon label, the library's name may be preprinted commercially on the label or the name may be stamped in house (using a curved stamp) on the curved portion of the label. To deter theft, ownership marks may also be placed on the sleeves, but it is not necessary to add call number labels.

Figure 4.11
Processing Disc with Minimal Labels

Album Jacket Labeling

Option a: Simplified label processing

On a label, print with a pen using permanent ink or type the call number, the disc or part number, the copy number, and the accession number (if used). Contents information (see Figure 4.13) is optional. Placement of this label on the album jacket in a location consistent with library policy guarantees patron and staff easy access while bin browsing or shelving.

Option b: Full label processing

On a label, print with a pen using permanent ink or type the call number, the disc or part number, the copy number and the accession number (if used), the author's name (if applicable), the title, and the accompanying material designation. The accompanying material may be either specific ("3 sound discs, 1 libretto, 1 program note") or it may be general ("Accompanying Materials"). This label may be placed in an area lacking important information (see Figure 4.14).

Spine labels. A call number label may be applied to the spine if it is wide enough for the number to be readable, or to the lower left front cover if the spine is too narrow for the call number label.

Figure 4.12
Processing Disc with Full Labels

Ownership marks. Ownership marks may be commercially preprinted on labels or stamped in house on a label and placed on the front and/or back cover of the album, being careful not to cover important information. However, labels are difficult to remove once they are in place for an extended period of time.

Pockets for Circulation

Option a: Inside the album jacket

Opaque pockets for circulation may be applied inside the album jacket opening along the side back edge (see Figure 4.15). Use double-stick tape, glue, or rubber cement to attach the pocket to the jacket.

Option b: Front top cover of the album jacket

A clear vinyl self-sticking pocket or an opaque pocket may be applied to the front of the album. Vinyl pockets allow the user to read information on the album cover underneath the pocket.

Option c: Multiple disc boxes

An opaque pocket may be hinged in the center on the inside front cover using ¾-inch clear tape. This will allow the pocket to be lifted so that information beneath the pocket on the box is readable. If this is not a concern, the pocket may be attached using glue, double-sided tape, or rubber cement.

Figure 4.13
Album Jacket with Simplified Label Processing

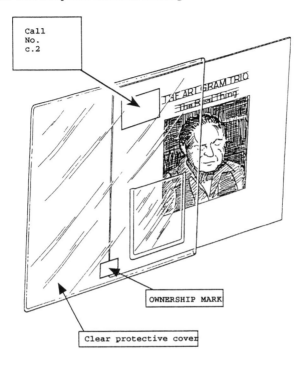

Barcodes

Individual library policy will determine placement of barcodes. When determining the location on items and/or their containers, consistency of placement is important.

Option a: Sound disc

Barcodes may be placed on either side of the disc, being careful to cover as little information as possible. If the curved ownership label has been applied to side 1, then the barcode may be applied to side 2 of the disc. Placement on the disc guarantees that staff know if the disc has been returned.

Option b: Album jacket

Several locations are possible when barcodes are applied to the album jacket or box. Some libraries may choose to apply the barcode to the upper right corner of the back of the container parallel to the spine. This position is easily accessible during shelf inventory. Exercise caution not to cover important information. Some libraries may prefer to locate the barcode on the upper center edge of the front or back cover of the container, where it is always easily accessible.

Figure 4.14
Album Jacket with Full Labeling

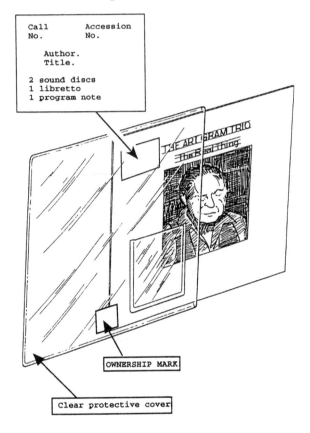

Placement directly adjacent to the circulation pocket is another favored location. Multiple barcodes may be placed under each other if library policy prescribes individual barcodes for each disc in a set (see Figure 4.16). This placement is ideal for inventory scanning and speeds up circulation because it does not require physical contact with each disc.

Option c: Disc and album jacket

This method requires duplicate barcodes, one for the disc and one for the disc jacket. The checkout process is speeded up because staff could scan the barcode on the album. At time of check-in, staff would be required to scan the barcode on the individual recordings, thus guaranteeing that staff know if each disc has been returned. This method provides the advantages of previous options, but it requires staff to have physical contact with each disc at check-in. Staff must be

Figure 4.15
Pocket for Circulation Located inside the Album Cover

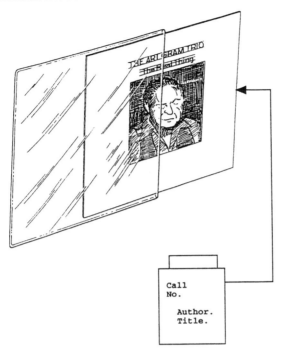

cautious in the handling of the disc, touching only its edges and thereby avoiding disc deterioration from finger oils.

Security Strips

For a more complete discussion, see the section on security in Chapter 1. Security strips or labels may be attached to the container or disc without affecting the stability of the information on the sound disc.

Option a: Security strips

The same security devices used on books may be placed on the interior edge of the slip case or the jacket where they are not easily detected. They may be applied on the inner spine of multiple-disc sets. Cover the strip with a piece of opaque colored tape or a label. Alternatively, security strips used on sound discs may be placed on the disc label under an ownership label or under a full processing identification label.

Option b: Security labels

Security devices embedded in labels come in several varieties, which include blank labels, date due labels, special information labels (e.g., HANDLE WITH

Figure 4.16
Barcode on Album Jacket

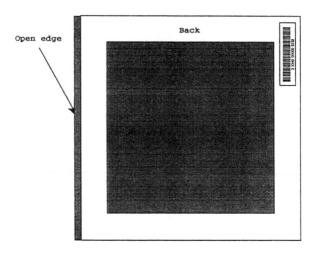

CARE), and ownership labels. Placement on the album cover should follow library guidelines for placement on other types of materials.

Accompanying Material

Accompanying materials, including program notes and librettos, usually are laid in sound disc boxes or inserted into jackets and should follow the guidelines discussed in Chapter 2. Larger pieces of accompanying material should receive more permanent covering. Accompanying material should always be secured with labels. A label with an identification or call number may be placed on the cover of the accompanying material so that it is linked to its sound disc. It is advisable to be consistent in placing ownership designations (stamps or labels) according to established guidelines. When accompanying material is stored separately and barcodes are in general use for the rest of the collection, a unique barcode should be placed on each piece of accompanying material. This practice will help the library keep track of each separate circulation.

Gift Plates

Gift plates may be attached inside the back of the jacket adjacent to the circulation pocket or inside the top cover of boxed albums. Some libraries may prefer attaching the gift plate to the outside front cover of both single and boxed albums with the hinging method to avoid covering significant information.

SOUND DISC: DIGITAL (CD)

Definition: A type of optical disc produced and read with laser technology on which . . . sound may be recorded. They are 4 ¾ . . . in. in diameter and contain up to 60 minutes of continuous playing time. *Also called* . . . **Compact audiodisc, Digital audiodisc, Laser optical disc.** (Olson 1988: 6)

General Information

Playing surfaces should be treated with care and kept free of grease, dust, and fingerprints. Compact discs are new enough that the long-term effect of any type of labeling on the disc is not known. Some librarians maintain that any labels affect the balance of the disc spinning at great speeds and distort the sound. Others believe that it is acceptable to attach a circular label to the clear plastic area immediately surrounding the center hole of the disc without affecting playback quality. All agree that labels should not be attached to any of the metallic areas of the disc. Therefore, it is important to keep up to date with the latest literature on the subject.

Considerations for Digital Disc (CD) Storage

- Compact discs may be stored upright in their original jewel cases and/or in vinyl or pressboard albums.
- Compact discs may be stored horizontally in their original containers in specially designed compartmentalized shelving.

Digital Disc (CD) Containers

CD containers are available as clear plastic jewel cases, vinyl albums, and pressboard binders. Each stores single and double discs.

Vinyl albums. Vinyl albums come in several varieties with and without molded inserts. Those without the inserts have sleeves or pockets which hold the discs and accompanying materials. Those with inserts hold either the jewel case or the disc itself. A hub similar to the one found in jewel cases secures the CD in the album. Albums provide an alternative to broken jewel cases.

Pressboard binders. Pressboard binders are less expensive than vinyl albums and provide some protection. Some libraries prefer vinyl albums because they are free standing and may even last longer than pressboard binders. Others prefer pressboard binders to vinyl packaging as ecologically more sound, more versatile, and less expensive.

Display sleeves. CD display sleeves provide additional protection for compact discs. Usually used in browsing bins, display sleeves or displayers have two separate sleeves—one that holds the disc and the other that holds its descriptive brochure.

Figure 4.17
Processing a CD without Labels

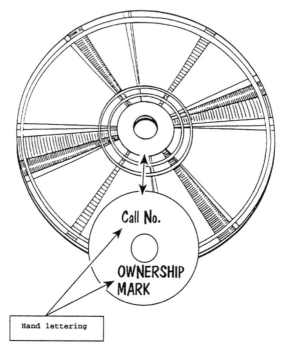

(See also sections on storage in Chapter 1 and packaging/repackaging in Chapter 2.)

Compact Disc Labeling

Most compact discs are labeled commercially and include the author/composer and title selections recorded on the disc.

Option a: Processing without labels

A library may prefer to use a permanent ink marking pen because it preserves commercially supplied information. However, the latest research indicates that chemicals used in marking pen ink may corrode the plastic covering and eventually damage the metallic surface. Water-based, felt-tipped markers will not accomplish the desired end because they are easily removable. A short identification or brief call number may be written on the clear inner gripping ring of the CD, thus linking the disc to the container (see Figure 4.17). Those who are more conservative tend to avoid marking the disc in any way and mark the container instead. This can create a problem if discs are returned in the wrong container.

Figure 4.18
CD with Embossed Ownership Mark on Clear Ring

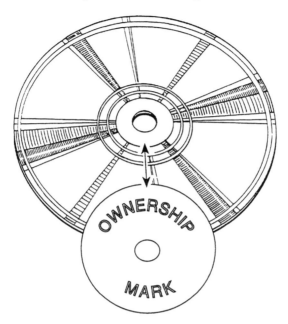

Ownership marks. Using a pen with permanent ink, an ownership mark may be put on the clear plastic portion of the disc's center but not on any of the surfaces covering the metallic layer (see Figure 4.17). Another option for ownership marks is an embossing device developed for use on the clear plastic portion of the disc (see Figure 4.18). However, because of the fragile nature of the laser disc, extreme caution should be used when considering any device that might cause a strain to the CD's protective lacquer coating.

Option b: Processing with labels on disc's clear center

Even though the CD was thought to be indestructible, we now realize that CD surfaces read by the laser beam should never have labels attached to their metallic surfaces. Some librarians are concerned that even the adhesive on circular center labels may cause corrosion of the disc. Such labels are available commercially and are designed to be placed over the inner clear gripping ring of the CD. The call number or a brief identification number may be written or typed on these labels (see Figure 4.19). Circular center labels come in sets with a rectangular container label and two spine labels, which work well for call numbers and/or spine titles. Each library will need to review the cost of the label sets and the efficiency of this method.

Ownership marks. Circular center labels may be commercially imprinted with an ownership mark or stamped in house with a circular stamp.

Figure 4.19
Processing a CD with Labels

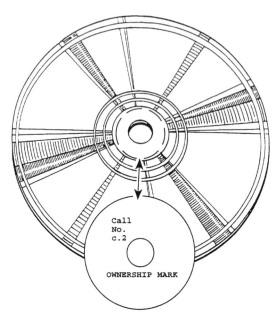

Compact Disc Container Labeling

The compact disc jewel box, album, or display sleeve are the primary locations for ownership marks and labels. The front cover of the container is a good location for the identification label. This label may contain the call number, the disc or part number, the copy number and/or the accession number (if used), the author's name (if applicable), a uniform title, the actual title, the number of discs in the container, and an accompanying material designation (see Figure 4.20). Various combinations are possible. Placement should be in a position consistent with library policy. A library may choose not to use this label if the container has a clear cover that shows the desired information.

Ownership marks. Ownership marks should be visibly placed on the front and/or back cover of the CD container. A library may choose to use a pen with permanent ink to print the library name or ownership mark on the plastic container. Another possibility includes using a small label stamped, imprinted, or embossed with the library's name or logo, which may be placed in a prominent place on the front or back cover (see Figure 4.20). However, labels are difficult to remove once they are in place for an extended period of time.

Spine labels. A brief call number label may be placed on the container cover in a position consistent with library policy (i.e., the lower portion of the spine

Figure 4.20
Processing a Compact Disc Container with Labels

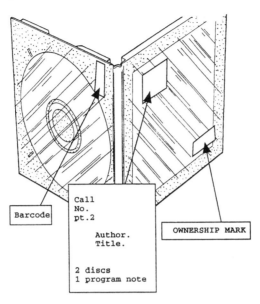

Barcode

Call
No.
pt.2

Author.
Title.

OWNERSHIP MARK

2 discs
1 program note

or the front cover not covering the manufacturer's record number or other unique information).

Pockets for Circulation

Traditional circulation pockets may be attached to the CD container on either the front or back, depending on local library guidelines. Self-sticking clear vinyl pockets allow the user to read information beneath the pocket. As an alternative, permanent pressure-sensitive date due labels may be placed on the front cover above the call number label.

Barcodes

Barcodes should never be placed on the disc itself. Several locations are possible for barcodes on the outside of the container, depending on institutional guidelines. Being sensitive not to cover important information, some libraries prefer placing the barcode adjacent to the circulation pocket. Other libraries prefer to locate the barcode in the upper center edge of the front or back of the container, where it is always easily accessible. Another possibility is the back of the container, parallel to the spine in the upper right-hand corner (see Figure 4.20). This location is easily accessible during shelf inventory. If libraries display cases without discs, they may decide to place barcodes inside the container.

When the case is returned and the disc removed, the barcode may be scanned to clear the CD. For multidisc sets, individual barcodes for each CD may be placed one above the other in volume number order on the container.

Security Devices

Security devices may be attached to the container. For security devices on discs, librarians may wish to check with security vendors before applying any security device to the CD in case the device would affect the discs. Spin wobble, or distortion of sound from unbalanced spinning, is to be avoided.

Option a: Security strips

1. Securing the disc. (For a more detailed discussion, see the section on security in Chapter 1.) A specially sized magnetic strip may be applied to the compact disc and covered by a transparent overlay. At this time there is some disagreement among experts as to whether the strips may cause distortion of sound and whether these adhesive overlays will protect or harm the CD surface. It is important to realize that overlays become permanent within a few hours and removal may damage the disc. Librarians are cautioned to review the latest literature and check with their security vendors to determine the usefulness of this method. Special equipment for desensitizing materials may be needed due to the small size of the strips. It is advisable to make sure that the new security devices are compatible with existing security systems.

2. Securing the paper liner cover or the container. One suggested location for the security strip is the paper cover under the molded plastic holder which secures the compact disc. Remove the compact disc and pop the plastic holder out. Attach the strip diagonally to the cover liner. Replace the plastic holder which covers the strip and the compact disc. Strips also may be placed in the spine of the container, making sure that they are not visible.

Option b: Security labels

Radio frequency labels are not an option for compact discs. The high metal content of the disc tends to shield the sensor tag, and the weight of the label itself could cause spin wobble (Dick 1990: 39). Security labels should be attached *only* to the CD container in a position consistent with library policy. They may be imprinted with an ownership mark or other information, or they may be blank. Blank security labels may be hidden under an ownership mark or any printed label.

Option c: Security boxes

Security boxes are available for storage of the CD and its container. These boxes are locked. Security strips or security labels may be placed on the box. The CD container is then locked in the box. It is removed from the security box at the time of circulation.

Accompanying Material

Accompanying material for compact discs, such as program notes or librettos, should follow the guidelines discussed in Chapter 2. If possible, the accompanying material should remain in the CD container. Larger pieces of accompanying material should receive more permanent covering. Accompanying material should always be labeled. A label with an identification or call number should be placed on the cover of the accompanying material so that it is linked to its compact disc. It is advisable to be consistent in placing ownership designations (stamps or labels) according to established guidelines. When accompanying material is stored separately and barcodes are in general use for the rest of the collection, a unique barcode should be placed on each piece of accompanying material. This practice will help the library keep track of each separate circulation.

Gift Plates

Traditional gift plates may be inserted into the circulation pocket. When boxed editions housing multiple CDs retain the boxes, the plates may be applied to the outside of the container. A hinge method of attachment may be necessary so useful information is not covered. Another possibility is to type on a blank label GIFT PLATE and the donor's name and date (if used) and apply the label to the CD container in an area devoid of information.

SOUND REEL TAPES

Definition: A sound recording tape wound on an unenclosed reel, and requiring a separate unenclosed take-up reel during playback. Standard characteristics include ¼ in. tape; reels of 5, 7, or 10½ in. diameter; playing speeds of 1⅞, ¾, 7½ and 15 ips. There are alternate tracks on stereophonic tapes. Also called **Sound reel.** (Olson 1988: 31)

General Information

A sound reel tape should have tape leader spliced to the beginning and end of each tape. If there is a side 1 and side 2 they can be differentiated by using different colors of leader. The outside loose end of the tape leader may be secured onto the reel of tape by attaching a narrow piece of masking tape or some other suitable pressure-sensitive tape to the tape leader.

Considerations for Sound Reel Tape Storage

• Sound reel tapes may be stored in plastic bags inside their boxes to protect the tape from dust and humidity.

Figure 4.21
Processing a Plastic Reel without Labels

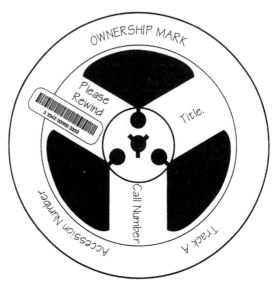

• Vertical storage of tape boxes allows for the most efficient use of storage space.

• Sound reel tapes should be stored away from all potentially damaging magnetic fields.

(See also sections on storage in Chapter 1 and packaging/repackaging in Chapter 20)

Sound Reel Tape Labeling

A library may choose to use the protective tape leader for labeling. The library's ownership mark may be written on the leader tape using a pen with permanent ink. Possible information to be added includes the call number, the reel or part number, the copy number, and the accession number (if used) and/or barcode number. This information must be kept to a minimum.

Plastic Reel Labeling

Option a: Processing without labels

Using a pen with permanent ink, write the call number on one of the arms between the openings of the tape reel. Write the title on another arm. The last arm may be left for barcode placement. Write the accession number (if used) on a curve of the reel, TRACK A or TRACK 1 on another curve, and the

Figure 4.22
Processing a Plastic Reel with Labels

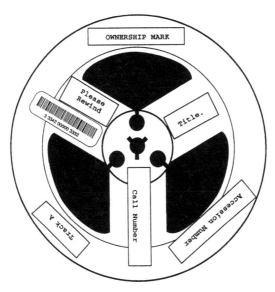

library's name in the last curve. All writing should face the same direction, as shown in Figure 4.21.

Option b: Processing with labels

Labels may need to be trimmed to fit the designated label location on the plastic arms located between the openings of the reel. On the first arm, attach the call number label. Trim to fit. Using a small label, type or print the title and the accession number (if used). Trim to fit and adhere to the second arm of the reel, making sure that all type faces the same direction. Trim two curved labels to fit in the curved spaces above the opening; on the first, type the accession number, and on the second label type TRACK A or TRACK 1. Affix all three labels to the spaces above the openings so that all letters face the same direction (see Figure 4.22).

Ownership marks. A curved label may be purchased commercially and imprinted with the library's ownership mark or made in house by stamping a curved label with the library's ownership mark. Attach the ownership label to the spaces above the openings so that all lettering faces the same direction (see Figure 4.22).

Informational labels. Place a REWIND label, SPEED label, and/or TRACK label on an outside curve where space is available. A label may be provided indicating whether the tape uses one, two, four, or eight tracks (see Figure 4.22). The proper choice of playback equipment is contingent on having this information (see Figure 4.22). Make a label that gives information about the tape speed.

Figure 4.23
Processing a Sound Reel Box with Labels

Sound tape reels can be recorded at 7½ inches per second (ips), ¾ ips, and 1⅞ ips.

Sound Reel Tape Box Labeling

On a label, type the call number, the author's name (if applicable), a uniform title (if used), the title, and the accompanying material (see Figure 4.23).

Ownership marks. The ownership marks should be visibly placed on the front and/or back cover of the container, using either a label, stamp, or marker to print the library's name.

Informational labels. A COPYRIGHT PROTECTION label may be placed in the lower right corner of the outside top cover. A REWIND label may be placed where space is available.

Pockets for Circulation

Circulation pockets may be applied to the inside lid of the sound tape reel box. They may be permanently attached to the top of the lid or hinged in place using tape. The hinge method of attaching pockets makes it possible to read information beneath the pockets.

Barcodes

Option a: Barcode on reel

Place the barcode on one arm of the reel (see Figure 4.21). If it is necessary to trim the barcode label, check with your vendor to see if trimming will cause problems. Attach the barcode so that all lettering faces the same direction as other labels.

Option b: Barcode on container

Placement should be consistent with library policy. Location of barcodes in the upper center edge of the front or back of the container is a convenient location, as is placement adjacent to circulation pockets. Barcode placement on the back of the container parallel to the spine in the upper right-hand corner allows for easy access during shelf inventory.

Option c: Barcode on container and reel

It is possible to use a barcode on both the reel and the container by combining both options a and b.

Security Devices

Apply security devices that come in strips to the inside spine of the container and cover with a long label or opaque strip of tape. If using security devices embedded in labels, apply them on the top front cover in a position consistent with library policy. It is advisable not to cover important information. Special equipment for desensitizing materials may be needed. It is advisable to make sure that existing security systems are compatible with the smaller security strips.

Accompanying Material

Accompanying material for sound reel tapes, including program notes, texts of speeches, and biographical or historical notes, may be laid in the box. When folding is required to fit the accompanying material into the box, it will be necessary to weigh the damage factor resulting from folding against the possibility of item loss. Larger pieces of accompanying material should receive more permanent covering. Accompanying material should also be secured with labels. A label with an identification number should be placed on the cover of the accompanying material so that it is linked to its reel. It is advisable to place ownership designations (stamps or labels) in a position consistent with library policy. When accompanying material is stored separately and barcodes are in general use for the rest of the collection, a unique barcode should be placed on each piece of accompanying material. This practice will help the library keep track of each separate circulation.

Gift Plates

Gift plates may be applied to the inside bottom or top of a sound reel tape box (if there is sufficient room). Hinged plates make it possible to read information beneath the plates.

REFERENCES

Anglo-American Cataloguing Rules, Second Edition, 1988 Revision, ed. by Michael Gorman and Paul W. Winkler for the Joint Steering Committee for Revision of AACR. Chicago: American Library Association.

Dick, Jeff T. 1990. "Laserdisc Redux." *Library Journal* (November 15): 37–39.

Olson, Nancy B. 1988. *Audiovisual Material Glossary.* Dublin, OH: OCLC Online Computer Library Center.

5

Motion Pictures
and Videorecordings

Motion pictures and videorecordings have the common characteristic of being able to present images that appear to be in motion, although each of the mediums is able to capture still images as well. Both formats appear in a variety of physical forms (e.g., cartridges, cassettes, loops, discs, and reels), and each form requires its own physical processing decisions.

MOTION PICTURE

Definition: A length of film, with or without recorded sound, bearing a sequence of images that create the illusion of movement when projected in rapid succession. (*AACR 2, 1988 rev.:* 620)

General Information

Although 35-mm and 70-mm film are used in the commercial production of motion pictures, neither are commonly found in circulating library collections. Instead, the motion pictures found in libraries are 16-mm film reels, 8-mm film reels, 8-mm film cartridges (often referred to as film loops), and film cassettes. The only one currently being marketed for libraries is the 16-mm format, but many library collections still circulate and process the other motion picture formats. Basic processing elements are similar for 16-mm and 8-mm reels, and the processing options for cartridges parallel those for cassettes.

Because motion picture film is an especially fragile medium, it is susceptible to anything that might scratch or damage its surface. It is a good idea to use cotton gloves whenever film is handled. Precautions should be taken not to have film near any sharp or jagged surfaces that could scratch the emulsion or tear the sprocket holes. Labels should not be attached to any type of film because they can be caught in a projector and cause major film damage. Label the film leader instead.

16-mm REEL FILM (OR 8-mm REEL FILM)

Definition: A thin sheet or strip of transparent or translucent material coated with a light-sensitive emulsion. The base is usually a plastic material such as cellulose acetate. (Olson 1988: 12)

General Information

Reel film comes in 16-mm and 8-mm widths with sprocket holes along one edge. Most film has either an optical or a magnetic sound track along the other edge of the film. Reel film should be secured with film leader at the head (beginning) and the tail (end) of the film to protect the film from projector damage. Different colors of leader are preferred for each (e.g., green for the head and red for the tail) to alert the user to how the film is wound on the reel. Self-cleaning varieties of leader are also available that are designed to pick up any dust or dirt that might be lingering in the film gate area of the projector.

Films should be inspected and cleaned after each use, because minor problems can turn into major problems if not taken care of prior to the next use. Some libraries will recommend that films be returned unwound so that the film will be in running position after its cleaning and inspection. This policy may necessitate supplying the take-up reel to certain users. Others will request that film be rewound after use because the film will be run through an inspection and then rewound (these libraries prefer their own rewind on the film to provide proper tension). An informational label that states the local winding policy should be placed on the film container during processing.

Considerations for Film Storage

- Because of its combustibility and dangerous fumes, nitrate-based film should not be stored in the library. For specific storage instructions, consult a film conservator.
- Archival safety film may be stored on large hubs in horizontal stacks of no more than two or three reels.
- Circulating safety film may be stored vertically in separator racks on baked enamel shelves.
- Reel film may be stored on enameled steel or heavy-gauge plastic reels in steel or

Figure 5.1
Film Leader Labeling

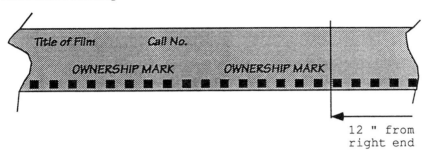

12 " from
right end

plastic film cans. Film reels also may be stored in heavy plastic locking cases that are stored vertically.

Film Labeling

It is advisable to use the film leader for labeling. Never label the film itself. Using a 6-foot piece of head leader with the sprocket holes down, print the call number, the film or part number (if there is more than one reel of film), and the copy number and/or accession number (if used) on the leader approximately 12 inches from the right end, allowing plenty of room for torn leader during use. To the left of the call number, print the name of the film and any part number which is considered part of the title (see Figure 5.1). Repeat the same type of marking on a 3-foot piece of tail leader, with the call number beginning approximately 10 inches from the left end of the tail (see Figure 5.2).

Ownership marks. If the library has not purchased preprinted leader with the library's name on it, the library's ownership mark may be written on the leader and the tail using a pen with permanent ink or a heat stylus and transfer tape. It is a good idea to repeat the ownership mark every 6 to 8 inches in case a large piece of leader or tail is damaged.

Film Reel Labeling

Libraries that rent films to patrons may choose not to label their film reels, especially if they have a policy that the borrower should not rewind the film. For libraries that wish to label their reels, the following options are available.

Option a: Processing without labels

Using a pen with permanent ink, write the call number on one of the arms between the openings of the film reel. Write the title on another arm. Write the copy number and/or accession number (if used) on a curve of the reel or on another arm, and write the library's name in the last curve or near the center

Figure 5.2
Film Tail Labeling

10 " from
left end

hole. All writing should face the same direction, as shown in Figure 5.3. One arm may be used for barcode placement, if that location seems appropriate.

Option b: Processing with labels

As noted earlier, some libraries may choose not to label reels. If used, labels may need to be trimmed to fit in the designated locations of the arms between the openings of the reel. Prepare a call number label and attach it to one arm of the reel. Using another small label, type the title and attach it to the next arm of the reel, making sure that all type faces the same direction. Type the copy number and/or accession number (if used), and place it on the curve of the reel or on another arm. One arm may be used for barcode placement also (see Figure 5.3).

Ownership marks. Preprinted ownership labels or blank labels with stamped or typed ownership marks may be placed on the curved spaces above the opening or near the center hole of the reel (see Figure 5.3).

Informational labels. Place a REWIND label or DO NOT REWIND label on the reel in a prominent place following library guidelines. If the format is 8 mm, specify whether the gauge is STANDARD 8 MM or SUPER 8 MM.

Film Can or Case Labeling

For films stored in film cans or cases, if the commercial label is lacking or is incomplete, type an identification label (as shown in Figure 5.4) with the title, call number, part number (if there is more than one container for the film), copy number and/or accession number (if used), and the contents of the accompanying material and place it in the center of the top of the film can or case or in the upper left corner of the top of the film case.

Spine labels. Various methods can be used to label the sides of film cans and cases. Hand lettering of the call number and title with a pen using permanent ink is one option. Another is to use a desktop electronic labeling system or a

Figure 5.3
Processing a Film Reel

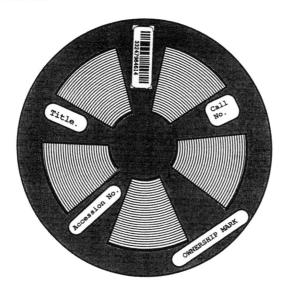

typewriter to generate narrow adhesive-backed labels. A third option is to generate an adhesive-backed, punch-type plastic label that will adhere to the edge of the can or case. Whichever method is chosen, letters and numbers should be large enough to read when the film is filed on the shelves. Some libraries may wish to place ownership marks on the spine.

Ownership marks. Ownership marks should be placed visibly on the top of the film container using either a label, stamp, or permanent marker to print the library's name.

Informational labels. A copyright restriction label may be placed near the title on the container. According to library policy, place either a REWIND label or DO NOT REWIND label on the top of the container in a prominent place. If the format is 8 mm, specify whether the gauge is STANDARD 8 MM or SUPER 8 MM.

Pockets for Circulation

Circulation pockets may be applied to the inside or the outside of the film container, but a protected location inside will usually prove to be the most durable. Pockets may be either attached permanently or hinged in place using tape. When the hinging method is chosen to allow access to information beneath the pocket, it should always be on an inside location.

Figure 5.4
Film Container Labeling

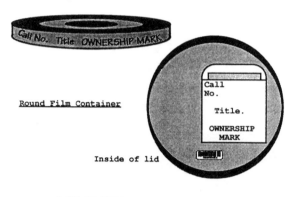

Round Film Container

Inside of lid

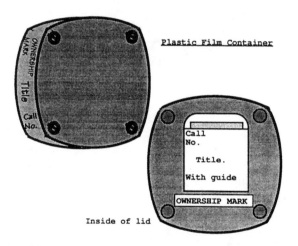

Plastic Film Container

Inside of lid

Barcodes

Option a: Barcode on reel

For libraries that have the policy of placing barcodes on the item itself whenever possible, the film reel could be used instead. However, because libraries may not always get their own reels returned, other locations may be preferred. If the reel is used, place the barcode on one arm of the reel, as shown in Figure 5.3. Attach the barcode so that all lettering faces the same direction as other labels.

Option b: Barcode on container

Placement should be consistent with library policy; several locations are possible. Some film libraries place the barcode on the outside front of the container, whereas others place the barcode on the inside of the container. If choosing the outside, the upper center edge of the front or back of the container or directly adjacent to the circulation pocket are convenient locations. Other libraries may prefer to place the barcode inside the container on the lid or on the bottom under the film to encourage circulation personnel to perform a visual check that the correct reel is in the container. If the circulation pocket is inside, locate the barcode on or near it for ease at check-out. The important thing is to be consistent with placement on similar kinds of containers so circulation personnel know where to look. At the same time, care should be taken not to place barcodes over ridges on the container or over important information.

Option c: Barcode on container and reel

If the library's policy is to use duplicate barcodes for the reel and container or one-and-a-half barcodes, it is possible to place one on the reel and the other on the container, thus matching the reel to the container.

Security Devices

Apply security devices that come in strips to the inside spine of the container and cover with a long label or opaque strip of tape. Security devices that are embedded in labels may be applied in a place consistent with library policy. It is advisable not to cover important information.

Accompanying Material

Accompanying material for film reels may include charts, posters, spirit masters, program notes, biographical or historical notes, scripts, teacher guides, etc. Materials that can be laid in a container should be kept with the film reel. When folding is required to fit the accompanying material into the box, it will be necessary to weigh the damage factor resulting from folding against the possibility of item loss. Larger pieces of accompanying material should receive more permanent covering. All accompanying material should be secured with labels. A label with an identification number should be placed on the cover of the accompanying material so that it is linked to its reel. It is advisable to be consistent in placing ownership designations (stamps or labels) according to established guidelines yet allow for flexibility if the choice is to cover important information. When accompanying material is stored separately and barcodes are in general use for the rest of the collection, a unique barcode should be placed on each piece of accompanying material. This practice will help the library keep track of each separate circulation.

Gift Plates

Gift plates may be applied to the inside of reel containers (top or bottom, wherever there is sufficient room). Plates also may be affixed to circulation pockets or hinged to the container, making it possible to read information underneath. Another option is to use a small pressure-sensitive label and type GIFT OF followed by the donor's name, if used, and apply it wherever space is available.

8-mm FILM CARTRIDGE (OR CASSETTE)

Definitions

Film cartridge: A standard 8-mm or super 8-mm film loop of short length or duration that is sealed in a plastic container in such a way that the beginning and end of the film are joined in an endless loop for continuous play. (Olson 1988: 12)

Film cassette: A motion picture film encased in a cassette which runs reel-to-reel. (Olson 1988: 12)

General Information

Motion picture cartridges are relatively easy to maintain, but the required equipment often malfunctions. A frequently encountered problem is that the projector jams and subsequently melts the film. Although 8-mm film can be spliced, splices tend to cause additional equipment malfunctions.

Considerations for Film Cartridge Storage

- Film cartridges come in small plastic boxes and may be stored vertically on baked enamel shelves. Because of the cartridge's small size, special shelf supports may be necessary to prevent them from falling through standard shelves.

Cartridge Labeling

Labels are never put on the film or leader but only on the integral container. Film loop cartridges are generally labeled by the producer on either the raised film side of the cartridge or the flat horseshoe side of the cartridge (see Figure 5.5). Libraries may want to add title and information labels to the same side. It is recommended that libraries be consistent with their own labeling and choose one of these sides on which to place their labels. Print or type a call number

Figure 5.5
Film Cartridge Labeling

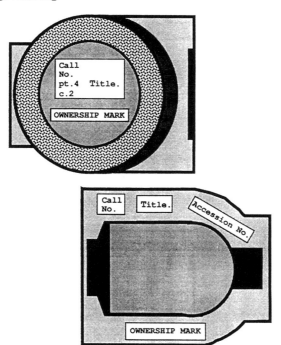

label, the part number (if the cartridge is part of a set), and the copy number and/or accession number (if used), and place the label close to the commercial label on the cartridge.

If no commercial label exists, type an identification label with the title, the call number, the part number (if the cartridge is part of a set, the copy number and/or accession number, if used), and the contents of the accompanying material and place the label in the center of the raised cartridge or in the upper left corner of the flat horseshoe side of the cartridge case. If necessary, trim to fit.

Ownership marks. Ownership marks should be placed visibly on the same surface of the film cartridge as the identification labels, using either a label, stamp, or permanent marker to print the library's name.

8-mm Film Cartridge Box Labeling

Film loop boxes generally have a commercial label on one of the flat sides of the box that includes a title, the running time, and often a synopsis of the contents. If such a label is lacking, the library may choose to create one. Or the library can prepare an identification label with the title, the call number, the cartridge or part number (if it is part of a set), the copy number and/or accession number (if used), and the contents of any accompanying material. The label should be placed on the flat side of the box to the right of the labeled spine (see Figure 5.6).

Spine labels. If the title of the film loop is commercially printed on the spine, letter or type a call number label to be placed on the lower portion of the spine. If there is no title label on the spine, prepare a title label to be placed on the upper portion of the spine, and make a call number label that includes part number (if the cartridge is part of a set) and the copy number and/or accession number (if used) for the bottom portion of the spine.

Ownership marks. Ownership marks should be placed visibly on the same surface of the film cartridge as the identification labels (see Figure 5.5).

Informational labels. A copyright restriction label may be placed near the title on the cartridge box. If the format is 8 mm, specify whether the gauge is STANDARD 8 MM or SUPER 8 MM.

Pockets for Circulation

Film loop boxes may be hinged so that they open completely, they may have a lid that is hinged so the cartridge can be slipped in and out of the box, or they may consist of an open-end slipcase. Circulation pockets may be mounted on the inside of hinged boxes and may need to be trimmed to fit. On boxes with the open or hinged top, circulation pockets may be permanently attached to the side of the box or hinged to retain access to information that would otherwise be covered. Clear self-adhesive pockets are also an option.

Barcodes

Option a: Barcode on cartridge

Place the barcode on the cartridge surface near the title of the film loop or in some other handy and consistent location.

Option b: Barcode on cartridge box

Placement should be consistent with library policy. Some libraries place the barcode on the outside front of the container in a consistent location where it is always accessible, such as the upper center edge of the front or back cover of the container. Others prefer placement directly adjacent to the circulation pocket for ease of access at the time of checkout. Another preferred location may be parallel to the spine in the upper right corner of the back of the container to allow for easy access during inventory. The important thing is to be consistent with placement on similar kinds of containers so circulation staff know where to look and at the same time be careful not to place barcodes over ridges on the container or over important information.

Figure 5.6
Film Cartridge Box Labeling

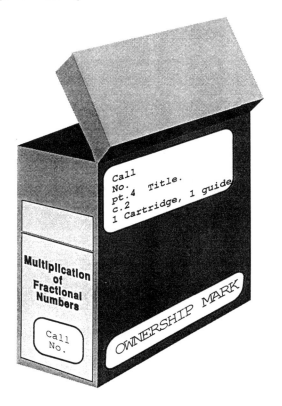

Option c: Barcode on cartridge and box

If the library's policy is to use duplicate barcodes or one-and-a-half barcodes for the cartridge and the box, one may be placed on the cartridge and the corresponding one on the container, thus matching the cartridge to the container.

Security Devices

Security devices that come in strips may be placed on the cartridge itself or on a flat surface of the cartridge box in a consistent place. The strips may be covered by a label or opaque piece of tape. Placement under the identification label would be a good choice or under the ownership label if such labels are used and are long enough to cover the security strips. If using security devices that are embedded in labels, attach them to the cartridge or box in a place consistent with library policy.

Accompanying Material

Accompanying material for film loops may include diagrams, charts, spirit masters, or teacher guides. Materials that can be laid in the container should be kept with the film cartridge. When folding is required to fit the accompanying material into the box, it will be necessary to weigh the damage factor resulting from folding against the possibility of item loss. Larger pieces of accompanying material should receive more permanent covering. All accompanying material should be secured with labels. A label with an identification number should be placed on the cover of the accompanying material so that it is linked to its cartridge. It is advisable to be consistent in placing ownership designations (stamps or labels) according to established guidelines yet allow for flexibility if the choice is to cover important information. When accompanying material is stored separately and barcodes are in general use for the rest of the collection, a unique barcode should be placed on each piece of accompanying material. This practice will help the library keep track of each separate circulation.

Gift Plates

Gift plates may be applied to the container which stores the film cartridge wherever there is sufficient room. They may have to be hinged to preserve access to written information underneath. They also may be attached to circulation pockets. Another option is to use a small pressure-sensitive label and type GIFT OF followed by the donor's name, if used, and apply the label wherever space is available.

VIDEORECORDING

Definition: A recording on which visual images, usually in motion and accompanied by sound, have been registered; designed for playback by means of a television set. (*AACR 2, 1988 rev.:* 624)

General Information

Three different standards for videocassette presentation exist in the world today; National Television Standards Committee (NTSC) is the one used in North America, Central America, Brazil, Sweden, and a few other places. The other two foreign standards, phase alternative line (PAL) and SEquential Color and Memory (SECAM), are used throughout the rest of the world. If a library collects other than what is standard for its part of the world, prominent labels should be affixed to the video and its container to alert the user to the need for special equipment.

The most common physical formats acquired in North American libraries are

½-inch videocassettes (VHS and Beta), the ¾-inch U-matic cassette, and the laser optical videodisc. Videoreels may be found in some libraries as well, but they are no longer available for commercial library purchase. Normally they have been replaced by videocassettes because of the cassette's availability on the commercial market, its ease of use, and the popular acceptance of cassette equipment over reel equipment.

VIDEOCASSETTE

Definition: A permanently encased videotape that winds from reel to reel. (Olson 1988: 35)

General Information

The videocassette is the most popular information format to be added to library collections over the last decade. This is because of its ease of use and because it is usually much less expensive than 16-mm film. Compared to film, however, maintaining video can be somewhat problematic. It cannot be spliced (except at the beginning or end of the tape) because splices can damage the heads of the video player. Replacement footage for damaged tape, therefore, is not an option, as it is with film. A videocassette tape's shelf life may be less than that for 16-mm film. If a videotape is not used at least once a year, it should be run forward and back at least once during that time to prevent the oxide particles from printing through to other layers. Ideally, libraries will have access to cleaning and inspection equipment after each circulation, but such equipment is both labor intensive and expensive. Thus, some libraries will choose to take their chances and plan instead to replace videocassettes as they become damaged. Procedures for processing videocassettes apply to all three formats (VHS and Beta ½-inch videocassettes and U-matic cassettes).

Considerations for Videocassette Storage

- Videocassettes should be stored in a dust-free environment that is neither too hot nor too cold.

- Videocassettes should be stored away from all potentially damaging magnetic fields, which can be caused by electrical motors or magnetic security systems.

- Videocassettes should be stored vertically, with tape rewound to the original supply reel. This keeps the weight of the tape on the lower reel, with the least potential for reel distortion.

- Videocassettes may be stored in their original cardboard packaging if it is reinforced and dust free or if it is cut apart and slipped into a snap-lock plastic video case.

• Videocassettes may be stored in vinyl albums and binders with preformed trays to hold the cassettes.

• Videocassettes may be stored in fiber and pressboard binders and boxes.

(See also sections on storage in Chapter 1 and repackaging/repackaging in Chapter 2.)

Videocassette Labeling

Labels are never put on the videotape itself but only on the integral cassette container.

Option a: Processing without labels

Commercial cassettes usually come with a producer's label on the flat portion of the top of the cassette between the clear windows. Using a pen with permanent ink, print identification information directly on the commercial cassette label. Print the call number, the tape and/or part number, and the copy and/or accession number (if used) on the commercial label as space provides. If the original label is too dark to show hand-printed markings, refer to option b.

Ownership marks. Ownership marks should be stamped on the commercial label as space permits or onto a blank label, which can be placed in a consistent place on the top of the videocassette away from the top edge of the cassette that goes into the VCR.

Option b: Processing with minimal labels

Type the call number, tape or part number (if the videocassette is part of a set), and copy number and/or accession number (if used) on a label. Attach to the front of the cassette above the commercial label. Avoid covering any important information on the commercial label (see Figure 5.7).

Ownership marks. Preprinted or stamped ownership labels may be placed on the bottom of the commercial label if space permits, or they can be placed in another consistent place on the top of the videocassette away from the top edge of the cassette that goes into the VCR (see Figure 5.7).

Option c: Processing with full labels

If cassettes are lacking commercial labels, it may be desirable to create one with the title, publisher, date, sound and color characteristics, format (VHS, etc.) and running time. Or an identification label can be prepared with the title, call number, part and video number (if the cassette is part of a set), copy number and/or accession number (if used), and contents of the accompanying material. Place this label on the slightly recessed flat surface of the top of the cassette between the two clear windows, as shown in Figure 5.8, being careful not to obscure the take-up reel if there is a clear protective window.

Spine labels. Spine labels may be needed for both the videocassette and the

Figure 5.7
Processing a Videocassette with Minimal Labels

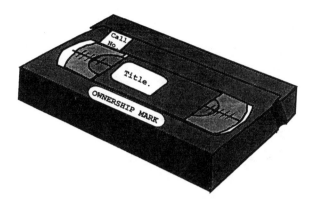

video packaging. The following procedure may apply to both the cassette spine and to the package spine, whether it is the original package or a replacement container. If the title of the videotape is commercially printed on the spine, letter or type a call number label to be placed on the lower portion of the spine consistent with library guidelines. If there is no title label on the spine, prepare a title label to be placed on the upper portion of the spine. Make a call number label that includes the tape part (if the video is part of a set) and the copy number and/or an accession number (if used) for the bottom portion of the spine.

Ownership marks. Ownership marks may be located on the identification label as space permits, or they may be placed in another consistent place on the top of the videocassette away from the top edge of the cassette that goes into the VCR.

Informational labels. There are several kinds of informational labels that a library may wish to use for videocassettes, but only a few need to be placed on the videocassette itself. To avoid jamming the playback equipment, labels should never be placed near the top edge of the cassette that is inserted into the VCR. If a copyright restriction label is not included on the commercial label, libraries may wish to apply one below the title in a consistent location on the top of the cassette. According to library policy, place a REWIND or DO NOT REWIND label near the clear window of the cassette as well.

Videocassette Container Labeling

Videocassettes stored in their original packages usually have commercial labels on the top of the box or case that include title, publisher, date, sound and color characteristics, format (VHS, etc.), running time, and a summary. If such packaging is of a permanent nature, only minimal additional labeling that includes call number, part number (if the tape is part of a set), copy number and/

Figure 5.8
Processing a Videocassette with Full Labels

or accession number (if used), and the contents of any accompanying material will be needed. If the packaging is not permanent, parts of it may be salvaged and placed into clear sleeves of replacement cases, albums, or binders.

When videocassettes come from small independent producers or are locally produced, little or no information about the program may be provided. In such instances one option may be to create a uniform customized template for the front and back of a cassette container, such as the one shown in Figure 5.9. Information specific to each videocassette can be filled in on the template through a word processing program, and the result can be printed and placed in the clear sleeves of a videocassette case.

Another option is to prepare an identification label with the title, publisher, date, special sound characteristics, and running time. Also include the call number, part number (if the tape is part of a set), the copy number and/or accession number (if used), and the contents of the accompanying material. Place label(s) on the top of the container in the upper center portion of the package or in the upper left corner of the package. If the latter location is chosen, both patron and staff can easily view the information when scanning the shelf or browse bin.

Informational labels. A large number of informational labels may be needed on any given videocassette. If a videotape has been recorded at other than regular speed, a label stating VARIABLE SPEED PLAYER REQUIRED may be needed. If a program is recorded in stereo or VHS hi-fi, it is helpful to alert the user to such special equipment needs. Other examples of informational labels that might be needed include a copyright restriction label, BETA or VHS designation, CLOSED CAPTIONED, LETTERBOX FORMAT, MASTER, MPAA RATING, RESTRICTED USE, etc.

If processing any kind of archival material or locally produced videos (e.g., teleconferences, class demonstrations, poetry readings), other special considerations should be noted on the container, such as 1ST GENERATION MASTER; 2ND GENERATION MASTER; 1ST GENERATION COPY, etc.

Figure 5.9
Processing a Videocassette Container with a Customized Template

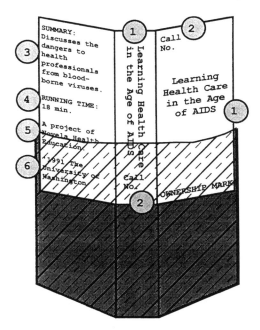

Ownership marks. Ownership marks should be placed visibly in a consistent place on the front or back of the videocassette container using either a label, stamp, or permanent marker.

Pockets for Circulation

If videocassettes are housed in albums, binders, or boxes that open and have a flat and protected inside surface, this area would be preferred for permanently attached circulation pockets. The least protected place for a pocket is the exterior of the container, but sometimes there is no alternative. In such cases pockets can be permanently attached to the outside of the container using double-sided tape, clear book tape, the permanent rubber cement method, etc. If important information will be covered, consider clear self-adhesive pockets or the hinging method as alternatives, keeping in mind that the hinging method may not be a permanent solution due to inevitable wear and tear during shelving.

Barcodes

According to each library's specifications, barcodes are placed either on containers or on the items themselves. Some libraries will strike out or remove the manufacturer's barcode that appears on the item or the container, thus assuring that there will be no confusion due to multiple barcodes.

Option a: Barcode on the cassette's edges

The edges or narrow sides of the cassette work well for barcodes. One option for the barcode location is the gate of the videocassette that goes into the VCR (see Figure 5.8). This location does not come in contact with any moving parts of the VCR and does not compete with other information. The opposite spine of the cassette is also a possibility, but it is more likely that competing title information will be located there. The two ends of the cassette are another possibility. Often the manufacturer has chosen one of these locations for its barcode. If that is the case, the manufacturer's code may be erased or removed to prevent confusion with the library's barcode.

Option b: Barcode on cassette

Place the barcode on the flat center portion of the front of the cassette below the title label, as shown in Figure 5.7.

Option c: Barcode on cassette packaging

Placement of barcodes should be consistent with library policy, being careful not to place barcodes over ridges of the container or over important information. Some libraries place the barcode on the outside front of the container in a consistent location, such as the upper center edge of the front or back cover of the container where it is always accessible. Others prefer placement directly adjacent to the circulation pocket for ease of access at the time of checkout. Another preferred location may be the upper right corner of the back of the container parallel to the spine, which allows for easy access during inventory. The important thing is to be consistent with placement on similar kinds of containers so circulation staff know where to look yet be careful not to place barcodes over ridges on the container or over important information.

Option d: Barcode on both cassette and container

If the library's policy is to use duplicate barcodes for the videocassette and the container or one-and-a-half barcodes (see the section on barcodes in Chapter 2 for a more complete discussion), one may be placed on the cassette and the corresponding one may be placed on the container, thus matching the cassette to the container.

Security Devices

Security strips or labels may be attached to the videocassette itself or the container. However, caution must be exercised if the security system is a magnetic one. In such cases special warning labels may be required to ensure that magnetic materials do not pass through regular desensitizing equipment. (For a more complete discussion of these concerns and the different types of security labels and strips, see the section on security in Chapter 1.)

Option a: Securing the cassette

A security device (i.e., label or strip) is available that may be applied to the cassette itself. If it is a magnetic strip, it may be placed on the inside of the gate that opens to expose the tape when it plays in the machine. Another location for the strip is under the identification label; or, if the strip is short, it may be placed under the barcode or ownership label. Security devices that are embedded in labels may be placed wherever they will not interfere with the operation of the cassette.

Option b: Securing the container

Security labels that are embedded in a date due label may be placed on the front cover of the cassette container or inside the container near the circulation pocket. Those embedded in property stickers may be placed on the container according to consistent library policy. Security strips may be placed in the spine or under the container's identification label or any other label large enough to cover the strip.

Option c: Security boxes

Locked security boxes eliminate the need to secure the cassette or its box. They are available for the storage of the cassette and its container. Security strips may be applied to the inside edge of the box. The cassette container is then locked in the box. It is removed at the time of circulation. It is advisable to store security boxes at the circulation desk, where they are readily available for use when the cassette is returned. This process requires storage space but is a good theft deterrent.

Accompanying Material

Accompanying material for videocassettes includes program notes, libretti, texts for plays and operas, biographical or historical notes, scripts, teacher's manuals, etc. Follow the guidelines in Chapter 2 for detailed treatment of such materials. If possible, accompanying material should remain in the container with the videocassette. For example, vinyl and plastic cases with clear plastic sleeves are an ideal location for accompanying material. When folding is required to fit the accompanying material into the sleeve, it will be necessary to weigh the damage factor resulting from folding against the possibility of loss of the item. Accompanying material should be labeled with an identification or call number so that it is linked to the videocassette. It is advisable to place ownership designations (stamps or labels) in consistent places according to established guidelines yet allow for flexibility if the choice is to cover important information. When accompanying material is stored separately and barcodes are in general use for the rest of the collection, a unique barcode should be placed on each piece of accompanying material. This practice will help the library keep track of each separate circulation.

Gift Plates

Gift plates may be applied to the container which stores the videocassette wherever there is sufficient room. They may have to be hinged to preserve access to written information underneath. They also may be attached to circulation pockets. Another option is to use a small pressure-sensitive label and type GIFT OF followed by the donor's name, if used, and apply the label wherever space is available.

VIDEODISC

Definition: A videodisc is a shiny, platter shaped silver disc, commonly made of polyvinyl chloride, usually 12 in. in diameter, without grooves, but with information printed on tracks that are imperceptible to the naked eye. (Ellison 1987: 355)

General Information

Videodiscs are analog and may contain motion, audio, still images, and/or combinations of all three. Originally there were two types of videodisc on the market—a capacitance electronic disc (CED), which required a stylus, and an optical disc, which required a laser. The CED is no longer produced, and because few libraries collected that format, the emphasis in this manual will be on optical videodiscs only. Videodiscs can be constant linear velocity (CLV) and/or constant angular velocity (CAV). Both types are collected by libraries. Although the 12-inch size currently seems to be the most popular, videodiscs also come in other sizes (e.g., 7¾ inch and 5 inch).

Care of videodiscs should be similar to that for sound discs and compact discs. Playing surfaces should be kept free of grease and dust and any sharp objects that might puncture them. Minor scratches are usually not a problem, but any mark that interferes with the reflection of the laser beam on either side of the disc can interrupt the playing signal. Studies have shown that if left on the surface, oil from a fingerprint is potentially the biggest danger to laser discs. Over time, the oils will deteriorate the plastic layers and corrode the protective metallic surface of the disc. When it is necessary to clean videodiscs, a simple solution of mild liquid soap can be used, followed by a rinse in tepid water and drip drying. If pressure must be used to remove grease, use a horizontal motion across the disc rather than a circular motion. If sticky substances are found on discs, rubbing a small portion of peanut butter on the surface works to remove them. This is followed by the mild soap solution (to remove any remaining grease), rinsing, and drying.

Considerations for Videodisc Storage

- Videodiscs should be stored in a dust-free environment that is neither too hot nor too cold.
- Videodiscs should be stored vertically away from direct sunlight or heat.
- Videodiscs may be stored in their original albums and cases or in replacement containers.

Videodisc Labeling

Labels should not be attached to any area of the disc that is read by the laser. Because there is some disagreement about the effects of putting marks or additional labels (which might affect the balance or speed of the disc) on the commercial videodisc label, the following instructions should be considered within that context. The latest available research should be examined before making a final processing decision.

Option a: Processing without labels

Using a pen with permanent ink, print the call number, the disc or part number (if the disc is part of a set), and the copy number and/or accession number (if used) on the commercial videodisc label (see Figure 5.10).

Option b: Processing with minimal labels

Type or print the call number, disc or part number (if the disc is part of a set), and the copy number and/or the accession number (if used) on a label to be placed on the commercial label. Be careful not to cover any important information (see Figure 5.11).

Ownership marks. Type or stamp the library name on the commercial videodisc label, or use preprinted regular or curved labels that may be attached to the commercial label where space allows (as shown in Figure 5.11).

Option c: Processing with full labels

Because of the controversy over the effects of label adhesives on videodisc, a more complete label is not recommended at this time.

Inner Sleeve Labeling

Videodisc recordings should always be kept in inner sleeves to assure maximum protection. It is not necessary to use identification labeling on them, but ownership marks may be placed on these sleeves to deter theft.

Figure 5.10
Processing a Videodisc without Labels

Album Cover Labeling

If a commercial label is lacking or is incomplete, the library may choose to create such a label, or it may prepare an identification label with the title, the call number, the disc or part number (if the disc is part of a set), the copy number and/or accession number (if used), and the contents of any accompanying material. Place the label in a consistent location on the front of the container (e.g., in the upper left corner). This location guarantees patrons and staff easy access to information on items that are on the shelves or in a browsing bin (see Figure 5.12).

Spine labels. If the spine is wide enough, a call number label may be placed on the bottom portion of the spine. If the spine is too narrow, the lower or the upper left corner of the front of the album is a good location for the call number so that all numbers in the call number may be visible for both patrons and staff. Libraries may choose either of these locations if they wish to place call numbers consistently for both print and nonprint materials.

Ownership marks. Ownership marks should be placed visibly in a consistent location on the front or back of the videodisc container using either a label, stamp, or permanent marker.

Informational labels. Because videodisc applications are sometimes referred to as level I, level II, level III, or level IV, it is important to provide SYSTEM REQUIREMENTS labels to alert the user and the library staff to the type of equipment and peripherals that are necessary for the disc's use. Examples might

Figure 5.11
Processing a Videodisc with Minimal Labels

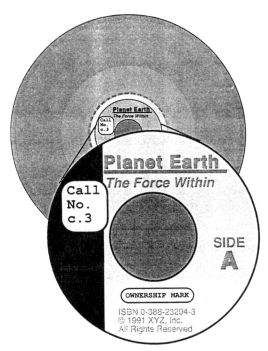

include REQUIRES EQUIPMENT WITH DIGITAL MEMORY, REQUIRES EQUIPMENT WITH MICROPROCESSOR, REQUIRES AN EXTERNAL COMPUTER AND MONITOR, or REQUIRES STILL-FRAME EQUIPMENT. Other labels might detail the need for accessories, such as REQUIRES USE OF PORTABLE SCANNER, or they might provide useful information, such as LETTERBOX, CAV (Constant Angular Velocity), CLV (Constant Linear Velocity), etc.

Protective Album Covers

Clear vinyl album jacket covers (similar to those used for sound discs) are an excellent choice for guaranteeing an extended life to commercial laser disc albums. Place the original labeled album jacket in a vinyl cover. Some covers have attached circulation pockets. If pockets are not supplied, follow the direction provided in the following section, ''Pockets for Circulation.'' To deter theft of clear covers, the album cover may be stapled to the album jacket. It also is a good idea to place ownership labels on the clear covers.

Figure 5.12
Videodisc Album Labeling

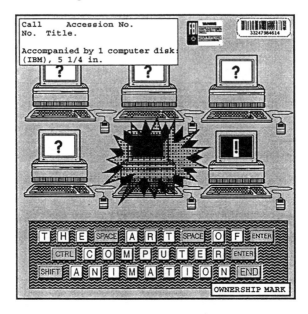

Pockets for Circulation

The least protected place for a pocket is the exterior of videodisc albums and boxes, but sometimes there is no alternative.

Option a: On album or box cover

An opaque pocket or clear vinyl pocket may be permanently attached to the front or back of the album or box in a consistent location according to library guidelines. If important information would be covered, use the hinging method for attaching opaque pockets or use a clear vinyl self-adhesive pocket that can be read through.

Option b: Inside the album

Self-adhesive vinyl or opaque circulation pockets may be attached to the inside of an album cover sleeve along the back edge. Use double-stick tape, glue, or rubber cement to attach opaque pockets permanently.

Option c: Inside a box or multiple album

For boxes or albums that open, some libraries will want to attach pockets to the inside of a box lid or a flat surface of the inside front or back album cover, because pockets in protected locations last longer.

Barcodes

Because of the disagreement about the effects of putting additional labels on the commercial videodisc label, the following instructions should be considered within that context. The latest available research should be examined prior to making a final processing decision.

Option a: Barcode on commercial videodisc label

A barcode may be placed on the videodisc's commercial label but not on either side of the disc's metallic surface.

Option b: Barcode on videodisc container

Placement of barcodes on videodisc containers should be consistent with library policy; several locations are possible. Some libraries place the barcode on the outside front of the container in a consistent location, such as the upper center edge of the front or back cover of the container where it is always accessible. Others prefer placement directly adjacent to the circulation pocket for ease of access at the time of checkout. Another preferred location may be the upper right corner of the back of the container parallel to the spine, which allows for easy access during inventory. The important thing is to be consistent with placement on similar kinds of containers so circulation staff know where to look yet be careful not to place barcodes over ridges on the container or over important information.

Security Devices

Security devices should not be placed on videodiscs themselves. Because laser discs can usually be played on both sides, security strips made for the compact laser disc and covered with a clear plastic overlay are not appropriate. The radio frequency type of labels are not feasible either because the high metal content of the disc tends to shield its sensor tags (Dick 1990: 39).

Security strips or labels may be attached to the container. For a more detailed discussion of security devices, see the section on security in Chapter 1.

Option a: Security strips

For the videodisc container, security devices that come in strips may be applied to any location where they are inconspicuous and can be covered with a long label or opaque strip of tape. Possible locations where they might not be detected easily (other than under identification labels) are the interior edge of the slipcase or jacket and the inner spine of multiple-disc sets. Cover the strip with a piece of opaque colored tape or a label in these locations.

Option b: Security labels

Security devices that are embedded in labels come in several varieties, which include blank labels, date due labels, special information labels (e.g., HANDLE

WITH CARE), and ownership labels. Placement on the album cover should follow library guidelines for placement of such labels on other types of materials. It is always advisable not to cover important information.

Accompanying Material

Accompanying material for videodiscs may include teacher's guides, manuals, textbooks with barcoded pictures, indexes, computer disks, posters, study prints, etc. Materials that can be laid in a container should be kept with the videodisc. When folding is required to fit the accompanying material into the box, it will be necessary to weigh the damage factor resulting from folding against the possibility of item loss. Larger pieces of accompanying material should receive more permanent covering. All accompanying material should be secured with labels. A label with an identification number should be placed on the cover of the accompanying material so that it is linked to the videodisc. Ownership designations (stamps or labels) should be placed on the items according to established library guidelines yet allow for flexibility if the choice is to cover important information. When accompanying material is stored separately and barcodes are in general use for the rest of the collection, a unique barcode should be placed on each piece of accompanying material. This practice will help the library keep track of each separate circulation.

Gift Plates

Gift plates may be attached directly to videodisc containers on either the inside or the outside, wherever there is sufficient room. Plates may be affixed to circulation pockets or hinged to the container, making it possible to read information underneath. Another option is to use a small pressure-sensitive label and type GIFT OF followed by the donor's name, if used, and apply the label wherever space is available.

VIDEOREEL

Definition: A reel containing magnetic tape upon which both sound and video signals of a television production are recorded for playback through a television receiver. (Olson 1988: 36)

General Information

Handling or creasing videotape should be avoided. Although splicing videotape at the beginning or end of a reel is possible, it should be done very carefully so that splices will not damage the recording heads of the video player. If a

Figure 5.13
Videoreel Tape Labeling

videotape is not being used frequently, it should be fast forwarded and rewound once a year to prevent bleed-through (oxide sticking to the next layer of tape).

Considerations for Videoreel Storage

- Videoreels should be stored in a dust-free environment that is neither too hot nor too cold.
- Videoreels should be stored away from all potentially damaging magnetic fields, which can be caused by electrical motors or magnetic security systems.
- Archival reels may be stored horizontally on shelves that allow only a couple of reels to be stacked on each other.
- Circulating reels may be stored vertically on single reels in plastic bags inside their boxes.

Videoreel Tape Labeling

It is a good idea to use the videotape leader for labeling rather than the tape itself. Because reel video is an older format, older methods of labeling are often used. Some libraries still use an electric stylus to engrave the call number and title directly onto the emulsion side of the leader. Another option includes using a pen with permanent ink to print the call number, the tape or part number (if there is more than one reel in the set), and the copy number or accession number (if used) a few inches in from the end of the shiny side of the tape leader. Some libraries will print the title of the tape just to the left of the call number (see Figure 5.13).

Videoreel Labeling

Option a: Processing without labels

Using a pen with permanent ink, print the call number on one of the arms between the openings of the tape reel and the part number (if the tape is part of a set). Write the title on another arm. The last arm may be left for barcode placement. Write the copy number and/or accession number (if used) on a curve

Figure 5.14
Videoreel Labeling

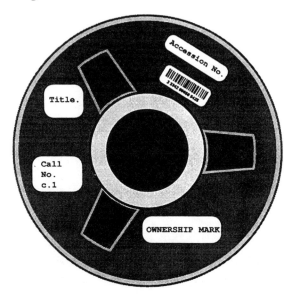

of the reel and the library's name in the last curve. All writing should face the same direction, as shown in Figure 5.14.

Option b: Processing with labels

On one arm attach the call number label. On another label type the title and attach this label to the next arm of the reel, making sure all type faces the same direction, as shown in Figure 5.14. One arm may be used for barcode placement if that location seems appropriate. Type the accession number (if used), and place it on the curve of the reel or on another arm. Preprinted ownership labels or blank labels with stamped or typed ownership marks may be placed on the curved spaces above the opening.

Informational labels. Place a copyright restriction and a REWIND label on the outside curve where space is available. For archival or master tapes, other special labels may be useful, such as 1ST GENERATION MASTER, 2ND GENERATION MASTER, 1ST GENERATION COPY, etc.

Videoreel Container Labeling

On a label type the call number, the reel or part number (if the tape is part of a set), the copy number and/or accession number (if used), the title, and the contents of the accompanying material. Place the label in a position consistent with library policy on the top of the box (see Figure 5.15).

Figure 5.15
Videoreel Container Labeling

Ownership marks. The ownership marks should be placed visibly on the front and/or back cover of the container using either a label, stamp, or marker to print the library's name.

Informational labels. A copyright restriction label may be placed in the lower right corner of the outside top cover. A REWIND label may be placed where space is available. For archival or master tapes, other special labels may be useful, such as 1ST GENERATION MASTER, 2ND GENERATION MASTER, 1ST GENERATION COPY, etc.

Pockets for Circulation

Circulation pockets may be applied to the inside of the reel box top. They may be permanently attached to the top or hinged in place using tape. Hinging pockets or using clear vinyl pockets makes it possible to read information on the lining of the cover.

Barcodes

Option a: Barcode on reel

Place the barcode on one arm of the reel (see Figure 5.14). If it is necessary to trim the barcode label, check with your vendor to see if this will cause problems. Attach the barcode so that all lettering faces the same direction as other labels.

Option b: Barcode on container

Placement should be consistent with library policy. Some libraries place the barcode on the outside front of the container, whereas others choose a location on the inside of the container. If the outside is chosen, the barcode should be in a consistent location, such as the upper center edge of the front or back cover of the container where it is always accessible. Others prefer placement directly adjacent to the circulation pocket for ease of access at the time of checkout. Another preferred location may be the upper right corner of the back of the container parallel to the spine, which allows for easy access during inventory. The important thing is to be consistent with placement on similar kinds of containers so circulation staff know where to look yet be careful not to place barcodes over ridges on the container or over important information.

Option c: Barcode on container and reel

If the library's policy is to use duplicate barcodes for the reel and the container or one-and-a-half barcodes, one may be placed on the reel and the other on the container, thus matching the reel to the container.

Security Devices

Apply security devices that come in strips to the inside spine of the container and cover with a long label or opaque strip of tape. However, caution must be exercised if the security system is a magnetic one. Special equipment for desensitizing magnetic materials may be needed, or special warning labels may be required to ensure that magnetic materials do not pass through regular equipment. (For a more complete discussion of these concerns, see the section on security in Chapter 1.) When using security devices that are embedded in labels, apply them on the top front cover in a place consistent with library policy. It is advisable not to cover important information.

Accompanying Material

Accompanying material for videoreel tapes may include program notes, texts of speeches, biographical or historical notes, etc., and it may be laid in the box. When folding is required to fit the accompanying material into the reel box, it will be necessary to weigh the damage factor resulting from folding against the possibility of item loss. Larger pieces of accompanying material should receive more permanent covering. Accompanying material should also be secured with labels. A label with an identification number should be placed on the cover of the accompanying material so that it is linked to its reel. It is advisable to be consistent in placing ownership designation (stamps or labels) according to established guidelines yet allow for flexibility if the choice is to cover important information. When accompanying material is stored separately and barcodes are in general use for the rest of the collection, a unique barcode should be placed on each piece of accompanying material. This practice will help the library keep track of each separate circulation.

Gift Plates

Gift plates may be applied to the inside of videoreel boxes or albums (top or bottom, wherever there is sufficient room). Hinged plates make it possible to read information printed underneath on the cover. Another option is to use a small pressure-sensitive label and type GIFT OF followed by the donor's name, if used, and apply the label wherever space is available.

REFERENCES

Anglo-American Cataloguing Rules, Second Edition, 1988 Revision, ed. by Michael Gorman and Paul W. Winkler for the Joint Steering Committee for Revision of AACR. Chicago: American Library Association.

Dick, Jeff T. 1990. "Laserdisc Redux." *Library Journal* (November 15): 37–39.

Ellison, John W. 1987. *Nonbook Media: Collection Management and User Services.* Chicago: American Library Association.

Olson, Nancy B. 1988. *Audiovisual Material Glossary.* Dublin, OH: OCLC Online Computer Library Center.

6

Graphic Materials

Definition: A graphic is a two-dimensional representation whether opaque (e.g., art originals and reproductions, flash cards, photographs, technical drawings) or intended to be viewed, or projected without motion, by means of an optical device (e.g., filmstrips, stereographs, slides).

(AACR 2, 1988 rev.: 618)

Graphic materials comprise a wide variety of nonprint materials, many of which are commonly found in libraries. For the purposes of this manual, graphics are broken down into the following four categories: two-dimensional opaque materials (e.g., art prints, art reproductions, charts, flash cards, photographs, pictures, posters, and study prints), filmstrips, slides, and transparencies.

TWO-DIMENSIONAL OPAQUE MATERIALS

Definitions

Art original—An original two-dimensional . . . work of art (other than an art print (q.v.) or a photograph) created by the artist (e.g., a painting, drawing, . . . , as contrasted to a reproduction of a painting, drawing, or sculpture). *(AACR 2, 1988 rev.: 615)*

Art print—An engraving, etching, lithograph, woodcut, etc., printed from the plate prepared by the artist. *(AACR 2, 1988 rev.: 615)*

Art reproduction—A mechanically reproduced copy of a work of art, generally as one of a commercial edition. (*AACR 2, 1988 rev.:* 615)

Chart—An opaque sheet that exhibits data in graphic or tabular form (e.g., a wall chart). (*AACR 2, 1988 rev.:* 616)

Flash card—A card or other opaque material printed with words, numerals, or pictures and designed for rapid display. (*AACR 2, 1988 rev.:* 618)

Photograph—An image recorded on photographic or other opaque photosensitive material, usually by a camera. (Olsen 1988: 24) [or] . . . a printed reproduction of that image. (Ellison 1987: 262)

Picture—A two-dimensional visual representation accessible to the naked eye and generally on an opaque backing. Used when a more specific term (e.g., art original, photograph, study print) is not appropriate. (*AACR 2, 1988 rev.:* 621)

Poster—The single or multi-sheet notices made to attract attention to events, activities, causes, goods, or services, generally for posting, usually in a public place, and chiefly pictorial. Intended to make an immediate impression from a distance. (Olson 1988: 25)

Study print—A picture or print, issued singly or in sets, with accompanying text, prepared specifically for teaching purposes; text might be printed on the verso of the print, in margins, or issued separately. The text might include descriptions, discussion questions, terms with definitions, and/or bibliography. (Olson 1988: 33)

Technical drawing—A cross section, detail, diagram, elevation, perspective, plan, working plan, etc., made for use in an engineering or other technical context. (Olson 1988: 33)

General Information

This group of materials includes both commercially produced graphic material as well as original two-dimensional art work (e.g., oil paintings, watercolors, gouache, pastels, drawings, and crafts), photographs and negatives, historical prints and posters, and art prints. Commercially produced graphics include art reproductions, charts, flash cards, pictures, posters, study prints, and technical drawings. Although much of the material is made up of still pictures, it also may be textual or technical in nature (such as flash cards and technical drawings) or it may combine both pictures and text (as in study prints). These materials are similar in that they require no special equipment to view or fully utilize them. Often, similar processing procedures may be used for these materials.

As with maps, there is no single correct way of storing two-dimensional materials. The size, format, type of library, and the collection's purpose must all be considered. It is also necessary to weigh the features of each storage option with the relative cost of each method, the amount of available storage space, and the desired patron accessibility for the collection. With these concepts in mind, various options are feasible, as discussed next.

Considerations for Two-Dimensional Opaque Material Storage

- Large items may be stored in wide horizontal storage cabinets with shallow drawers or in shallow boxes stored on wide deep shelves. Heavy materials should be well separated with corrugated fiberboard.

- Smaller items may be stored in folders, portfolios, boxes, or individually in filing cabinet drawers. Some master images should never be put in envelopes or portfolios but should be placed in archival boxes with dividers so rubbing is avoided.

- Framed items may be stored vertically in browse bins or hung on walls, on sliding screens hung from tracks, on metal mesh panels, or on pegboard suspended from the ceiling or wall.

- Graphic materials should be stored away from direct sunlight or fluorescent lighting, and extremes of heat and humidity should be avoided.

- Original unframed art work may be wrapped in acid-free lining paper and stored in padded boxes, portfolios, or other flat files with separate acid-free guard sheets. Avoid folding art work because items will crack and degenerate along the fold.

- Art reproductions may be stored similarly to art originals but often can be treated in more practical terms. Depending on their purpose and use, they may not require protective sheets and special packing in browse bins, drawers, or filing cabinets.

- If art reproductions are on paper and are to be circulated unframed, they may be mounted on some type of rigid backing, matted, laminated, encapsulated, or covered with some other type of clear covering. Matte finish laminations may be preferable to diminish light reflection when the reproduction is hung for viewing by the user. Fixative sprays may be another alternative.

- Smaller reproductions may be placed in acid-free folders or portfolios and placed in filing cabinet drawers or interfiled on regular library shelving.

- Charts and posters that are single-sided may be laminated or mounted on cloth backing.

- Charts and posters may be rolled and stored in tubes, laid flat in large shallow drawers or boxes, hung vertically by clamps or in hinged panels, or kept in large portfolios (which can be made from fiberboard and hinged with bookbinding tape).

- Flash cards may be stored in their original boxes or bags or in replacement containers on regular library shelving.

- Storage conditions for photos depend on whether they are considered ephemeral or archival in nature. All photo materials, however, are especially sensitive to light.

- Original photographs and photographic negatives may be kept in individual acid-free protective envelopes or mylar sleeves or folders and should be housed in dark, dry storage areas such as vertical files, boxes, or file cabinet drawers.

- Large and fragile photos may be housed in packets in suspended files in metal cabinets. This method of storage provides less wear and tear than horizontal methods.

- Photographs may be stored mounted within a hinged mat or unmounted and housed more than one to an envelope or file. Very small photos may be mounted on larger paper for easier retrieval.

- If pictures are to be available to users in a browsing collection, it may be advisable to mount them on card stock, foam core, railway board, or unbleached muslin using the wet mounting process.

- Pictures may be stored in vertical files, cabinets, or large shallow drawers. Large pictures may be stored in shallow flat drawers such as those designed for maps or X-rays.

- Study prints may be kept in folders, envelopes, three-ring binders, boxes, hanging bags, or other containers. These various methods lend themselves to file drawers, vertical files, and/or regular library shelving.

- Technical drawings may be housed between protective sheets in envelopes, folders, binders, boxes, and pamphlet boxes.

Two-Dimensional Opaque Material Labeling

Some graphic items are issued in sets or collections. A decision must be made regarding whether items should be identified individually or as units. Such decisions should be based on the needs of the library, needs of the users, other resources available in the library, and whether items can be used independently of the rest of the unit.

Labeling of two-dimensional opaque items will vary according to individual library needs. Recommended placement of identification labeling depends on whether it is archival, how it is stored, whether it is mounted, whether it has borders, etc. For nonarchival material stored in drawers, one choice may be to place call number labels in the lower left- or right-hand corner of the item so the call number is readily visible when the drawer is opened. When horizontal images are interfiled with vertical images, call numbers that are placed in the lower right corner of horizontal images and call numbers that are placed in the upper right corner of vertical images filed in the drawer to their right allow all call numbers to be viewed in the same position in the lower right corner of the drawer.

If images are stored in files accessible from the top, labels attached to the upper left corner of horizontal images and labels attached to the upper right corner of vertical images filed to their left will display call numbers for all images, both horizontal and vertical, in the same upper left position.

Other choices may be to put identification numbers on the item's mount or on the back of material so that numbers do not detract from the visual contents of the item. In every instance it is important to avoid covering important information, whether it be on the front or the back of the item.

Option a: Processing without labels

Using a pen with permanent ink, print the call number, part number (if there are multiple items in a set), the copy and/or accession number (if used), the title (if needed), and the accompanying material designation on either the front or back of the item, according to local guidelines.

Option b: Processing with minimal labels

Print with a pen using permanent ink or type a call number label and place it on the front or the back of the item. Label placement should avoid covering any important information and should be in a position consistent with library policy.

Option c: Processing with full labels

Prepare an identification label consisting of call number, part number (if there are multiple items in a set), the copy and/or accession number (if used), the author (if appropriate), the title, and the accompanying material designation (see Figure 6.1). Place the label on the front or back of the item in a position consistent with library guidelines. Placement on the reverse side of one-sided opaque material assures that important information is not covered.

Ownership marks. Placement of ownership designations should depend on the type of storage and preservation that is chosen for this kind of material. Preprinted labels or stamped ownership marks may be placed in a position consistent with library guidelines for this type of material (e.g., center top or bottom of backside or lower right-hand corner of the back or front).

Informational labels. It may be desirable to add special informational markings to the matting of an art original, an art print, an art reproduction, or a picture or photograph. The name of the work and the location or subject of a photograph or picture may be important information that makes the item useful. Such marking can be done in pencil if the item is archival in nature. If the items are not original or rare, typed labels or permanent ink lettering on the back of flat materials may be preferred. Other kinds of information may include the number of sheets in a flip chart, the size of an item when framed, or the location and size of original art.

Two-Dimensional Opaque Material Container Labeling

Commercial materials such as art reproductions, flash cards, pictures, study prints, and technical drawings may come to the library in containers. Usually such containers have preprinted identification labels with the title and publisher's name on them. They also may include a copyright date, name of a series if applicable, and a contents note. If such a commercial label is lacking or is incomplete, prepare an identification label with the title and any other information the library deems important. Either hand letter or type a label which includes the call number, part number (if there are multiple items in a set), copy number and/or accession number (if used), and the contents of any accompanying material (see Figure 6.2). Place this label on the outside front cover of the container where space permits.

Spine labels. The spine of the packaging may display the title and the call number. If the title of the opaque material is already commercially printed on the container spine, letter or type a call number label to be placed on the lower portion of the spine consistent with library guidelines. If there is no title label

Figure 6.1
Processing Opaque Material with Full Label

on the spine, prepare a title identification label to be placed on the upper portion of the spine, and make a call number label that includes a part number (if there are multiple items in a set) and a copy and/or accession number (if used) for the bottom portion of the spine (see Figure 6.2).

Ownership marks. Ownership marks should be placed visibly on the front of the container using either a preprinted label, permanent stamp, or marker to print the library's name.

Pockets for Circulation

Option a: Single-sided two-dimensional materials

Flat materials that are not housed in their own containers present special challenges in terms of preparing them for circulation. If pockets are to be used,

Figure 6.2
Two-Dimensional Container Labeling

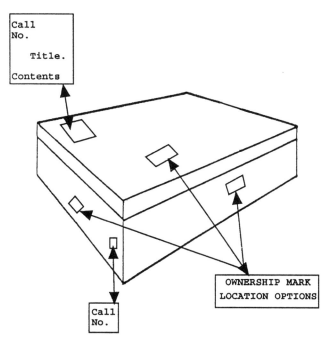

a variety of solutions are available. Paper or self-adhesive clear pockets may be attached to the back of single-sided flat materials if they are not archival in nature. Pockets may be spaced at intervals on the reverse side to prevent pocket buildup when materials are stored horizontally in drawers and boxes. (See Chapter 3 for a more detailed discussion of this method.) If materials are matted, pockets may be attached to the back side of mats. For pictures and other materials to which pockets should not be attached, special circulating envelopes or folders with pockets may be used. In such cases, individual labeling would not be needed because the envelopes and folders may be reused for various types of materials.

Option b: Double-sided two-dimensional materials

Pockets may be hinged using clear tape so that information may be read when the pocket is lifted. Attach these pockets in a position consistent with library policy. An alternative would be to attach to one of the surfaces a clear self-adhesive pocket that will allow the user to see information beneath the pocket.

Option c: Two-dimensional materials stored in containers

The least protected place for the pocket is on the exterior of the container. Consistency of placement is important but will be affected by the availability of a flat surface void of important information. Pockets also may be applied to the inside front cover of boxes, albums, and folders that open and have flat surfaces.

Barcodes

Option a: Barcode on individual two-dimensional material

If two-dimensional material is to be checked out individually, barcodes may be attached directly to each item. Choose a consistent place on the front or the back of the material for barcode placement. If pockets are used, some libraries may find it convenient to locate the barcode adjacent to the pocket. Others may prefer to locate the barcode near the call number, where it is always easily visible.

Option b: Barcode on two-dimensional material container

Placement of barcodes on flat material containers should be consistent with library policy. Barcodes should not be placed over any ridges of the container or over important information. Some libraries may prefer to locate the barcode on the upper center edge of the front or back cover of the container, where it is always easily accessible. Another favored location is directly adjacent to the circulation pocket for ease of access at the time of checkout. Other libraries may choose to apply the barcode to the upper right corner of the back of the container parallel to the spine. This location is easily accessible during shelf inventory.

Security Devices

If two-dimensional opaque materials are to be checked out individually, it may be a good idea to attach a security device directly on each individual item. Security strips may be attached to the back of the item in a consistent location and should be covered with opaque tape or a small narrow label. If using security devices that are embedded in labels, attach them to the flat material in a place consistent with library policy, exercising caution not to cover important information.

For two-dimensional materials housed in their own containers, security devices may be placed on the inside of the container in an inconspicuous location or on the outside in a place consistent with library policy. If using strips which would otherwise be visible, cover them with a label or opaque piece of tape (such as an identification label or an ownership label). For security devices that are embedded in labels, attach them to the flat material container in a place consistent with library policy. For a more complete discussion of security devices, see the section on security in Chapter 1.

Accompanying Material

Accompanying material for opaque two-dimensional materials is often a study guide or identification document. For materials that have no original container and are housed in drawers, some type of label or marking should be attached to the individual piece to indicate the availability and location of the accompanying material. When materials are stored in containers that are too small to include their accompanying materials, labels are needed for the containers to indicate the remote location of the accompanying material. Various methods for doing this are detailed in the section on accompanying material in Chapter 2. Materials housed in their original or replacement containers should be kept together with the flat materials. When folding is required to fit the accompanying material into the container, it will be necessary to weigh the damage factor resulting from folding against the possibility of item loss. Larger pieces of accompanying material should receive more permanent covering. A call number should be placed on the covering of accompanying material so that it is linked to its two-dimensional material. It is advisable to be consistent in placing ownership designations (stamps or labels) according to individual libraries' established guidelines yet allow for flexibility if the alternative would be to cover important information. When accompanying material is stored separately and barcodes are in general use for the rest of the collection, a unique barcode should be placed on each piece of accompanying material. This practice will help the library keep track of each separate circulation.

Gift Plates

Two-dimensional single-sided materials not housed in their own containers may have gift plates attached to their reverse side if they are not archival or one-of-a-kind art originals. Pockets may be hinged to the back of the item to prevent covering important information. Gift plates may be applied to containers which store flat materials wherever there is sufficient room. If necessary, gift plates may be hinged to preserve access to written information. Gift plates also may be attached to circulation pockets. Another option is to use a small pressure-sensitive label and type GIFT OF followed by the donor's name, if used, and apply the label wherever space is available.

FILMSTRIP

Definition: A length of film containing a succession of images intended for projection one at a time, with or without recorded sound. (*AACR 2, 1988 rev.:* 618)

General Information

Since the 1950s, filmstrips have been a popular and relatively inexpensive format for libraries to collect, especially in educational settings. Originally filmstrips came in either short flat strips or in long rolls wound into small round metal or plastic canisters. Relatively few libraries collected the flat strip, and it is no longer commercially available. Various educational producers and distributors continue to issue the 35-mm filmstrip roll.

Filmstrips may be silent or have sound accompaniment. The silent ones contain captions printed on the frames below the images. For filmstrips with sound, an accompanying sound disc or sound cassette supplies a narrative that also contains an audible and/or an inaudible signal, which manually or automatically causes the filmstrip projector to advance the filmstrip. At one time a few 16-mm filmstrips were issued with integral sound in a cartridge that included a sound tape reel, but this format required a special type of projector and was never distributed widely.

Filmstrips are made of a fragile film medium and are susceptible to anything that might scratch or damage their surfaces. Because they have sprocket holes on both sides, they are especially vulnerable to sprocket hole cracks and tears. It is recommended that cotton gloves be used whenever the filmstrip is handled or repaired. A filmstrip may be spliced, but care must be taken not to crease the splice or the filmstrip itself, because either can cause further damage to the filmstrip during projection. Filmstrip projectors must be kept clean and in good repair to prevent harm to the filmstrip.

Considerations for Filmstrip Storage

- Filmstrips may be housed individually in shallow compartmentalized drawers in free-standing stacking units. Accompanying materials are stored separately.
- Filmstrips may be housed in free-standing canister holders, which are designed to be used on standard library shelving. (Store accompanying materials separately.)
- Filmstrips may be housed individually or as sets in the original containers in which they come (e.g., boxes, albums, hanging bags, etc.) or in similar replacement packaging. These containers usually lend themselves to intershelving on regular library shelving. Accompanying materials can usually remain with the filmstrips with this option.

Filmstrip Labeling

Although many libraries prefer not to label the filmstrip itself, there are acceptable methods of identification labeling which do not involve attaching labels that might jam in a projector. Permanent ink film markers are an option for writing on film, as are sharp instruments such as an electric stylus, which can

Figure 6.3
Filmstrip Labeling

be used to etch a call number and an ownership designation onto the emulsion side of the filmstrip leader (see Figure 6.3).

Filmstrip Canister Labeling

Most commercial filmstrips have a preprinted identification label on the lid with the title and publisher's name on it. The lid may also include the name of the series, the number of frames, and/or a date. If the commercial label is lacking or is incomplete, an identification label may be prepared that includes the title and any other information the library deems important (e.g., number of frames, color or black and white, etc.). Small blank circular labels are available commercially, or small rectangular ones may be used. Either hand letter or type the label, including the call number, the filmstrip or part number, the copy number and/or accession number (if used), and the contents of any accompanying material. Place this label on the top of the film canister where space permits (see Figure 6.4).

Ownership marks. Ownership marks should be placed visibly on the side of the filmstrip canister using either a preprinted label, permanent stamp, or marker with the library's name.

Filmstrip Package Labeling

Packages for filmstrip canisters are usually either boxes with round cutout holes or plastic albums with round molded holes to house the film canisters. If filmstrips are accompanied by sound cassettes or sound discs, cutouts are usually present for holding the sound medium.

Often commercial labels are attached to the front surface of the filmstrip album or box. Such labels may include a set or series title (if more than one filmstrip is included), the publisher, individual filmstrip titles, and the number of frames for each filmstrip. If no such label exists, the library may choose to create such a label. Or the library may choose to prepare an identification label with the title, call number, filmstrip or part number, copy number and/or accession number (if used), and the contents of any accompanying material. Place

Figure 6.4
Filmstrip Canister Labeling

such a label on the front cover in a consistent location, such as the upper left corner (see Figure 6.5).

Spine labels. If the title of the filmstrip(s) has been commercially printed on the spine, letter or type a call number label to be placed on the lower portion of the spine. If there is not a preprinted title label on the spine, prepare one to be placed on the middle portion of the spine, and make a call number label which includes the filmstrip part (if the filmstrip is part of a set) and the copy number and/or an accession number (if used) for the bottom portion of the spine.

If hanging bags are used to house filmstrips, an identification label may be prepared for those as well. Labels featuring the title, call number, filmstrip part, copy number and/or accession number (if used), and the contents of any accompanying material should be attached near the top of the bag in a location consistent with library policy.

Ownership marks. Ownership marks should be placed visibly on the same surface of the filmstrip container as the identification labels using either a preprinted or typed label, stamp, or permanent marker to print the library's name.

Informational labels. If special equipment is required, a label may be made that indicates exactly what is needed (e.g., REQUIRES INAUDIBLE SIGNAL EQUIPMENT). A copyright restriction label also may be placed near the title on the filmstrip container.

Pockets for Circulation

The least protected place for the pocket is on the exterior of the container. Consistency of placement is important but will be affected by the availability of a flat surface void of important information. Pockets may be attached to the inside front

Figure 6.5
Filmstrip Package Labeling

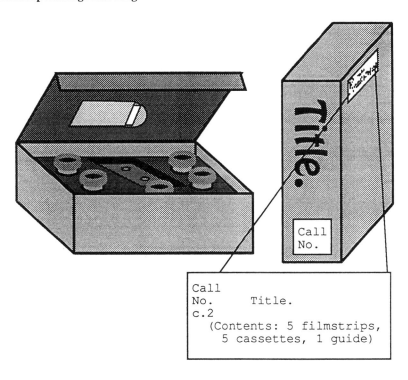

cover of boxes and albums that have lids that open and have flat surfaces. If film-strips are housed in boxes that slide in and out of their outside covering, as shown in Figure 6.6, pockets may have to be attached to an outside surface.

Barcodes

A barcode should never be placed on the filmstrip itself because this could cause the filmstrip to jam in the projector.

Option a: Barcode on filmstrip can

The barcode may be placed on the side of the filmstrip can or, if the barcode is small enough, on the lid of the filmstrip can.

Option b: Barcode on filmstrip container

If a larger container is the preferred location for barcodes, several locations are possible. Some libraries place the barcode on the outside front of the container in a consistent location, such as the upper center edge of the front or back cover of the container where it is always accessible (see Figure 6.6). Others prefer place-

Figure 6.6
Pocket for Filmstrip Container That Slides Open

ment directly adjacent to the circulation pocket for ease of access at the time of
checkout. Another preferred location may be the upper right corner of the back of
the container parallel to the spine, which allows for easy access during inventory.
It is important to be consistent with placement on similar kinds of containers so
circulation staff know where to look, but one must also be careful not to place barcodes over ridges on the container or over important information.

When a container houses multiple filmstrips that have been cataloged individually, the library may choose to place a barcode for each filmstrip on the
outside of the container. If each barcode is scanned at the time of checkout, this
practice assures that the circulation status for each filmstrip appears correctly in
the online catalog when the container is checked out.

If the library's policy is to use duplicate barcodes for each filmstrip in the
container or one-and-a-half barcodes, one barcode may be placed on the filmstrip
and the corresponding part on the container, thus matching the filmstrip to the
container.

Security Devices

Security devices that come in strips may be placed on the filmstrip cans
themselves or on a flat surface of the filmstrip container in a consistent place.

In either location, the strip should be covered by a label or opaque piece of tape (such as an identification label or an ownership label). If security devices are embedded in labels, attach them to the filmstrip can or filmstrip container in a location consistent with library policy. For a more complete discussion of security devices, see the section on security in Chapter 1.

Accompanying Material

Accompanying material for filmstrips is often a sound cassette or a sound disc, a set of spirit masters, study prints, and/or a teacher's guide. If filmstrips are housed in drawers, identification labels should indicate that accompanying material is available. Various methods for doing this are detailed in the section on accompanying material in Chapter 2. Materials housed in original or replacement containers should be kept with the filmstrip(s). When folding is required to fit the accompanying material into the container, it will be necessary to weigh the damage factor resulting from folding against the possibility of item loss. Larger pieces of accompanying material should receive more permanent covering. A label with an identification number should be placed on the covering of accompanying material so that it is linked to its filmstrip. For sound cassette and sound disc labeling, see Chapter 4 for specific details. It is also advisable to be consistent in placing ownership designation (stamps or labels) according to established guidelines. When accompanying material is stored separately and barcodes are in general use for the rest of the collection, a unique barcode should be placed on each piece of accompanying material. This practice will help the library keep track of each separate circulation.

Gift Plates

Gift plates may be applied to the container which stores the filmstrip(s) wherever there is sufficient room. They may have to be hinged to preserve access to written information underneath. They also may be attached to circulation pockets. Another option is to use a small pressure-sensitive label and type GIFT OF followed by the donor's name, if used, and apply the label wherever space is available.

SLIDE

Definition: Transparent material on which there is a two-dimensional image, usually held in a mount, and designed for use in a projector or viewer. (*AACR 2, 1988 rev.:* 623)

General Information

Historically speaking, slides are one of the oldest forms of nonprint material found in libraries. Although it is recognized that many libraries may house and circulate some older slide forms (such as glass plate lantern slides, 2¼-inch by 2¼-inch slides, or View-master 3D or non-3D discs), the emphasis for this manual is on the 2-inch by 2-inch 35-mm slide that is common today.

The 2-inch by 2-inch slide is usually mounted in a plastic or cardboard mount. Neither is totally satisfactory. Cardboard mounts tend to bend and get caught in carousel trays or projectors; plastic mounts can warp from the heat of projectors and cause slides to jam projectors or trays. An alternative for heavily used slides is to remount them between glass in plastic or metal mounts. Glass mounts, however, are usually too thick for carousel trays and may jam or stick in certain types of equipment.

Whenever a problem arises with an existing mount, it should be replaced immediately to prevent any potential harm to the slide image. Use of cotton gloves is recommended whenever slides are being handled or remounted to protect the slide film from body oil and fingerprints. Projectors should be kept clean and in good repair to help prevent any potential damage to slides during projection. Color slides are particularly sensitive to light, heat, and humidity, but all slides are fragile and susceptible to anything that might scratch or damage their surfaces.

Considerations for Slide Storage

- Slides may be stored in nonacidic, inert plastic or acrylic sleeves in loose-leaf binders on shelves, or in pouches in filing drawers.
- Slides may be stored in plastic carousel trays housed in boxes or albums that protect slides from dust and light.
- Slides may be stored in secure compartments within large locking cases that can be stored on regular library shelving.
- Slides may be stored in visual racks that hold up to 100 slides each and are illuminated when the cabinet is open.
- Slides may be stored in small original producer boxes if they are secured on shelves in some way or slipped into hanging bags or envelopes that will be filed in drawers.
- Master slides should be kept in a cold storage area for maximum protection from heat, humidity, and light.

Slide Labeling

Commercial slide mounts are labeled in one of three ways. When compared to the image on the slide film, they either correspond to the image on the slide, are upside down compared to the film image, or are sideways to the image. These varied labeling methods often cause confusion for the user about how slides should be put into a slide tray for proper projection. One solution to this confusion is to use a thumbspot on the slide mount. Thumbspots are uniform stickers or ink marks that are always placed on the lower left-hand corner of

Figure 6.7
Labeling Slide Mounts with Thumbspots for Placement in Projectors and Trays

the slide mount when one is looking at the slide image in its upright position. If slides are mounted properly, this will also be the nonemulsion side of the slide film. If the thumbspot is placed correctly on the mount, the thumbspot will always be in the user's right hand when the slide is placed upside down into the projector. Library-provided thumbspots help a user load slides into a slide tray or projector so that images will not be backward or upside down when projected (see Figure 6.7).

Slides are often issued in sets or collections. The librarian needs to decide whether slides are to be identified individually or as a unit. Such decisions will depend on the needs of the users, what other library resources are available, whether the slides are accompanied by other materials such as sound recordings, and whether the library allows a slide to be used independently of the rest of the set. For example, a set of Renaissance painting slides may consist of individual paintings by various painters. The slides may be housed in browsing cases from which users can pick and choose various slides according to their special needs; or they may be housed in a carousel tray with an accompanying sound cassette and be checked out only as a unit.

In the former instance, each slide may require an identification label that includes the painter, name of painting, an identification number for the set as

Figure 6.8
Slide Marking for a Carousel Tray

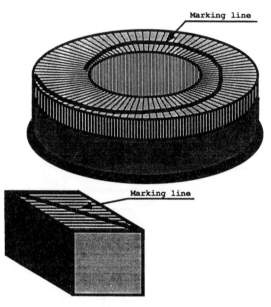

well as one for the individual slide, and an ownership mark. If slides are circulated as a unit in a tray, each slide may only need a call number for the set and an individual slide number on each slide. For slides that will be housed in a carousel tray, it is a good idea to make a diagonal line along the bottoms of the mounts before they are placed in the tray (see Figure 6.8). Later this kind of marking will identify missing or out-of-order slides when they are placed upside down in carousel trays or stacking trays.

Library labeling of slide mounts should be consistent and usually done so it corresponds with the upright image on the slide itself. Because of the small size of the slide mount, most libraries will stamp and/or print slide identification marks on the mounts themselves rather than on labels to be attached to the mounts. Another reason for not using labels is that labels can come loose and cause the projector to jam. If slides are mounted in plastic, metal, or glass mounts, a pen with permanent ink is recommended for marking. If property stamps are used, permanent ink for the stamp pad is also recommended. When slides are mounted in cardboard mounts, care must be taken to use a very fine pen point and an ink that does not bleed into the cardboard.

The library's call number should be placed in either the upper left or the upper right corner of the slide mount, according to library policy. Sequence numbers can be included as part of the call number or placed on the opposite corner from the call number. If copy and/or accession numbers are used, they

Figure 6.9
Individual Location Markings for Slides Housed in an Illuminated Display Cabinet

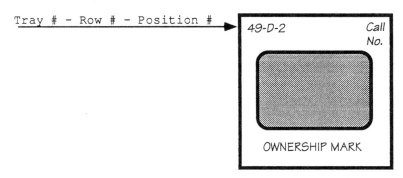

may appear below the call number, in the middle of the upper portion of the mount, or on the back of the mount.

Ownership marks. A stamp with ownership identification is recommended for use on slide mounts. A good location for this marking is on the middle of the lower frame below the slide film itself.

Informational labels. It may be necessary to add special informational markings to the slide mount such as THIS SIDE UP or HANDLE BY MOUNTS ONLY. Other information, such as name and/or location of the subject on the slide itself, may also be useful, especially if the slides are to be housed in lighted slide trays or in plastic sleeves which allow browsing by library patrons. For slides housed permanently in carousel trays, this type of labeling may not be necessary because accompanying information that provides such detailed identification is usually available.

For slides that are housed in special illuminated cabinet trays or other locked cases, providing an exact slide location mark for each slide is also helpful (see Figure 6.9). The location includes a cabinet number (when more than one cabinet is in use), the tray number, and the space number in the tray, as well as the call number for the individual slide. Sometimes it may be advantageous to house more than one set or more than one part of a set in the same carousel tray. In this case, a detailed contents label may be needed for the tray, such as the one shown in Figure 6.10.

Slide Container Labeling

As noted earlier in this section, there are several storage options for slides. For slides stored in boxes (large or small), binders, hanging bags, envelopes, etc., basic identification labeling is needed. If commercial labeling is lacking or is incomplete, type an identification label with the title, call number, part number (if there is more than one container in a set), copy number and/or accession

Figure 6.10
Carousel Tray Labeling for More Than One Set of Slides

number (if used), and the contents of the accompanying material. Place this type of identification on the front of the container in a location consistent with library policy (see Figure 6.11).

Spine labels. If the title of the slide set is commercially printed on the spine, letter or type a call number label to be placed on the lower portion of the spine. If there is no title label on the spine, prepare a title identification label to be placed on the middle portion of the spine, and make a call number label that includes part number (if appropriate) and copy number and/or accession number (if used) for the bottom portion of the spine.

Ownership marks. Ownership marks should be placed visibly on the same surface of the slide container as the identification labels using either a preprinted label, a stamped or typed label, or a permanent marker to print the library's name.

Informational labels. A copyright restriction label may be placed near the title on the slide container. If special equipment is required, prepare a special label indicating what is required (e.g., REQUIRES INAUDIBLE SIGNAL EQUIPMENT).

Pockets for Circulation

Circulation pockets may be attached to the inside or the outside of slide containers, but an inside protected location will usually be the most durable. Often pockets may be applied to the inside front cover of boxes or binders that open and have flat surfaces. If slides are housed in containers that have important writing on the inside cover, pockets may have to be attached to an outside surface or hinged on the inside to allow access to what lies underneath. Consistency of placement is important but will be affected by the availability of a flat surface that is void of important information.

Figure 6.11
Slide Container Labeling

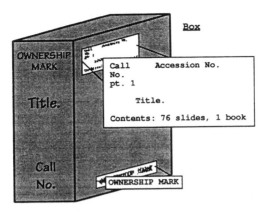

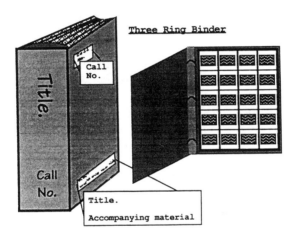

Barcodes

Option a: Barcode on individual slide

If slides are to be checked out individually, it is a good idea to order small barcodes that can be attached directly to the individual slide mounts. Because the front of the slide mount is already being used for various types of labeling, it is recommended that the barcode be placed on the back of the mount in a consistent location.

Option b: Barcode on slide container

Placement of barcodes on slide containers should be consistent with library policy, being careful not to place them over any ridges of the container or over

important information. Some libraries place the barcode on the outside front of
the container in a consistent location, such as the upper center edge of the front
or back cover of the container where it is always accessible. Others prefer placement directly adjacent to the circulation pocket for ease of access at the time of
checkout. Another preferred location may be the upper right corner of the back
of the container parallel to the spine, which allows for easy access during inventory.

Option c: Barcode on carousel tray

Barcodes may be placed on the outside edge of a carousel tray.

Security Devices

If slides are to be checked out individually, it may be a good idea to attach
a security device directly to the individual slide mount. Security strips that have
been trimmed to keep only the magnetic portion of the strip may be attached to
the back of the mount in a location consistent with library policy but should be
covered with opaque tape or a small narrow label. At this time, radio frequency
labels are not small enough to fit on slide mounts.

Security devices that come in strips may be placed on slide containers in a
consistent location. The strip should be covered by a label or opaque piece of
tape (such as an identification label or an ownership label). Security devices that
are embedded in labels may be attached to the slide container in a place consistent with library policy. For a more complete discussion of security devices,
see the section on security in Chapter 1.

Accompanying Material

Accompanying material for slides is often a sound cassette or a sound disc,
a set of spirit masters, study prints, and/or a teacher's guide. If slides are housed
in drawers, trays, or cabinets, identification labels should indicate that accompanying material is available. Various methods for doing this are detailed in the
section on accompanying material in Chapter 2. Materials that fit in the original
or replacement container should be kept together with the slides. When folding
is required to fit the accompanying material into the container, it will be necessary to weigh the damage factor resulting from folding against the possibility
of item loss. Larger pieces of accompanying material should receive more permanent covering. A label with an identification number should be placed on the
covering of accompanying material so that it is linked to its slide(s). For additional information about labeling sound cassettes and sound discs, refer to Chapter 4. It is also advisable to be consistent in placing ownership designations
(stamps or labels) according to established guidelines. When accompanying material is stored separately and barcodes are in general use for the rest of the
collection, a unique barcode should be placed on each piece of accompanying

material. This practice will help the library keep track of each separate circulation.

Gift Plates

Gift plates may be applied to the container which stores the slides wherever there is sufficient room. They may have to be hinged to preserve access to written information underneath. They also may be attached to circulation pockets. Another option is to use a small pressure-sensitive label and type GIFT OF followed by the donor's name, if used, and apply the label wherever space is available.

TRANSPARENCY

Definition: A sheet of transparent material bearing an image and designed for use with an overhead projector or a light box. It may be mounted in a frame. (*AACR 2, 1988 rev.*: 624)

General Information

Overhead transparencies may be purchased from commercial sources or produced locally from diazo or thermal transparency film. Images can also be hand drawn on acetate or plastic sheets. Transparencies may be clear with contrasting black or colored images, tinted with colored or black images, or opaque with images portrayed in clear or transparent colored outlines. Transparencies are generally created on 8½-inch by 11-inch sheets and can be used in a mounted or unmounted format. Unmounted transparencies may be single sheets or have overlays that have either an opaque border or are clear. Some may come in book form to be torn out as used, whereas others may be attached permanently in spiral-type binders. Many single transparencies have overlays with additional detail that are attached to the transparency itself or to its paper or plastic mount. Others may have manually operated movable parts such as clock hands or meshing gears. A final type of transparency requires a motion adapter attachment on the overhead projector that creates an illusion of motion by utilizing light-polarizing materials in the rotating disc of the attachment and on the transparency itself.

Transparency mounts come in different styles and materials. They can be made from card stock, white fiberboard, or plastic; and each comes with different sized openings depending on specific needs. The mount itself is usually about 10 inches by 12 inches. Those with wider borders allow for more marking room on the mounts but less inside dimension. When attaching a mount to the transparency, care should be taken not to cover any information on the transparency. With fiberboard and card stock mounts, the inside can be trimmed if necessary

Figure 6.12
Transparency Mounting with Masking Tape

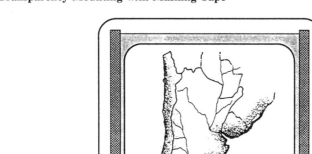

to enlarge the transparency opening. Mounts may be attached to the transparency
with masking tape (see Figure 6.12).

Placing the mount face down on the table, center the transparency face down
on the mount. Use masking tape to attach the transparency to the mount, over-
lapping the tape along the edge of the transparency and the mount. Figure 6.13
shows the self-adhesive style mount. Place the front side of the mount face
down on the table. Open the back part of the mount and center the transparency
face down onto the inside front of the mount. When it is positioned correctly,
close the back of the mount onto the front of the mount, making sure that all
adhesive surfaces are pressed together.

Although diazo dyes used in many transparencies may be more durable than
photographic dyes, basic transparency care should include the following.

Considerations for Transparency Storage

- Secure transparencies in containers that will protect them from dust, direct sunlight,
  heat and humidity, or contact with anything that might stain or mark them.
- Handle the transparency surface as little as possible to prevent fingerprints, scratches,
  dust, and other marks from showing up on the projected image.

Figure 6.13
Transparency Mounting with Self-Adhesive Mounts

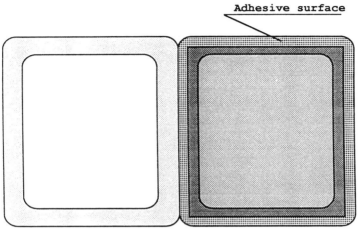

Place transparency on adhesive surface.

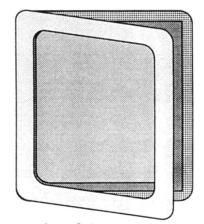

Fold over and seal transparency.

- Unmounted transparencies may be stored in nonacidic plastic or paper folders or envelopes, separated by acid-free sheets of paper or fiberboard. Folders and envelopes may be stored in vertical file drawers, divided shelves, pullout racks, bins, hanging folders, and bags.

- Unmounted transparencies may be punched and stored in three-ring binders with a protective sheet of paper between each transparency.

- Single mounted transparencies may be housed in large envelopes with top and bottom protective sheets and be stored in legal or X-ray size file drawers, hanging folders or bags, and divided shelves.

* Sets of transparencies may be housed in their original containers (boxes, books, folders, binders, hanging bags, etc.) or in replacement containers and be stored on regular library shelving.

Transparency Labeling

It is preferable to label transparencies on their mounts or their containers. However, if a library has a large collection of unmounted transparencies, the librarian may choose to use some sort of brief labeling on each transparency itself. A heat stylus may be used or a pen with permanent ink. It is important to remember, however, that any labeling placed directly on the transparency will show up on the projected image. If a label is attached to the transparency, it will show up as an opaque blank area on the projected image.

Transparency Mount Labeling

Most commercial transparencies have preprinted identification markings on the transparency mounts with the name of the transparency, a sequence number (if the transparency is part of a set), and perhaps the name of the publisher. If the commercial label is lacking or is incomplete, hand letter or type an identification label with the title and any other information that the library deems important. Transparency mounts should be labeled when the image on the transparency is facing up, as it would appear on the screen when it is projected. If transparencies are mounted in plastic mounts, a pen with permanent ink is recommended for marking. When property stamps are used, permanent ink for the stamp pad is recommended as well. If transparencies are mounted on card stock or fiberboard mounts, care should be taken to use a fine pen point and an ink that does not bleed into the paper or fiberboard.

Print with a pen using permanent ink or type a label (see Figure 6.14) which includes the transparency call number, the part number (if the transparency is part of a set), the copy number and/or accession number (if used), and an indication of accompanying material. Place this labeling in either the upper left or the upper right corner of the transparency mount according to local library policy. Sequence numbers may be included as part of the call number or placed on the opposite corner from the call number. If copy or accession numbers are used, they may appear below the call number or in the middle of the upper portion of the mount or on the back of the mount.

Ownership marks. Ownership marks should be placed visibly on the front of the transparency mount using either a preprinted label, permanent ownership stamp, or marker to print the library's name. A good location for this marking is on the middle of the lower frame below the transparency film itself.

Informational labels. It may be necessary to add special informational mark-

Figure 6.14
Transparency Mount Labeling

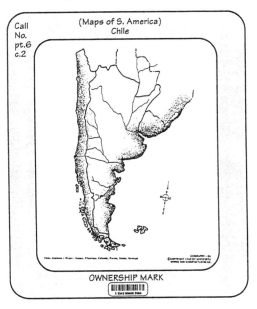

ings to the transparency mount, such as the name of the series or more information
about the transparency itself. This is especially useful if the transparencies are to
be housed in folders or plastic envelopes which allow browsing by the library patrons. For transparencies that are housed permanently in books or binders, this
type of labeling may not be necessary because accompanying information is usually available that provides such detailed identification.

Transparency Container Labeling

As noted earlier in this section, there are several storage options for transparencies. For transparencies stored in boxes, binders, hanging bags, envelopes,
etc., basic identification labeling is needed. If commercial labeling is lacking or
is incomplete, type a label (see Figure 6.15) with the title, the call number, the
part number (if there is more than one container in a set), the copy number and/
or accession number (if used), and the contents of any accompanying material
and place it on the front of the container in a consistent location.

Spine labels. If the title of the transparency set is commercially printed on
the spine, letter or type a call number label to be placed on the lower portion
of the spine. If there is no title label on the spine, prepare a title label to be
placed on the middle portion of the spine, and make a call number label that

Figure 6.15
Transparency Container Labeling

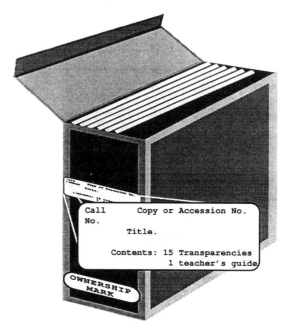

Call   Copy or Accession No.
No.
                Title.

            Contents: 15 Transparencies
                      1 teacher's guide

OWNERSHIP
MARK

includes part number (if applicable) and copy number and/or accession number (if used) for the bottom portion of the spine. For containers too thin to have the call number marked on the spine, mark the call number on the front in the lower or upper left-hand corner, consistent with library policy for other formats.

Ownership marks. Ownership marks should be placed visibly on the same surface of the transparency container as the identification labels using either a preprinted label, a stamped or typed label, or a permanent marker to print the library's name.

Informational labels. A copyright restriction label may be placed near the title on the transparency container. If special equipment is required, prepare a special label indicating what is required (e.g., REQUIRES MOTION ADAPTOR ATTACH-MENT).

Pockets for Circulation

The least protected place for the pocket is on the exterior of the container. Consistency of placement is important but will be affected by the availability of a flat surface void of important information. Pockets may be applied to the inside front cover of boxes and binders that open and have flat surfaces and inside envelopes near the top of the opening. If transparencies are housed in boxes that have important writing on the inside cover, pockets may have to be attached to an outside surface or hinged on the inside to allow access to what lies underneath.

Barcodes

Option a: Barcode on individual transparency

It is not recommended that barcodes be attached to unmounted transparencies. As already stated, any labeling placed on the transparency film itself will show up on the projected image. If a barcode label is attached to the transparency, it will show up as an opaque blank area on the projected image.

Option b: Barcode on transparency mount

If transparencies are to be checked out individually, barcodes may be attached directly to individual transparency mounts. Choose a consistent place for barcodes on the front or back of the mount that is usually void of other important information.

Option c: Barcode on transparency container

Placement of barcodes on transparency containers should be consistent with library policy, being careful not to place them over any ridges of the container or areas with important information. Some libraries place the barcode on the outside front of the container in a consistent location, such as the upper center edge of the front or back cover of the container where it is always accessible. Others prefer placement directly adjacent to the circulation pocket for ease of access at the time of checkout. Another preferred location may be the upper right corner of the back of the container parallel to the spine, which allows for easy access during inventory.

Security Devices

If transparencies are to be checked out individually, it may be a good idea to attach a security device directly to the individual transparency mount. Security strips can be attached to the back of the mount in a consistent location and should be covered with opaque tape or a small narrow label. If mounts are made in house, the strip could be hidden between the layers at that time. If using security devices that are embedded in labels, attach them to the mount in a place consistent with library policy.

For transparencies housed in their own containers, security devices may be placed on the container in a location consistent with library policy. If the strips would otherwise be visible, cover them with a label or opaque piece of tape (such as an identification label or an ownership label). For security devices that are embedded in labels, attach them to the transparency container in a place consistent with library policy. For a more complete discussion of security devices, see the section on security in Chapter 1.

Accompanying Material

Accompanying material for transparencies is often a set of transparency masters and/or a teacher's guide. If transparencies are housed in containers too small to include their accompanying materials, identification labels should indicate that accompanying material is available. Various methods for doing this are detailed in the section on accompanying material in Chapter 2. Materials that can be housed in their original or replacement containers should be kept together with the transparencies. When folding is required to fit the accompanying material into the container, it will be necessary to weigh the damage factor resulting from folding against the possibility of item loss. Larger pieces of accompanying material should receive more permanent covering. A label with an identification number should be placed on the covering of accompanying material so that it is linked to its transparency. It is also advisable to be consistent in placing ownership designation (stamps or labels) according to established guidelines. When accompanying material is stored separately and barcodes are in general use for the rest of the collection, a unique barcode should be placed on each piece of accompanying material. This practice will help the library keep track of each separate circulation.

Gift Plates

Gift plates may be applied to the container which stores the transparencies wherever there is sufficient room, or they may be affixed to circulation pockets. To preserve access to written information underneath, it may be necessary to hinge gift plates to one of the surfaces. Another option is to use a small pressure-sensitive label and type GIFT OF followed by the donor's name, if used, and apply the label wherever space is available.

REFERENCES

Anglo-American Cataloguing Rules, Second Edition, 1988 Revision, ed. by Michael Gorman and Paul W. Winkler for the Joint Steering Committee for Revision of AACR. Chicago: American Library Association.

Ellison, John W. 1987. *Non-print Media: Collection Management and User Services.* Chicago: American Library Association.

Olson, Nancy B. 1988. *Audiovisual Material Glossary.* Dublin, OH: OCLC Online Computer Library Center.

Weihs, Jean. 1991. *The Integrated Library: Encouraging Access to Multimedia Materials.* Phoenix: Oryx Press.

7

Computer Files

Definition: A file (data and/or program) encoded for manipulation by computer.

(*AACR 2, 1988 rev.:* 617)

GENERAL INFORMATION

Library computer collections have evolved and changed dramatically over the past thirty years. During the late 1960s, if libraries collected computer files at all, collections consisted of large reels of magnetic tape and/or paper punch cards that were designed to run on large mainframe computers. By the 1980s, mainframe computers were competing with microchip technologies and the development of minicomputers and microcomputers. Formats called microcomputer software began to emerge, and libraries began to collect computer cassettes, cartridges, and floppy disks. Today's computer technology continues to evolve and change. Libraries are adding new formats all the time (e.g., high-density floppy disks, CD-ROMs, CD-Is, etc.).

For the purposes of this processing manual, the discussion applies to files that are stored on, or contained in, carriers physically located in the library. Computer files that are available by remote access are not considered, nor are large computer-center kinds of collections. Files considered include computer cassettes, computer cartridges, computer disks, computer laser optical discs (e.g., CD-ROMs), and computer reels. For purposes of distinction between computer disks and computer laser optical discs, *disk* spelled with a *k* refers to magnetic computer disks and *disc* spelled with a *c* refers to computer laser optical discs such as the CD-ROM or CD-I discs. This distinction is based on Library of Congress Rule Interpretations for Chapter 9, rule 9.5B1, which states "(The term 'disc' reflects the standardized spelling used by the computer industry for optical storage devices. The term 'disk' reflects the spelling for magnetic storage devices.)" (Library of Congress *Cataloging Service Bulletin,* Spring 1994: 13).

Because of the vulnerability of computer files, where practical and when legal a library may decide to maintain a noncirculating backup collection of files. Many computer disks come with their own backup disks or with directions for making backups. In other cases, permission for making backup copies is obtained at the time of purchase. When data is in the public domain, a solution to multiple programs on one diskette or cassette is to copy individual programs from the original to other diskettes or cassettes, thus enabling programs to be grouped by subject or curriculum area. It may be desirable for libraries to purchase only computer software for which they have computers; otherwise they have no way to make backups or check software for erasure and damage.

An additional consideration for computer files is that United States law requires that all computer files in a library must have labels placed on them cautioning against illegal copying. According to Kent Dunlap, Principal Legal Advisor of the U.S. Copyright Office,

The implementing regulation does not specifically specify size, or other requirements. It merely provides: "the notice shall be printed in such a manner as to be clearly legible, comprehensible, and readily apparent to a casual user of the computer program." . . . The implementing regulation provides the notice "shall be affixed to the packaging that contains the copy of the computer program which is the subject of a library loan to patrons, by means of a label cemented, gummed, or otherwise durably attached to the copies *or* to a box, reel, cartridge, cassette, or other container used as a permanent receptacle for the copy of the computer program." . . . It is clear under the regulations that only one warning need be placed on the carrier (disk, tape, etc.) or the packaging. . . . The warning does not have to be placed on both the carrier and the container-packaging. However, if the container-packaging is not lent to the patron, then the warning must be placed on the carrier. (A description of the requirements of the Computer Rental Amendments Act of 1990 as they pertain to copyright for software lent by nonprofit libraries, explained by Kent Dunlap, Principal Legal Advisor, Copyright Office, Library of Congress, in a letter to Eric Childress, Special Materials Cataloger, Elon College, North Carolina, January 1992)

Computer formats may be limited in use by special licenses and signed agreements or by a library's own decision to require security deposits, to restrict the computer formats to special types of patrons, or to restrict them to use only within the library. If a signed agreement is required by the vendor who sells the software, it may stipulate specific limitations such as use on only one machine at a time and no use on a network of any kind. Some licenses prohibit rental or lending of software. For software purchase orders, it is a good idea to include a statement that alerts the vendor to the fact that the item is being ordered for patrons in a circulating library.

Computer files are generally accompanied by some sort of documentation (i.e., user manuals, data dictionaries, code books, charts, demonstration disks, backup disks, information sheets, or other descriptive guides). This documentation provides crucial information for using the computer file, because external descriptive labels on computer files are often brief and incomplete. In some libraries the documentation may be the only item cataloged and held on site, with the actual computer file housed somewhere else. In such cases, informational labeling on the documentation serves as a link to the actual computer file. Labels should include the remote location and call number of the computer file, the system requirements for the file (including its physical characteristics), the make and model of the required computer and any required peripherals, and information about any use restrictions.

Several questions regarding storage come to mind when both the computer file and its documentation are housed in the library. Should they be stored together or separately? A related but different question is, What should the library do with computer software that comes as accompanying material to a book? For answers to both of these questions, the same issues that apply to making other general nonprint processing decisions should be considered.

- Is the entire collection open to users on an unrestricted basis or does the library have a policy of in-house use only?
- Does the library maintain open or closed shelving?
- Are various formats of material intershelved, or are book materials shelved in one place and other formats (including computer files) shelved in separate areas?
- Does the library utilize a magnetic security system? If so, does it erase magnetic materials?

Decisions should be based on answers to these considerations. When the decision is made that books accompanied by computer files or computer files accompanied by written documentation are to be kept together, shelving and packaging choices must be made that ensure user accessibility and security of the materials. If the library has a magnetic security system, another decision will be needed regarding how circulation personnel will be alerted to the fact that the book or package contains a magnetic computer file and should not be passed through the regular desensitizing equipment. Some libraries choose to house magnetic materials in specially colored containers. Others choose large fluorescent warning labels that are attached to containers or the outside of books, such as WARNING: DO NOT DESENSITIZE or WARNING: REQUIRES SPECIAL HANDLING.

If items are kept separately, the computer file and its accompanying documentation or the book and its accompanying computer file should be identified so there is no doubt that the items go together. Detailed informational labeling is necessary to make both patron and circulation personnel aware of the other item's availability and separate location. Special technical details labeling is also helpful for the use of computer files. Such specific information should be attached to the book, the package, and/or to the software itself (e.g., "System requirements for computer files: 386 system or higher; min. 4 MB (8 MB recommended); Windows 3.0 or higher, hard drive"). If barcodes are used, a barcode should be placed on the accompanying material as well as on the main item. This allows the library to track the circulation of all separately housed materials.

The formats (cassette, cartridge, magnetic disk, computer laser optical (CD-ROM) disc, or magnetic tape reel) that a library collects and their intended use will determine the types of processing that are appropriate. Generally the same general guidelines used for similar nonprint formats may be followed. Libraries that promote browsing and open access to all formats will find detailed computer system requirements labeling to be helpful to patrons using computer files. On the other hand, libraries in which patrons depend on the catalog for choosing computer files may believe that detailed labeling is too labor intensive to justify its use.

COMPUTER CASSETTE AND COMPUTER CARTRIDGES

Definitions

Computer cassette—A device consisting of permanently encased magnetic computer tape that winds and rewinds from reel to reel. (Olson 1988: 7)

Cartridge—A container used to protect and facilitate the use of various computer-related media such as . . . magnetic disk, . . . optical disk, integrated circuitry, or printer ink . . . ribbon. It is usually designed so that the medium remains permanently within the cartridge or at least attached to it, and the medium itself is not touched by an operator. *See* magnetic tape cartridge, disk cartridge, ROM cartridge, caddy. (*Dictionary of Computing*, 3rd ed. 1990: 59–60)

Computer cartridge—A device consisting of either magnetic tape (computer tape cartridge), disk (computer disk cartridge), or chip (computer chip cartridge), encased in a container. (Olson 1988: 7)

> *Computer tape cartridge*)—A device consisting of magnetic tape permanently encased in a plastic container. (Olson 1988: 8)
>
> *Computer disk cartridge*—Single or multiple hard or floppy disks encased in a container, usually made of plastic. The disk unit may be removable, in that it can be taken in and out of the disk drive and replaced with other disk units; or it may be fixed, in that it is permanently sealed by the disk drive inside a clean airtight space. Disk cartridges vary in dimensions, depending upon the size of the disk. They are sometimes called disk modules, and often in the case of multiple disks, disk packs. (Olson 1988: 7)

Computer chip cartridge—A device consisting of a permanently encased computer chip mounted on a printed circuit board. A plug with metal contacts extends out of the bottom of the container, which is mated with a connector found on the computer itself or a console, usually at the bottom of the cartridge slot. Computer chip cartridges are used extensively in arcade and video games. (Olson 1988: 7)

General Information

Several definitions related to computer cassettes and computer cartridges are presented because these terms have been and are sometimes used interchangeably by both librarians and vendors. In addition, confusion has resulted from the similar appearance of some computer cassettes (e.g., Commodore, Tandy, and PET) and standard sound cassettes. Both cassettes and cartridges come in various sizes, varying from the game-type cassettes or cartridges to the full-size and mini-size data system cassettes or cartridges of high-density tape found in computer centers. For the most part, physical processing procedures for cassettes and cartridges are similar except for labeling.

Considerations for Storage

- Computer cassettes and cartridges should be stored in areas that have stabilized temperatures and are free of dust, oil, and magnetic fields.
- Cassettes may be stored upright on baked enamel or wooden shelves in their original plastic boxes, with the tape rewound to the original supply reel. (Due to the small size of cassettes, special shelf supports may be necessary to prevent them from falling through standard shelves.)
- Cartridges may be stored upright on specially divided baked enamel or wooden shelves.
- Cassettes and cartridges may be stored in cabinet drawers or catalog tray files.
- Cassettes and cartridges may be stored in hanging bags, the pockets of binders and albums, or sturdy boxes.

Computer Cassette Labeling

Option a: Processing without labels

Commercially produced computer cassettes come with a producer's label on the flat portion of the top of the computer cassette. Using a pen with permanent ink, print the call number, the computer cassette or part number (if there are multiple cassette tapes in a set), and the copy number and/or accession number (if used) directly on the cassette label as space allows (see Figure 7.1).

Ownership marks. The library name may be written or stamped on the commercial label as space permits or onto a blank label that can be placed on the

Figure 7.1
Processing a Computer Cassette without Labels

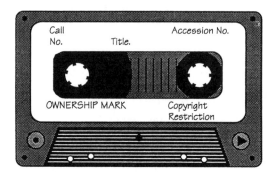

cassette in an area that will not cover important information or cause the cassette or the label to become stuck in the computer.

Informational labels. A handwritten copyright restriction statement may be added where space permits. Refer to the first section of this chapter for specific copyright requirements.

Option b: Processing with minimal labels

Print with a pen using permanent ink or type the call number, computer cassette and/or part number (if there are multiple cassette tapes in a set), and copy number and/or accession number (if used) on a label. Trim if necessary and apply to the upper left or right portion of the commercial label. Avoid covering any important information.

Ownership marks. Preprinted or stamped ownership labels may be placed on the bottom of the commercial label or on another area of the cassette that will not cover important information or cause the cassette to become caught in the computer.

Informational labels. A copyright restriction label may be attached where space permits. Refer to the first section of this chapter for specific copyright requirements.

Option c: Processing with full labels

If computer cassettes are lacking commercial labels, it may be desirable to use full cutout cassette or face labels similar to those used for sound cassettes. They may be purchased as blank labels or commercially imprinted with the library's logo or ownership mark. Over time, the adhesive on some cassette labels may dry up and cause the labels to loosen. If this happens, the label or the cassette could jam in the computer.

Prepare a label that includes the author (if there is one), the title, the version (if applicable), the call number, the part and tape number (if there are multiple cassette tapes in a set), the copy number and/or accession number (if used), and

Figure 7.2
Processing a Computer Cassette with Full Labels

the contents of the accompanying material. Place this label on the top of the computer cassette in the recessed area around the tape path rollers (see Figure 7.2).

Ownership marks. Preprinted or stamped ownership labels may be placed on the identification label as space permits or placed on another area of the cassette that will not cause the cassette to become stuck in the computer.

Informational labels. A copyright restriction label may be attached as space permits. Refer to the first section of this chapter for specific federal copyright requirements.

Computer Cassette Box Labeling

Original computer cassette boxes are the preferred vehicles of storage because they are durable and keep cassettes free from dust. Informational labels may be placed on these boxes depending on the completeness of the commercial labeling on the cassette itself and the library's labeling policy.

Option a: Processing without labels

Supplied data on cassette liners does not have to be repeated, although title labeling may be appropriate for both the front of the cassette box and its spine if otherwise lacking. Using a pen with permanent ink, print the call number and

Figure 7.3
Computer Cassette Box Labeling

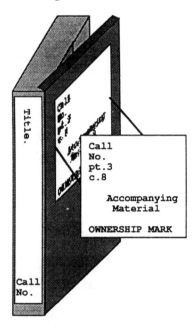

title on the front of the box in a consistent location (e.g., in the upper left corner, or next to the hinged spine near the bottom).

Spine labels. Print the title vertically on the hinged spine beginning near the top, and print the call number near the bottom of the box.

Ownership marks. The library name may be written or stamped with permanent ink on the cassette box as space permits. It is advisable to develop a simple clear ownership designation if using this method.

Option b: Processing with minimal labels

If the box is transparent, labels on the cassette itself may be sufficient. If author and/or title information is needed on the box, print with a pen using permanent ink or type a label with that information, the call number, the cassette or part number (if the cassette is part of a set), and the copy number and/or accession number (if used). Place the label in a consistent location on the front of the box (see Figure 7.3).

Spine labels. Print or type the title on a label and attach it to the center of the hinged spine. Print or type the call number on a label and place it on the box spine near the bottom of the spine.

Ownership marks. A small ownership label stamped or imprinted with the library's name or logo may be placed in a position consistent with library policy on the front or back of the box.

Informational labels. Informational labels (e.g., copyright restrictions) may be placed visibly on the front and/or back cover of the cassette box.

Option c: Processing with full labels.

If a computer cassette box is lacking a commercial liner or label, it may be desirable to prepare a label that includes more detailed information, including the author (if there is one), the title or titles, the version (if applicable), the call number, the part and tape number (if there are multiple cassettes in a set), the copy number and/or accession number (if used), and the physical contents of the accompanying material (manuals, reference cards, instructions, etc.). Place this label on the front of the computer cassette box. Follow the instructions for spine labels and ownership marks under "Option b: Processing with minimal labels."

Informational labels. It is helpful to include system requirements notes that give the make and model of the computer on which the cassette will run, the memory requirements of the computer, the operating system, and any peripherals that are required for using the cassette. Additional special labels may point out such things as title variations from the cassette label, special use restrictions, or a brief statement of what the program does (e.g., "A game designed to teach basic Japanese grammar skills"). A label for the intellectual contents is also helpful if more than one program is on a cassette.

If copyright information is not on the cassette itself, a copyright restriction label should be attached to the cassette box where space permits. Refer to the first section of this chapter for specific copyright requirements.

Computer Cartridge Labeling

Computer cartridges come in different sizes depending on whether they are game-type computer chip cartridges or high-density data disk or tape cartridges. Labeling specifications may be applied to all of them.

Option a: Processing without labels

Commercial cartridges usually come with a producer's label on the flat portion of the front of the computer cartridge. Using a pen with permanent ink, print the call number, the computer cartridge or part number (if there are multiple cartridges in a set), and the copy number and/or accession number (if used) directly on the cartridge label as space allows (see Figure 7.4).

Ownership marks. The library name may be written or stamped on the commercial label as space permits or onto a blank label, which can be placed on another area of the cartridge that will not cause it to become stuck in the computer (i.e., above or below the commercial label or on the edge of the cartridge opposite the edge placed into the computer; see Figure 7.4).

Informational labels. A copyright restriction statement should be added where

Figure 7.4
Processing a Computer Cartridge without Labels

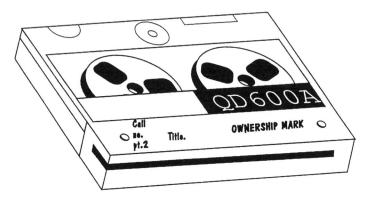

space permits if it is not already supplied. Refer to the first section of this chapter for specific copyright requirements.

Option b: Processing with minimal labels

Print with a pen using permanent ink or type the call number, computer cartridge and/or part number (if there are multiple cartridges in a set), and copy number and/or accession number (if used) on a label. Trim as necessary and apply to the upper left portion of the commercial label. Avoid covering any important information.

Ownership marks. Preprinted or stamped ownership labels may be placed on the bottom of the commercial label or on another area of the cartridge that will not cover important information or cause it to become stuck in the computer (e.g., the edge of the cartridge opposite the edge placed into the computer).

Informational labels. A copyright restriction label should be attached to the cartridge if one is not already supplied. Refer to the first section of this chapter for specific copyright requirements.

Option c: Processing with full labels

If computer cartridges are lacking commercial labels, it may be desirable to prepare one that includes the author (if there is one), the title or titles, the call number, the part and tape number (if there are multiple cartridges in a set), the copy number and/or accession number (if used), and the physical contents of the accompanying material: disks, manuals, reference cards, keyboard templates, guides, etc. Place this label on the front of the computer cartridge (see Figure 7.5). Follow the instructions for ownership marks under "Option b: Processing with minimal labels."

Informational labels. It is helpful to include system requirements notes that give the make and model of the computer on which the software will run, the memory requirements of the computer, the operating system, and any peripherals

Figure 7.5
Processing a Computer Cartridge with Labels

that are required for using the cartridge. If space is not available on the cartridge itself, such information can be included on the accompanying documentation. A copyright restriction label should be attached if not already supplied. Refer to the first section of this chapter for specific copyright requirements. In addition, some libraries may also use other types of special labeling to point out such things as title variations from the cartridge label, special use restrictions, or a brief statement of what the program does (e.g., ''A motorcycle racing simulation designed to teach safety skills''). A label for the intellectual contents is also helpful when more than one program is on the cartridge.

Pockets for Circulation

Pockets cannot be attached directly to computer cassettes or cartridges. One option is to attach a small pocket to the outside front or back of cassette boxes, although the exterior of these small containers is the least protected place for pockets. Another option for both cassettes and cartridges is to house them inside albums, binders, bags, or corrugated boxes. Pockets may be attached to the inside of such containers with permanent rubber cement or two strips of double-stick tape. Self-sticking vinyl pockets are also an option and work well on hanging bags. Consistency of placement is important, but it will be affected by the availability of a flat surface that is lacking important information. Hinging a pocket may be the only alternative to not covering important information. A final option is to use only circulation cards and keep them at the circulation desk.

Barcodes

If the library's policy is to use duplicate barcodes or one-and-a-half barcodes for the computer cassette and its container, one part may be placed on the cassette and the other part on the cassette box, thus matching the computer cassette to the container. As long as the placement is consistent, barcodes may be placed on either side 1 or side 2 of computer cassettes, where space is available. Another option is to use a small barcode that may be placed on an edge of the cassette that does not touch the computer when the cassette is inserted into the machine.

When barcoding cartridges, place the barcode on the cartridge surface in a place consistent with library policy. Some libraries place the barcode on the front of the cartridge on the upper center edge, where it is readily accessible, or on the upper right corner of the back of the cartridge to allow for easy access during inventory. Another preferred location may be on the spine or on one of the ends of the cartridge.

Security Devices

Security strips or labels may be attached to the computer cassette or its box and to the computer cartridge. Radio frequency labels will not affect the stability of information on either. Blank radio labels may be placed under identification and ownership labels, and those encoded as informational or ownership labels may be placed on the front of the cassette or its container or on the cartridge. If albums or boxes are used, security strips may be covered by labels or a piece of opaque tape and placed inside the spines of these containers. Caution must be exercised when using magnetic security labels or strips. Some systems utilize a newer and smaller magnetic strip or label that can be demagnetized without affecting magnetic library material. However, special demagnetizing equipment is required for these devices. One must be certain that existing security systems are sensitive enough to be triggered by the newer and smaller security devices and still render the computer data safe. Special warning labels and/or specially colored containers will be required to alert circulation personnel that an item should not pass through the regular desensitizing equipment. Studies have shown that there is no risk of data alteration from passing magnetic materials through exit sensor gates. For a more complete discussion of security systems and problems, refer to Chapter 1.

Accompanying Material

There are a variety of accompanying materials associated with computer files, as detailed in the preceding "General Information" section of this chapter. Follow the guidelines discussed in Chapter 2 for treatment of such materials. When possible, the accompanying material should remain in the container with the computer cassette or cartridge. For most cassettes and cartridges, this would be possible only if the cassettes and cartridges were housed in larger albums, bags, binders, or boxes. When folding is required to fit the accompanying material into the same container, it will be necessary to weigh the damage factor resulting from folding against the possibility of item loss. When using three-ring binders, it may be necessary to punch holes in the accompanying material for placement in the binder. Larger pieces of accompanying material should receive more permanent covering.

Accompanying material should always be given complete identification labeling that includes the call number so that it can be linked easily to its companion computer cassette or cartridge. Consistent ownership designations (stamps or labels) should also be included according to locally established guidelines. When accompanying material is stored separately and barcodes are in general use for the rest of the collection, a unique barcode should be placed on each piece of accompanying material. This practice will help the library keep track of each separate circulation.

Gift Plates

Gift plates may be applied to the cassette or cartridge container. They may be glued or cemented to the outside of the container if room is available or be attached to the inside or outside of the circulation pocket. Another option is to use a small pressure-sensitive label and type GIFT OF followed by the donor's name (if used). This may be applied to the container or the circulation pocket depending on the availability of space.

COMPUTER DISK

Definition: A circular, flat device with one or both sides coated with a magnetic material on which information and/or instructions for the computer are written or stored. Disks are direct access storage devices, in that the computer can reach the desired information without having to scan all the information that precedes it. Disks can be rigid or flexible. Flexible disks (diskettes, floppy disks) are available in 3 inch, 3½ inch, 5¼ inch, and 8 inch sizes. Also called **Diskette, Floppy Disk, Magnetic Disk.** (Olson 1988: 7)

General Information

Five and one-quarter inch floppy disks should be "write protected" by covering side notches with special labels made for that purpose (usually included in boxes of new disks; see Figure 7.6). To rewrite a floppy disk, the label is removed. Three and one-half inch disks come with a movable tab. When the tab is in the raised position (with the hole open), the disk is write protected. When it is in the lowered position (with the hole covered), the disk can be rewritten.

For the purposes of this manual, processing techniques may be applied to all sizes of floppy disks. The only difference is that one may write directly on the hard plastic-encased 3½-inch disk, but writing on the flexible 5¼ inch casing with anything other than a felt tip pen can cause damage to the computer data.

Figure 7.6
"Write Protecting" Computer Disks

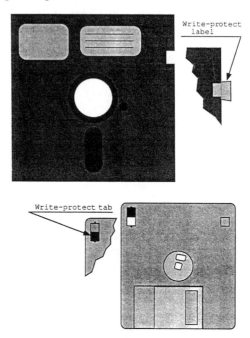

Stamps should not be used on flexible disks either. Computer disks should be touched minimally during processing and only on the casing. Touching exposed areas of the disk, such as the open slot, may cause permanent damage to encoded information. Care should be taken when applying labels to disks. Do not bend or apply undue pressure to the carrier. If labels become loose or torn, remove them before adding new ones. Label buildup can cause a disk to become stuck in the disk drive.

Considerations for Storage

- Computer disks should be stored in areas that have stabilized temperatures and are free of dust, oil, and magnetic fields from central processing units (CPUs), televisions, telephones, fans, or any other machine that has an electric motor.

- Disks should be placed in individual sleeves or dust jackets to protect them from dust, fingerprints, scratches, or loose objects such as paper clips.

- Disks may be stored in storage drawers, hanging bags, plastic cases, diskette folders, corrugated boxes, original storage containers, three-ring binders, pamphlet binders, hanging file folders, and locking disk files.

- To avoid warpage, flexible disks should be stored upright and not leaning. They should not be stored too closely to one another, because imprinting from disk to disk may occur.

Computer Disk Containers

The preferred packaging choice is to retain the original container if it is durable, because it may contain essential information that is not available elsewhere. When the package is not durable, there are several repackaging options. (See also the section on storage in Chapter 1 and the packaging/repackaging section in Chapter 2.)

Option a: Plastic containers

One option is the diskette library case that stores multiple titles and may provide color-coded dividers. These cases come in different sizes and store from 10 to 150 disks. One advantage of this type of storage is that it keeps disks dust free and it stands alone on shelves. A disadvantage is that an additional container is needed for circulation of individual disks outside the library. Another disadvantage is that all accompanying material must be stored separately.

Option b: Albums, hanging bags, student folders, and three-ring loose-leaf binders

These options allow for individual and multiple storage of computer disks and their accompanying material. Albums have pockets for disks and a compartment to house accompanying material. Albums snap shut and keep disks dust free. Hanging bags may be able to accommodate disks and their accompanying material but are not recommended for housing flexible floppy disks because of their pliant characteristics. Student folders and binders with either soft or hard covers may be another solution for multiple disks and documentation. Both come with inside pockets for storing accompanying material, and optional disk pages can be added. Soft-sided pamphlets or student folders are inexpensive, but they are not a good choice for flexible 5¼-inch disks if they are to be circulated outside of the library. Rigid loose-leaf binders may accommodate several disk pages as well as large amounts of accompanying material and are free standing on shelves. They have the further advantage of being multifunctional and can be used to store other types of media as well.

Option c: Diskette cabinets

Diskette cabinets are good for storing large disk collections in a restricted library environment. They provide expandability because units can be stacked one upon the other. They do not allow the intershelving of computer software with other media formats or with their own accompanying material. If disks circulate outside of the library, additional circulating packages must be provided.

Figure 7.7
Processing a Computer Disk without Labels

COPYRIGHT RESTRICTIONS

Computer Disk Labeling

Libraries that retain both archival copies and circulating copies will need to decide how much labeling is necessary for the archival copies. For some libraries a call number may be all that is deemed necessary, whereas others will prefer complete labeling, including system requirement notes in case the circulating copy is destroyed.

Option a: Processing without labels

Commercially produced computer disks often come with a producer's label on the upper portion of the front of the computer disk. Using a soft felt tip pen with permanent ink, print the call number, the computer disk or part number (if there are multiple disks in a set), and the copy number and/or accession number (if used) directly on the disk label as space allows (see Figure 7.7).

Ownership marks. Using a felt tip pen with permanent ink, print the library name on the commercially produced label as space permits or onto a blank label, which can be placed in another area on the top of the disc.

Option b: Processing with minimal labels

The call number, the computer disk or part number (if there are multiple disks in a set), the copy number and/or accession number (if used), and a backup copy note (if used) may be printed using a pen with permanent ink or typed on

Figure 7.8
Processing a Computer Disk with Labels

small labels and applied to the commercially produced label, taking care not to cover important information.

Ownership marks. Preprinted or stamped ownership labels may be placed on the bottom of the commercial label or on another area on the top of the disk that will not cause it to become stuck in the computer.

Option c: Processing with full labels

If computer disks are lacking commercial labels or have only brief ones, it may be desirable to create one that displays the author (if there is one), the title or titles, the version (if applicable), the call number, the computer disk or part number (if there are multiple disks in a set) the copy number and/or accession number (if used), and a backup copy note (if used). Apply in the upper left corner of the floppy disk (see Figure 7.8) or on the recessed area of the 3½-inch disk.

Ownership marks. Follow the instructions given in "Option b: Processing with minimal labels."

Informational labels. It is helpful to include system requirements notes such as the required make and model of the computer on which the software will run, the memory requirements for the computer, the operating system, and any required peripherals if they are not already printed on the commercially produced label (e.g., REQUIRES LOTUS SOFTWARE or REQUIRES VIDEODISC PLAYER AND CONNECTING CABLES). A copyright restriction label also must be attached if it is not already there. Refer to the first section of this chapter for a discussion of the copyright requirements. If the disk is a backup copy, the same information should be included on that disk as well.

Diskette Sleeve Labeling

Disks usually come in inner sleeves to protect them from dust and other destructive elements. It is a good idea to stamp or label these sleeves with an ownership mark to deter theft. Other labeling is not necessary.

Disk Container Labeling

If commercial computer containers are lacking commercial labels or if the library is supplying some sort of repackaging, full container labeling may be desired. Prepare a label that displays the author (if there is one), the title, the call number, the part and tape number (if there are multiple disks in a set), the copy number and/or accession number (if used), and the physical contents of the accompanying material. Place this label on the top of the computer disk container.

Spine labels. If the title of the computer disk is commercially printed on the spine, using a pen with permanent ink print or type a call number label to be placed on the lower portion of the spine. If there is no title on the spine, prepare a title label to be placed on the upper portion of the spine, and make a call number label that includes the part number (if there is more than one container for the set) and the copy number and/or accession number (if used) for the bottom portion of the spine.

Ownership marks. Preprinted or stamped ownership marks may be located on the same identification label if space permits or on another area of the package.

Informational labels. It is useful to include system requirements notes on the container that give the make and model of the computer on which the software will run, the memory requirements of the computer, the operating system, and any peripherals that are required for using the disks. A copyright restriction label must be attached also if it is not already there. Refer to the first section of this chapter for detailed copyright requirements.

If the disk is a backup or has some other restriction, a library may choose to put this information on the container label also (e.g., LIBRARY OWNS EVALUATION COPY ONLY, CONTACT COMPUTER CENTER FOR DISTRIBUTION COPY). Additional labels may note such things as title variations from the computer screen, special use restrictions (e.g., RESTRICTED TO FACULTY AND THEIR RESEARCH ASSISTANTS), or a brief statement of what the program does (e.g., FORMATS AND PRINTS CATALOG CARDS). Intellectual contents labels are also extremely helpful when more than one program is in the package (see Figure 7.9).

Pockets for Circulation

Although the exterior of disk containers is the least protected place for pockets, one option is to attach a small pocket to the outside front or back. Another option for disks is to house them in albums, binders, bags, or boxes. Pockets

Figure 7.9
Disk Container Labeling

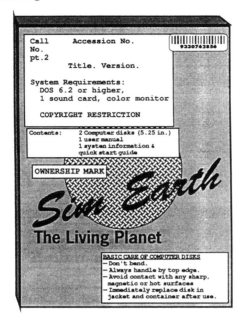

may be attached to the inside of the front cover or to the lid of these containers. Permanent rubber cement or two strips of double-stick tape will secure the pocket. Self-sticking vinyl pockets are another option and work well on hanging bags. Consistency of placement is important, but it will be affected by the availability of a flat surface that is void of important information. Hinging a pocket may be the only alternative to not covering important information. Pockets also may be stored in the vinyl pockets available on some disk packaging. A final option is to use only circulation cards and keep them at the circulation desk.

Barcodes

Barcodes may be placed on the disk and/or its container. If the library's policy is to use duplicate barcodes or one-and-a-half barcodes (also known as double barcodes) for both the disk and the container, a disk can be matched easily to its container or its accompanying material. Barcodes may be placed on the top edge of the disk, where it is held during insertion into the disk drive. If space is lacking on the labeled side, the barcode may be placed on the unlabeled side. For barcodes on containers, place the barcode on the surface in a place consistent with library policy. Some libraries place the barcode on the front of the container on the upper center edge, where it is readily accessible. Others prefer placement directly adjacent to the circulation pocket for ease of access at time of checkout.

Another preferred location is parallel to the container spine on the upper right corner of the back of the container to allow for easy access during inventory.

Security Devices

Radio frequency security labels may be attached to either the disk or its container without affecting the stability of the information on the computer disk. When such devices are embedded in a date due label, they may be placed on the front of the disk or on the front cover of the disk container. Blank radio labels may be placed under identification or ownership labels. Magnetic security strips may be covered by labels or a piece of opaque tape and placed inside the spine of albums or folders. However, caution must be exercised if the security system is a magnetic one. Some systems have newer and smaller magnetic strips or labels that can be demagnetized without affecting magnetic library material. However, special demagnetizing equipment is required for these devices. One must be certain that existing security systems are sensitive enough to be triggered by the newer and smaller security devices and still render computer data safe. Special warning labels and/or specially colored containers will be required to alert circulation personnel that an item must not pass through the regular desensitizing equipment. Studies have shown that there is no risk of data alteration from passing magnetic materials through exit sensor gates. For a more complete discussion of security systems and problems, refer to Chapter 1.

Accompanying Material

There are a variety of accompanying materials associated with computer files, as detailed in the preceding "General Information" section of this chapter. Follow the guidelines discussed in Chapter 2 for treatment of such materials. When possible, the accompanying material should remain in the same container with the computer disk. This would only be possible if the disks were housed in larger albums, binders, or boxes. For example, vinyl disk albums with clear plastic sleeves are an ideal location for accompanying material. If folding is required to fit the accompanying material into the sleeve, it will be necessary to weigh the damage factor resulting from folding against the possibility of loss of the item. When using three-ring disk binders, it may be necessary to punch holes in the accompanying material for placement in the binder. Larger pieces of accompanying material should receive more permanent covering.

Accompanying material should always be given complete identification labeling, including the call number, so that it can be linked easily to its companion disk. Consistent ownership designations (stamps or labels) should also be included. When accompanying material is stored separately and barcodes are in general use for the rest of the collection, a unique barcode should be placed on each piece of accompanying material. This practice will help the library keep track of each separate circulation.

Gift Plates

A gift plate may be applied to the container which stores the disk. It may be glued or cemented to an outside surface or to the inside of the front cover if room is available. When disks are stored in catalog trays or in their plastic boxes, some innovation is required. The plate may be cut to size and applied to an available area, or it may be inserted into the circulation pocket. Another option is to use a small pressure-sensitive label and type GIFT OF followed by the donor's name (if used). This may be applied to the container, the disk, or to the outside or inside of the circulation pocket, depending on the availability of space.

COMPUTER LASER OPTICAL DISC

Definitions

Computer laser optical disk—An optical disk designed to store computer data. (Olson 1988: 8)

Optical disk—A generic term for a disk produced and read with laser technology and used for storage of computer files. These disks may be 4¾, 5, 8, 12, or 14 inches in diameter. [Author's note: 3½-inch discs also are now available.] *Also called* **Laser disk, Laser optical disk, Optical digital data disk (OD3).** (Olson 1988: 23)

Compact disk (CD)—A type of optical disk produced and read with laser technology on which computer files are recorded. Compact disks are 4¾ or 5 inches in diameter. Types include **CD-ROM** (compact disk-read only memory), **CD-I** (compact disk interactive, developed by Philips International), **CD-PROM** (compact disk-programmable read only memory), **DataROM** (Sony's 5 inch disk), and **OROM** (3M's 5 inch disk). (Olson 1988: 6–7)

General Information

The preceding definitions illustrate the ongoing discussion about the spelling of computer disc(k)s that was discussed at the beginning of this chapter. Olson's definitions coincide with the 1978 *AACR 2* spelling of *disk* with a *k* when it refers to computers, whether it is a magnetic computer disk or an optical computer disc. As discussed at the beginning of this chapter, the Spring 1994 *Library of Congress Cataloging Service Bulletin* (LC,CSB) makes the distinction of using *disc* for any laser optical disc and *disk* for any magnetic computer disk (LC,CSB 1994:13).

There is one other CD-ROM that has not been mentioned. It is the PhotoCD. It consists of a laser optical disc with a collection of computer files on it that correspond to images on a disc. It differs from a regular CD-ROM in one way: It can be created incrementally. In other words, additional images can be added to it, week after week. It requires a multisession CD-ROM reader. Libraries may begin to collect this format from locally produced sources.

Considerations for Computer Optical Disc Storage

- Computer optical discs may be stored upright in their original jewel cases and/or in vinyl or pressboard albums and boxes.
- Computer optical discs may be stored horizontally in their original containers in specially designed compartmentalized shelving.
- Computer optical discs may be stored in protective sleeves that are placed inside other containers with accompanying materials.
- Computer optical discs may be stored in CD-ROM caddies and stored vertically or horizontally on shelves.
- Computer optical discs may be stored in lockable security boxes and be intershelved with other materials.

Computer Optical Disc Labeling

Most computer optical discs are commercially labeled directly on the surface of the disc with special inks. Such labeling usually includes the author (if there is one), the title, the publisher, and the date.

Option a: Processing without labels

The latest research indicates that chemicals used in marking pen ink may cause corrosion to the plastic coating that covers the metallic surface of the disc and may, in time, cause eventual damage to the metallic surface. At this time it seems appropriate to exercise caution in using pens with permanent ink for writing directly on laser optical discs. Water-based felt tip markers are not a solution because their marks are easily removable. Some people believe it is safe to write a brief call number and/or ownership mark on the clear inner gripping ring of the computer optical disc. This practice allows the disc to be identified uniquely and linked to a container that can provide more complete information (see Figure 7.10). Another option for ownership marks is an embossing device (described in Chapter 4) that was developed for use on the clear plastic portion of the disc. However, because of the fragile nature of the computer optical disc, caution should be exercised when considering any device that might cause a strain to the disc's protective lacquer coating. Those who are more conservative may tend to avoid marking the disc in any way and prefer to mark only the container. However, this practice can create problems if discs are returned in the wrong containers.

Figure 7.10
Processing a Computer Optical Disc without Labels

Option b: Processing with labels on the disc's clear center

Even though the computer optical disc has been thought to be indestructible, we know that labels should not be attached to the plastic coating over the metallic surface read by the CD-ROM drive. Distortion of data can result from the slightest weight differential, often referred to as spin wobble. Commercial suppliers make a circular center label that is available for placement over the inner clear gripping ring of the computer optical disc. These labels can be commercially preprinted with an ownership mark or stamped with a circular stamp. A brief call number may also be added to the label before placement on the disc (see Figure 7.11). Center labels come by themselves or in sets with rectangular container labels and two narrow spine labels that can be used on the container for call numbers and/or spine titles. Librarians who fear that the adhesive on the back of circular center labels may cause corrosion of the disc will not want to use these labels.

Computer Optical Disc Container Labeling

A jewel box is usually the original container for a computer optical disc, although other containers may include fiber or vinyl albums, CD-ROM caddies, security boxes, and binders. A brief label may be all that is necessary if the container has a cover that already provides the desired bibliographic information. If a more detailed label is desired, the front cover of the container is a good location or the recessed area on the underside of a disc caddy. Labels may

Figure 7.11
Processing a Computer Optical Disc with Labels

contain the author's name (if applicable), title, version (if applicable), call number, disc or part number (if the disc is part of a set), copy number and/or the accession number (if used), and the number and type of accompanying materials (see Figure 7.12).

Spine labels. A brief call number label may be placed on the lower portion of the spine if it is wide enough for the number to be read, or the number may be applied to the upper or lower left front cover consistent with library policy, being careful not to cover important information.

Ownership marks. Ownership marks should be placed visibly on the front and/or back cover of the computer disc container. A library may choose to use a pen with permanent ink to print the library name on the container or use a small label that is stamped, imprinted, or embossed with the library's name or logo.

Informational labels. It is useful to include system requirements notes on the container that give the make and model of the computer on which the disc will run (e.g., MULTISESSION CD-ROM PLAYER), the required computer memory and operating system (e.g., SYSTEM 7.0 OR HIGHER), and any peripherals required for using the discs. A copyright restriction label should be attached if one is not already present. Refer to the first section of this chapter for more detailed copyright requirements.

Pockets for Circulation

Although the exterior is the least protected place for pockets, one option for optical disc containers is to attach a small pocket to the outside front or back

Figure 7.12
Computer Optical Disc Container Labeling

depending on local guidelines. If computer optical discs are housed in albums, binders, or boxes, pockets may be attached to the inside of the front cover or lid of containers. Self-sticking clear vinyl pockets allow the user to read information beneath the pocket, although there may be some distortion. Hinging a pocket is another alternative to allow access to important information. An alternative to pockets are permanent pressure-sensitive date due labels, which may be placed on the front cover of containers.

Barcodes

Barcodes should *never* be placed on a computer optical disc itself. Several barcode locations are possible on the outside or inside of the container depending on institutional guidelines. Some libraries prefer placing the barcode adjacent to the circulation pocket. Other libraries may prefer to locate the barcode in the upper center edge of the front or back of the container, where it is always easily accessible. Another possibility is the back of the container, parallel to the spine on the upper right corner of the back of the container to allow for easy access during inventory. One other option is on the inside of the front cover. When libraries display cases without discs, they may decide to place barcodes inside the container. The barcode is scanned when the disc is placed in the container, and at the time the case is returned and the disc removed, the barcode is scanned to clear the disc. For multidisc sets in one container, individual barcodes for each disc may be placed one above the other in volume number order on the outside of the container.

Security Devices

Librarians may wish to check with security vendors before applying any security device to computer optical discs.

Option a: Security strips

1. Securing the disc. (For a more detailed discussion, see the section on security in Chapter 1.) A specially sized magnetic strip is available for application on the top of the computer optical disc and is to be covered by an adhesive transparent overlay. At this time there is some disagreement among experts as to whether these adhesive overlays will protect or harm the disc's surface. It is important to realize that overlays become permanent within a few hours and removal or attempted removal may damage the disc. This is especially worrisome for very expensive CD-ROMs. Distortion of data, resulting from imbalanced spinning, may also be a problem with this method. Librarians are cautioned to review the latest literature and check with their security vendors to determine the long-range safety of using this method. Special equipment for desensitizing these materials may be needed due to the small size of the strips. It is also advisable to make sure that these security devices are compatible with existing security systems.

2. Securing the container. If a jewel box container is used, one location for the security strip is the paper cover under the molded plastic holder which secures the computer optical disc. Remove the disc and pop out the plastic holder. Attach the strip diagonally to the cover liner. Replace the plastic holder that covers the strip and the optical disc. Strips may be placed in the spine of the container, making sure that it is not visible.

Option b: Security labels

Security labels come as blank labels, date due slips, ownership labels, or other specially printed messages. Security labels should never be attached to the computer optical disc itself. Instead, both magnetic and radio frequency labels may be placed on the disc container in a consistent location.

Option c: Security boxes

Security boxes may be used for the storage of both the computer optical disc and its container, and security strips or labels may be placed directly on them. The disc and its original container may be locked in the box. They are removed from the security box at the time of circulation.

Accompanying Material

Treatment of accompanying documentation for computer optical discs should follow the guidelines discussed in Chapter 2. Accompanying material should always be labeled with its appropriate call number and enough other information to make sure that wherever it is stored, it will be easily identifiable and readily evident regarding what it accompanies. The call number should be visible on the outside and the inside of accompanying material. When possible, accompanying material should remain in the same container as the optical disc. Larger pieces of accompanying material, such as user manuals or videodiscs, will require more permanent handling. If such items cannot be housed with the optical disc in an original container, either provide substitute packaging to accommodate both or provide extensive labeling on both the CD-ROM disc container and its accompanying material. Ownership designations (stamps or labels) should also be placed in consistent locations on all parts according to established local guidelines. When accompanying material is stored separately and barcodes are in general use for the rest of the collection, a unique barcode should be placed on each piece of accompanying material. This practice will help the library keep track of each separate circulation.

Gift Plates

A gift plate may be applied to the container which stores the disc. It may be glued or cemented to an outside surface or to the inside of a front cover if room is available. The hinge method of attachment may be necessary so that useful information is not covered. A gift plate may be cut to size and applied to an area void of important information, or a plate may be inserted into the circulation pocket. Another option is to use a small pressure-sensitive label and type GIFT OF followed by the donor's name (if used). This may be applied to the container or to the outside or inside of the circulation pocket depending on the availability of space.

COMPUTER REEL

Definition: A length of computer tape wound onto an unenclosed flanged holder or reel. *See also* **Computer tape reel.** (Olson 1988: 8)

General Information

Standard computer tape is ½ inch wide, 2400 feet in length, and wound on 10½-inch computer reels, though reels may vary in size and hold from 300 to 3600 feet. Ten years ago reels of computer tape were the most common carriers for computer information. Today few libraries or computer centers collect reel tapes, but they may be asked to catalog, index, or process older computer reel collections for storage.

Considerations for Computer Reel Storage

• Computer reels should be stored in areas that have stabilized temperatures, are free of dust and oil, and are away from any potentially damaging magnetic fields or other conditions that may damage them.

• Computer reels may be stored vertically on specially divided computer shelves or in racks on baked enamel steel or wooden shelves.

• Computer reels may be stored vertically in fiberboard boxes with corrugated storage compartments, a lift-off lid, and tote handles.

(See also sections on storage in Chapter 1 and packaging/repackaging in Chapter 2.)

Computer Reel Tape Labeling

Computer tape itself should not be labeled. Reels that hold the tape may be identified with hand lettering or labels, but hand lettering directly on clear reels may not be easily visible. Labels may be hand lettered, typed, or printed. Labeling may include the reel number, the rack number, and the shelf number in addition to standard library computer file identification. Other types of information to be provided are the number of tracks or channels, the density, the parity, the required operating system, the make and model of the computer, and any required peripherals or usage restrictions. Ownership marks may also be placed on the plastic reel.

Computer Reel Labeling

Option a: Processing with labels

Using a pen with permanent ink, print or type the call number, the part number (if the reel is part of a set), and the copy number and/or accession number (if used), and place it on the top of the reel (see Figure 7.13). Libraries also may want to add title information if it is not already there.

Ownership marks. A preprinted or stamped ownership label may be placed on the same surface.

Informational labels. It is useful to include system requirements notes that give the make and model of the computer on which the reel will run, the required operating system, the number of tracks or channels, the density, the parity, and any usage restrictions. A copyright restriction label should be attached if it is not already present. Refer to the first section of this chapter for more detailed copyright requirements.

Figure 7.13
Computer Reel Labeling

Computer Reel Container Labeling

If reels are stored in containers instead of open shelves, print with a pen using permanent ink or type a label with the call number, author's name (if applicable), title, version number (if applicable), and availability of any accompanying material (see Figure 7.14). Place the label on the side of the box which will be facing out when it is placed on a shelf.

Spine labels. A brief call number label may be placed on the lower portion of the spine if it is wide enough for the number to be read. If not, the number may be applied to the upper or lower left front cover of the container in a position consistent with library policy, being careful not to cover important information.

Ownership marks. The ownership mark should be placed visibly on the box in a position consistent with library guidelines and that will not cover important information.

Informational labels. A copyright restriction notice should also be attached if it is not present on the computer reel itself. Refer to the first section of this chapter for more detailed copyright requirements.

Figure 7.14
Computer Reel Container Labeling

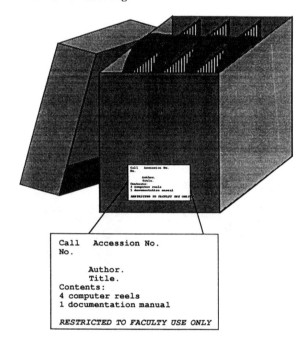

Call	Accession No.
No.	
	Author.
	Title.
Contents:	
4 computer reels	
1 documentation manual	
RESTRICTED TO FACULTY USE ONLY	

Pockets for Circulation

Circulation pockets may be attached permanently to the inside lid of a computer tape container. Self-sticking vinyl pockets are another option. The hinge method of attaching pockets may be the only alternative to not covering important information. Circulation pockets are not practical for computer reels themselves. A final option is to use circulation cards only and keep them at the circulation desk.

Barcodes

Option a: Barcode on reel

Barcodes may be placed on computer reels in a consistent location.

Option b: Barcode on container

If computer reels are placed in containers, placement should be consistent with library policy for other similar containers. Location of barcodes in the upper center edge of the front or back of the container is convenient, as is placement adjacent to the circulation pocket.

Option c: Barcode on container and reel

If one-and-a-half or double barcodes are used, it is possible to place a barcode on both the reel and the container by combining options a and b.

Security Devices

Radio frequency security labels may be attached to computer reels or their containers without affecting the stability of the information on the computer reel. Blank radio labels may be placed under identification and ownership labels, and those encoded in informational or ownership labels may be placed on the front of the computer reel or on its container. Caution must be exercised when the library security system is a magnetic one. Some systems have newer and smaller magnetic strips or labels that can be demagnetized without affecting magnetic computer data. However, special demagnetizing equipment is required for these devices so that magnetic library materials are not harmed. One must be certain that existing security systems are sensitive enough to be triggered by the newer and smaller security devices and still render the computer data safe. Special warning labels and/or specially colored containers will be required to alert circulation personnel that an item should not pass through the regular de-sensitizing equipment. For a more complete discussion of security systems and problems, refer to Chapter 1.

Accompanying Material

Accompanying material for computer reels is likely to be documentation in the form of a user manual, dictionary, or code book. These larger pieces of accompanying material should receive permanent covering and be labeled with enough information that the companion computer file can be used easily.

An identification label with the call number, title, version (if applicable), and reel location should be placed in a prominent position on the accompanying material so that it is linked easily to its reel. Ownership designations (stamps or labels) should also be included according to established guidelines. When ac-companying material is stored separately and barcodes are in general use for the rest of the collection, a unique barcode should be placed on each piece of ac-companying material. This practice will help the library keep track of each separate circulation.

Gift Plates

Gift plates may be applied directly to the computer reel or to a computer reel box (if one exists). A small pressure-sensitive label may be typed, with GIFT OF followed by the donor's name (if used), and attached to the reel, the container, or a circulation pocket. Plates may be glued or cemented to the inside lid of a box or inserted into a circulation pocket. Another option is to use hinged plates, which make it possible to read information beneath the plates.

REFERENCES

Anglo-American Cataloguing Rules, Second Edition, 1988 Revision, ed. by Michael Gorman and Paul W. Winkler for the Joint Steering Committee for Revision of AACR. Chicago: American Library Association.

Dictionary of Computing. 1990. 3rd ed. Oxford: Oxford University Press.

Dunlap, Kent. Letter to Eric Childress, Special Materials Cataloger, Elon College, North Carolina, January 6, 1992.

Library of Congress. Collection Services. *Cataloging Service Bulletin.* No. 64 (Spring 1994): 13.

Olson, Nancy B. 1988. *Audiovisual Material Glossary.* Dublin, OH: OCLC Online Computer Library Center.

8

Three-Dimensional Artifacts and Realia

The materials discussed in this chapter are both diverse in nature and in where they can be found. They include toys and games (including puzzles and simulations), braille cassettes, three-dimensional art objects, instructional models and dioramas, microscopic slides, and realia (e.g., real objects such as instruments, clothing, and tools). Libraries of all kinds as well as art and history museums may be the repositories for such material. Because museum curators have developed detailed registration systems for many of these objects, librarians who collect these materials may want to review their many fine manuals. Common features of museum processing include giving the name of the item, an extensive description, its physical makeup, the size, an account of its origin or source, and a summary of its past history and condition.

GENERAL INFORMATION

Determining the type of processing that is appropriate in a library setting for such varied formats will depend on the intended use of the materials.

- Are such materials to be used only for display, as they would be in a museum?
- Are they to circulate under limited circulation provisions?
- Will they circulate like any other library materials?

Each library will have to decide how extensively it wishes to mark its materials. Titles frequently need to be supplied, and labeling the items themselves can be difficult. Often such objects are accompanied by documentation such as original advertisements, news clippings, and/or correspondence. If preservation is a primary consideration, a few basic principles should be followed. Only soft lead pencils are to be used for identification and ownership marks, and the use of water-soluble paste (e.g., wheat paste) is recommended for attaching pockets and gift plates.

Considerations for Storage of Realia and Other Three-Dimensional Objects

- Three-dimensional items may be displayed as decorative items rather than on special shelves.

- Three-dimensional items may be stored on standard library shelving or in oversize areas and covered with cloth dust covers or clear plastic material.

- Three-dimensional items may be stored on regular library shelving in their original containers or in supplied enclosures, which help keep them dust free and protected from physical damage.

- Small objects may be stored in separate boxes close to the item's original size. Clear plastic boxes (available in hobby shops) provide for patron viewing of objects such as rocks, jewelry, flatware, shells, and similar objects.

- Padding may be used to protect fragile items. Foam cut to the box size may be hewn on one side to the shape of the item to create a space to protect the item. To further protect fragile items, foam may be covered with 100 percent cotton fabric such as muslin or linen, and a layer of netting may be laid on top of the item.

- Large items may be placed on bottom shelves to help prevent damage to items as they are removed and replaced on the shelves.

- Multiple items such as stones, individual beads, nails, or similar artifacts may be stored in trays lined with foam, with individual indentations cut to the size of the object to protect items from damaging each other. Alternatively, pieces may be placed in boxes lined with foam cut to the shape of the piece and the boxes may be placed in drawers. For the purposes of this manual, the following four formats will be used as examples for processing: games, models, realia, and toys.

GAME

Definition: A set of materials designated for play according to prescribed rules. (*AACR 2, 1988 rev.:* 618)

Figure 8.1
Individual Game Pieces Labeling

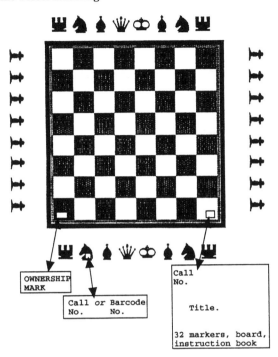

General Information

A library may decide to protect the surfaces of materials by covering them with clear contact paper or by painting the surface with polyurethane. A picture of the game (including individual pieces) attached to the box top or bottom will allow patron and staff to know the game's contents.

Individual Pieces Labeling

Larger game pieces. The library may choose to label game boards, larger plastic pieces, and replicas with some type of identification label. Using a pen with permanent ink, write the call number, copy and/or accession number (if used), barcode number, author (if appropriate), and/or the title on the item or on a label. The size of the item will determine the most effective size and method of labeling (see Figure 8.1).

Ownership marks. Ownership marks may be printed or stamped on larger game pieces in an area that lacks information.

Smaller game pieces. Libraries may want to print, using a pen with permanent ink, an identification number (call number, copy and/or accession number, or

Figure 8.2
Game or Toy Container Labeling

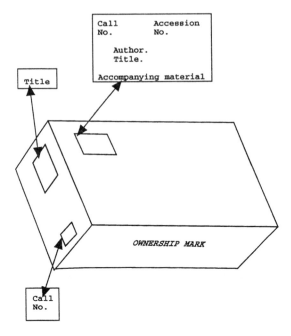

barcode number) on each piece, thereby linking individual pieces to their title and container. The size of the piece will determine how much information may be written on each piece (see Figure 8.1).

Ownership marks. Larger pieces and boards should receive ownership marks. Glossy surfaces may not hold the ink unless permanent ink is used. A label stamped with permanent ink or imprinted with the library's ownership mark may be preferred on these surfaces. Individual pieces, if large enough, may also receive ownership marks. Again, the surface may determine whether a stamp or label may be used. For smaller pieces, a decision will need to be made regarding the importance of the unique number (e.g., call number or accession number) and the importance of an ownership mark (see Figure 8.1).

Game Container Labeling

The game's original box from the manufacturer is the preferred container for storage. A library may want to reinforce the corners and the edges with clear plastic tape if the box sits on its edges on the shelf (see Figure 8.2).

Call number labels. The location of the label will be determined by the shelving method. If the box is shelved on its side, the label should be visible to patrons and staff when the label is placed on the outside edges approximately

½ inch from the base. This choice of label placement saves wear and tear during the shelving process.

Spine labels. The library may find that the game manufacturer's title printed on the box will meet its needs. If the title is lacking or a uniform look is desired, the library may want to create an in-house label by printing (using a typewriter or hand lettering) the title and attaching it approximately ½ inch from the top outside edge (see Figure 8.2).

Identification labels. A library may want to develop a label for the top of the container which includes the call number, copy and/or accession number (if used), author, title, contents, and accompanying material (see Figure 8.2).

Ownership marks. Using a pen with permanent ink, the library's name may be written on the side edges and the top of the box (see Figure 8.1). Another option is to use ownership stamps or labels on the box edge and/or top. Permanent ink should by used to avoid smudging on glossy surfaces. A label stamped or imprinted with the library's ownership mark may be preferred.

Pockets for Circulation Cards

Pockets may be attached to the inside box top using glue, cement, or tape. If instructions are printed on the inside box top, the pocket may be hinged with clear tape so that the pocket can be lifted and instructions read. Self-adhesive vinyl pockets are another alternative when instructions are printed on the inside top, although small print may not be legible.

Barcodes

A barcode may be attached to the top or bottom of the game container in a standard position (e.g., exterior upper left corner). These locations allow for accessible scanning during inventory. Another preferred location is adjacent to the circulation pocket. Attaching individual barcodes on each piece would require more work at the point of processing and additional work for circulation staff.

Security Devices

A security strip may be placed on the inside bottom of the box under dividers, if they are easily removable. This device may be covered with a label or an opaque piece of tape to camouflage it. Security labels are usually placed on the box top.

Accompanying Material

Accompanying material for games should follow the guidelines discussed in Chapter 2. If possible, the accompanying material should remain in the game box. Accompanying material may be placed in a large envelope to protect it. Attach a call number identification label. Larger pieces of accompanying material should receive more permanent covering and should also be labeled. A label with an identification number may be placed on the cover of the accompanying material so that it is linked to its game. It is advisable to place ownership designations (stamps or labels) in a position consistent with library policy. When accompanying material is stored separately and barcodes are in general use for the rest of the collection, a unique barcode should be placed on each piece of accompanying material. This practice will help the library keep track of each separate circulation.

Gift Plates

Traditional gift plates may be attached to the inside top of the box or container near the circulation pocket. Another choice includes typing GIFT OF and the donor's name on a small rectangular label and attaching the label to the inside top of the box or container near the circulation pocket. An additional option includes attaching the plate to the inside bottom of the box or container. Placement in this area may be preferred if instructions or other significant information are printed on the inside top.

MODEL

Definition: Three dimensional representation of a real thing. (*AACR 2, 1988 rev.:* 620)

General Information

It is advisable to retain a picture of the model either from the original advertisement or a photograph of the actual item. An in-house file containing the picture and/or a parts list may be helpful in case of missing parts or loss of the whole item. A duplicate picture of the model, including a parts listing, may be attached to the container so patrons know what they have borrowed.

Model Labeling

Option a: Processing without labels

Using a pen with permanent ink, write the library's name, the call number, and the copy and/or the accession number in an area void of information or in an area on the base of the model. An identification number (the accession number, the item number portion of the barcode, or a unique call number) may be printed on each piece so the individual part will be returned to its container.

Figure 8.3
Processing Model without Labels

Call No.   Accession No.
OWNERSHIP MARK

Unique call numbers give the location; however, they may be too long to fit on the item (see Figure 8.3).

Option b: Processing with labels

It is possible to use an identification label on larger items, such as a model of a tooth or an item that lacks parts. The label may be placed on the base of the item if it has parts. The call number, the part number, the copy and/or accession number (if used), the title, the parts listing (if appropriate), and the accompanying material may be typed or printed on a label to be used as the identification label (see Figure 8.4). The label may be attached to the item on the base or in an area that will not detract from its functioning. As necessary, trim to fit. If there is not a flat surface, the label may be placed around a portion of the model and the end pieces of the label may be backed to each other. This will reinforce the ends and stabilize the label.

Ownership marks. Ownership marks may be printed or stamped on the model or its base in an area that lacks information.

Option c: Processing with twill tape

Using a pen with permanent ink, print the part number and/or the library's name on a piece of twill tape. Using another piece of twill tape, print the call number, the copy number and/or accession number (if used), the title, and the barcode number (see Figure 8.5). Twill tape is fabric tape with a textile weave that gives the appearance of diagonal lines in the material. It is possible to

Figure 8.4
Processing Model with Labels

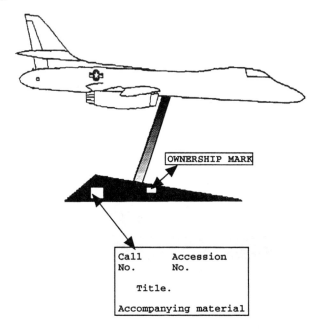

purchase twill tape with your library's name commercially printed on it. This tape may be looped over a portion of the model, and the ends may be sewn or glued to each other. Attach to the model by sewing or gluing.

Container Labeling

Option a: Processing without labels

Using a pen with permanent ink, write the call number, the part number (if the model has various parts), the copy and/or accession number (if used), the title, and the accompanying material designation (these may be available on the container already) on a prominent place. A good location is the upper left corner of the container top because it is easily seen by both patron and staff.

Option b: Processing with labels

The identification label, as shown in Figure 8.2, may be attached to the container top in a readily visible place for the patron and staff. The upper left corner is a good place because it is visible for browsing and shelving purposes. If the model is stored in a bag or under a covering, the label should be attached in a prominent place. If the label will not adhere to the bag or cover, it may be

Figure 8.5
Processing Model with Twill Tape

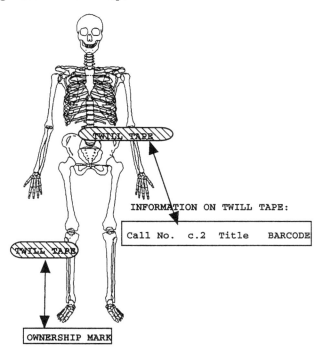

INFORMATION ON TWILL TAPE:

Call No.   c.2   Title   BARCODE

attached to a shipping label and tied (see the "Toy" section later in this chapter for more details) or stapled to the cover.

Pockets for Circulation

Option a: Models in boxes

Attach the pocket to the inside of the box top or bottom. It may be glued, cemented, or hinged to the top. Hinging with clear tape is the preferred method if information is printed in this area because it allows the user to raise the pocket and read the information underneath it.

Option b: Models on bases

One option is to attach the circulation pocket to the underside of the base, although this may cause the base to be unstable. Another option is to attach the circulation pocket to the model using florist wire. (See the section on globes in Chapter 3.) A third option consists of attaching the circulation pocket to a shipping label and tying it to the model.

Barcodes

Barcodes may be attached to the item itself. If there are multiple parts to the model in a container, consider using duplicate barcodes or one-and-a-half barcodes. Attach one to the major portion of the item and one to the container. Another option is to write the barcode number on each part to ensure that the model and its parts return to the container. This aids in inventory and shelving, but it may not be worth the effort if the parts are numerous or very small.

Security Devices

The security device may be attached to the container directly or by attaching it to a shipping label and tying the shipping label to the container. It may not be necessary to attach a security device if the model is housed in a locked case or in a secure area.

Accompanying Material

Accompanying material for models should follow the guidelines discussed in Chapter 2 and should remain in the original container whenever possible. Larger pieces of accompanying material should receive more permanent covering. A label with an identification number should be placed on the cover of the accompanying material so that it is linked to its model. It is advisable to place ownership designations (stamps or labels) in a position consistent with library policy. When accompanying material is stored separately and barcodes are in general use for the rest of the collection, a unique barcode should be placed on each piece of accompanying material. This practice will help the library keep track of each separate circulation.

Gift Plates

Gift plates may be attached to the inside of the box top or bottom adjacent to the pocket for circulation. Another option is to attach the gift plate to a stringed shipping tag and tie it to the model in a visible area. Some models can have an accompanying metal or special gift plate which may be attached directly to the model or to its base. Another choice is to type GIFT OF and the donor's name on a rectangular label and attach the label to the item.

REALIA

Definition: An artifact or a naturally occurring entity, as opposed to a replica. (*AACR 2, 1988 rev.:* 621)

General Information

When dealing with realia, the library must decide if ownership or other marks will be placed on the item to prevent theft. Another factor to consider is minimal marking for preservation. A library may wish to use conservative methods and not label items of an archival nature (such as a model of the library or the hockey puck of a local team).

Realia Labeling

Option a: Processing without labels

Using a pen with permanent ink, write the call number, the copy and/or accession number (if used), and the title in an area void of important information. An area may need to be painted white if the item is the same color as the writing instrument's ink.

Option b: Processing with tags

If the item is small or you do not want to write on it, the call number, the copy and/or accession number (if used), the barcode number, and/or the title may be printed on a jeweler's or shipping tag and tied to the item or laid in the box with the item. Ownership marks may be placed on the reverse side of the tag. More than one jeweler's tag may be needed depending on the amount of information. The use of multiple tags may prove unwieldy, and information should be kept to a minimum. This is a good method for jewelry, skeletons, and pieces of furniture (see Figure 8.6).

Option c: Processing with twill tape

This method involves printing the library's name, the call number, the title, and the copy and/or accession number (if used) on a piece of white twill tape. For items such as skeletons, necklaces, bracelets, and handles of handbags, loop the ends of the tag over the item. Glue the ends together or use a needle and thread to take a couple of stitches in the ends. Twill tape tags may be sewn into the seam of an article of clothing or onto a more prominent place. White twill tape ownership strips are excellent for identifying fabric pieces, rugs, costumes, and household fabric decorations (see Figure 8.7). They may be sewn to a seam, a hem, or a binding.

Option d: Processing with varnish

When processing nonporous substances such as ceramics, wood, marble, and metal, a library may choose to brush the surface with a strip of naphtha-based varnish. Using acrylic paint or a pen with acrylic ink, print the call number, title, and copy and/or accession number (if used) in this sealed area. Seal with

Figure 8.6
Processing Realia with Tags

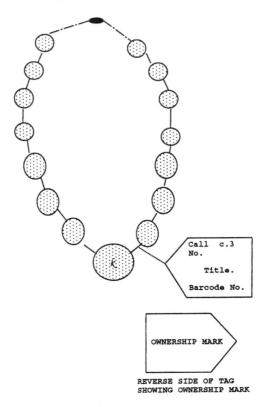

another coat of varnish. This may be removed with acetone. Varnish should not be used on plastic surfaces because the preparation will damage the surface.

Ownership marks. The library's name may be printed on the item where space is available, or the library may prefer to attach an ownership label to available space. Another option is to print the name on a strip of twill tape, loop the tape over the item, and glue or sew the ends to secure.

Informational labels. If an instrument such as a stethoscope is used by patrons, the library may wish to include washing directions for the staff upon its return. Such a note may say WASH WITH RUBBING ALCOHOL AFTER EACH RETURN FROM CIRCULATION.

Container Labeling

The preferred storage is the box the item came in because it usually contains important information. The item should be stored so that it does not move once it is placed in the box. Foam pieces cut to size or bubble sheets may be used

Figure 8.7
Processing Realia with Twill Tape

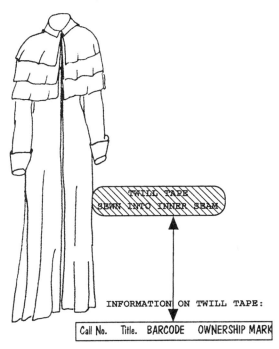

INFORMATION ON TWILL TAPE:

| Call No. | Title. | BARCODE | OWNERSHIP MARK |

to protect the item. The placement of the label depends on the method of shelving. It is best to place the label where it is read easily by patron and shelver. If the box is stored so that there is an outside edge, this would be a likely place for attaching the label. If not, the upper left corner of the box top is a good location for readability.

Option a: Boxes

An identification label with the call number, copy and/or accession number (if used), title, and contents of the box may be attached to the box top on the outside (see Figure 8.8).

Ownership marks. Ownership stamps and labels may be placed on the container where space is available.

Option b: Trays or drawers

The contents may be listed on the trays so that items are identified readily. Call numbers (if used) may be listed on the tray. If trays are stored in a cabinet or box, an identification label similar to the one shown in Figure 8.8 may be created and attached to the cabinet or box. Cabinets or boxes may need a finding list detailing their contents if realia is not arranged in call number order. Each

Figure 8.8
Realia Container Labeling

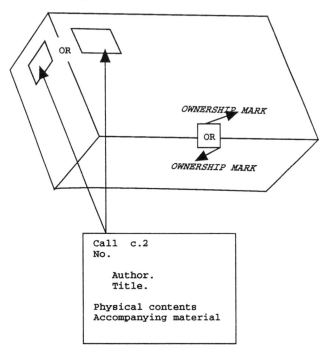

drawer may have a finding list for the holdings at points where the patron may ask for help (e.g., the reference and/or loan desk). One option is to label the drawer listing the contents. Another option is to print individual item identification numbers on a piece of white twill tape and lay it in the indentation that the item rests in or next to it.

Option c: Larger items

Larger items may need to be stored in cabinets or cupboards. The procedures recommended for globes may be helpful in labeling these items (see Chapter 3).

Option d: Bags

An item such as a basket stored in a bag to protect it from dust may have a jeweler's tag or a shipping label tied to it that details the call number, copy and/ or accession number (if used), and the title. An identification label showing this same information may be attached to the bag in which the realia is stored (see Figure 8.9).

Ownership marks. Realia stored in plastic bags may have ownership marks placed on both the item and the bag.

Figure 8.9
Realia Bag Labeling

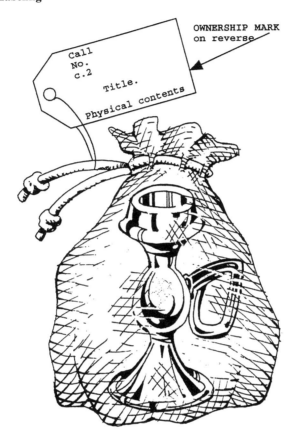

Pockets for Circulation

Option a: Attached to container

Pockets may be attached to the inside of the box top. If there is important information in this area, the pocket may be hinged to the inside of the box top using clear plastic tape.

Option b: Attached to item

Using the florist wire method described in ''Pockets for Circulation'' in the globe section of Chapter 3, pockets may be attached wherever possible. This method is good for handbags, clothing with buttons or straps, and other similar items.

Option c: Desk storage

Pockets may be stored at the circulation desk.

Barcodes

Barcodes may be attached in a variety of ways. If the item has a base, this would be a good location. Another option is to attach the barcode to the reverse side of the shipping tag used as an identification label (see Figure 8.9). A third option is to attach the barcode to the container in which items circulate.

Security Devices

Security devices may be placed on the top or bottom of the storage container or the item itself if a surface large enough to secure the device is available. Those devices which are not hidden behind a book pocket or ownership label may be hidden behind a strip of opaque tape.

Accompanying Material

Accompanying material for realia should follow the guidelines discussed in Chapter 2 and should remain in the original storage container whenever possible. Larger pieces of accompanying material should receive more permanent covering and should always be labeled. A call number should be placed on the cover of the accompanying material so that it is linked to its realia. It is advisable to place ownership designations (stamps or labels) in a position consistent with library policy. When accompanying material is stored separately and barcodes are in general use for the rest of the collection, a unique barcode should be placed on each piece of accompanying material. This practice will help the library keep track of each separate circulation.

Gift Plates

Traditional gift plates may be attached to items which have a space large enough to hold them. For items using the florist wire or shipping tag methods, the gift plates may be attached to the reverse side. Another option is to type GIFT OF and the donor's name on a small rectangular label and attach the label to the item.

TOY

Definition: A material object for children or others to play with (often an imitation of some familiar object); a plaything; also, something contrived for amusement rather than for practical use. (Olson 1988: 34)

Figure 8.10
Large Toy Piece Labeling

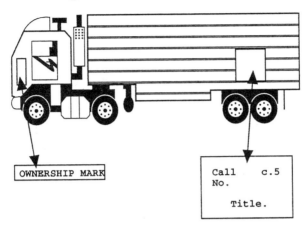

OWNERSHIP MARK

Call   c.5
No.

Title.

General Information

Retain a picture of each toy either from an advertisement or an actual photograph. This will be helpful in case of loss of parts or the whole item. Count the number of pieces in each box or container. Store the picture and the number of pieces in an in-house file. It is desirable to have a photocopy of the picture and contents attached to the inside bottom of the box or container so that the patron knows what has been borrowed. The preferred storage container is the box or bag in which the toy was acquired. If the original container is unavailable, use a durable box, a media storage box, a hanging bag, or a drawstring bag. Drawstring fishnet bags are preferred over opaque bags because the former allow the toys to be visible.

Individual Toy Labeling

Larger toy piece. The library may choose to label larger pieces with some type of identification label. The call number, copy and/or accession number (if used), barcode number, author (if appropriate), and/or the title may be printed on the item or on a label. The size of the item will determine the most effective size and method of labeling (see Figure 8.10).

Smaller toy pieces. Libraries may want to print an identification number detailing the call number, the copy and/or accession number, or the barcode number on each toy piece, thereby linking individual pieces to their title and container. The size of the piece will determine how much information may be written on each piece (see Figure 8.11).

Ownership marks. Both large and small pieces should receive ownership marks. Glossy surfaces may not hold the ink unless permanent ink is used. A

Figure 8.11
Small Toy Pieces Labeling

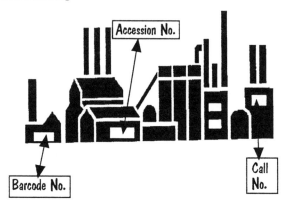

label stamped with permanent ink or imprinted with the library's ownership mark may be preferred on these surfaces. Individual pieces, if large enough, may also receive ownership marks. Again, the surface may determine whether a stamp or label may be used. For smaller pieces, a decision will need to be made regarding the importance of the unique number (e.g., call number or accession number) and the importance of an ownership mark.

Toy Container Labeling

Option a: Processing without labels

Using a pen or marker with permanent ink, write the call number, the copy and/or accession number (if used), the title, and the number of pieces on the container top so that they can be seen easily by both patron and staff. The library will determine the amount of specificity needed in the contents section. Should the contents area read "6 wooden people and 4 wooden cars" or "6 people and 4 cars" or simply "10 pieces"? This label may be placed in a prominent place so that it is seen easily by users and staff. If a drawstring bag is used, print or type this information on a strung shipping tag (see Figure 8.12). To preserve shipping tags, place them in a plastic holder or cover with clear contact paper.

A good-sized tag is 4¾ inches by 2⅜ inches because it will accommodate the aforementioned information without looking cramped. The tag may be attached to the drawstring or the bag itself by punching two holes in the bag and drawing the string through both holes and back over the label. When using a fishnet bag, an additional hole will not be needed. For larger toys, tags may be attached either by taping them to an area where they will not be abused or by tying them to a part of the toy that will not be subjected to stress.

Figure 8.12
Toy Bag Labeling

Option b: Processing with labels

Type the call number, copy number and/or accession number, title, and parts designation on a label (see Figure 8.8). Attach the label to the box in a location that is readily visible to both shelvers and patrons. If the toy is stored in a drawstring bag, attach the label to a shipping tag and tie it to the bag or attach the label to the bag itself.

Pockets for Circulation Cards

When toys are stored in boxes, the pocket may be attached to the inside box top or bottom. For toys stored in bags, the pocket may be attached by punching a hole in the circulation pocket. Attach the florist wire to the pocket, as described in the globes section in Chapter 3. Attach the other end of the florist wire to the hanging or drawstring bag. Pockets for free-standing toys, riding toys, or play houses may be placed in an area where they will receive as little abuse as possible. They may be taped to the item or attached by using the florist wire method. Another option is to keep circulation pockets at the circulation desk.

Barcodes

Option a: Toys in boxes

Attach the barcode to the box top or bottom (e.g., in the upper right corner or to the box bottom in the upper left corner). These areas facilitate circulation and inventory scanning.

Option b: Free-standing toys or toys in bags

The barcode may be attached to the reverse side of the strung shipping tag or to the bag or item itself.

Security Devices

If the toy consists of only one piece, the security device may be attached directly to it, as long as the device adheres to the toy's surface. If not, the device can be affixed to the toy's identification tag or circulation pocket. When dealing with boxed items, it is best to attach the security device to the container itself.

Accompanying Material

Accompanying material for toys should follow the guidelines discussed in Chapter 2. If possible, the accompanying material should remain in the box or bag with the toy. Accompanying material may be placed in a large envelope to protect it if the toy lacks a box or bag. A hole may be punched in the envelope and then attached to the toy with the florist wire method. Large pieces of printed accompanying material should receive more permanent covering. A label with an identification number or call number should be placed on the cover of the accompanying material so that it is linked to its toy. It is advisable to place ownership designations (stamps or labels) in a position consistent with library policy. When accompanying material is stored separately and barcodes are in general use for the rest of the collection, a unique barcode should be placed on each piece of accompanying material. This practice will help the library keep track of each separate circulation.

Gift Plates

Gift plates may be attached to the inside box top (if sufficient room is available) or to the box bottom. If the circulation pocket is attached by the florist wire method, the gift plate may be attached to the reverse side of the circulation pocket. Gift plates may be attached to the toy itself if space is available. Cover with tape or clear contact paper if protection is necessary. Another option is to type GIFT OF and the donor's name on a rectangular label and attach the label to the toy or the reverse side of the circulation pocket.

REFERENCES

Anglo-American Cataloguing Rules, Second Edition, 1988 Revision, ed. by Michael Gorman and Paul W. Winkler for the Joint Steering Committee for Revision of AACR. Chicago: American Library Association.

Museum Registration Methods. 1979. 3rd ed. Washington, DC: American Association of Museums.

Olson, Nancy B. 1988. *Audiovisual Material Glossary.* Dublin, OH: OCLC Online Computer Library Center.

9

Kits and Interactive Multimedia

With the publication of the *AACR 2* in 1978, the terms *kit* and *multimedia* were simultaneously adopted by the Anglo-American library cataloging community to describe various combinations of library materials made up of more than one category of material in which no one media item was predominant. The term *kit* was adopted by North American catalogers, and the term *multimedia* was adopted by catalogers of British origin. The term *multimedia* apparently was not adopted within the North American library community because it was already being used by educators and librarians to describe instructional presentations that utilized two or more components of audiovisual media (e.g., a slide presentation with synchronized sound).

Today the term *multimedia* has taken on yet another connotation with the addition of the word *interactive*. Multimedia is still a combination of more than one category of material, but the distinction is that a traditional kit or multimedia package is made up of two or more actual physical formats, whereas interactive multimedia is a computer-based technology made up of two or more categories of material that may or may not constitute one or more physical formats. Multimedia available only by remote access will not be considered in this discussion.

Today the term *interactive multimedia* conveys an additional meaning related to the development of interactive technologies. In a way, this latest connotation combines the two earlier meanings: (1) more than one category of information, none of which is predominant; and (2) a multimedia instructional presentation. It adds a third dimension of computerized technology and interactivity. Use of the term *multimedia* by manufacturers and distributors is becoming the most prominent among several terms (i.e., hypermedia, new media, CD-interactive [CD-I], digital video interactive [DVI], interactive media, intermedia, hypervideo) to describe this new computer-based technology, which includes two or more media categories that the user is able to control in terms of order and nature of presentation.

To quote from Eldon J. Ullmer in the introduction to *Interactive Technology* (February 1990),

The key instrumental ingredients of interactive technology are microcomputers, optical disc systems, input and display devices, and software programs for authoring and delivering instructional programs. The key conceptual ingredients that underlie instructional program development are the consolidation of information resources on disc media, multimedia presentation, the individualization of instructional delivery, and, most importantly, interactivity and adaptivity in lesson design.

For the purposes of this chapter, processing procedures for both kinds of multimedia are covered in two sections. The traditional kit or noninteractive multimedia combination of materials will be treated in the first section. Interactive multimedia will be covered in the second section.

KIT

Definition: An item containing two or more categories of material, no one of which is identifiable as the predominant constituent of the item; also designated "multimedia item," (q.v.). (*AACR 2, 1988 rev.:* 619)

General Information

Kit materials arrive in the library in one or in several containers. The first processing decision is whether to keep these materials together in one container or to split them up according to the individual formats which make up the kit. If items may be used independently from the kit as a whole, library personnel must decide how to package the items for circulation. Recommendations for the processing of individual nonprint formats are found elsewhere in this manual. Processing for print materials should follow the options discussed in Chapter 2 (in the section on accompanying material) or the library's local standard procedures for print materials.

Other processing considerations include the handling of consumable parts such as tests or score cards. Some libraries choose to make masters of such material and house the masters separately. All libraries will need to determine if consumable items such as pads should be individually labeled. One option is to stamp and label the backs of pads rather than each sheet. Stamping each sheet is time consuming, but a library's policies may justify doing so.

Considerations for Storage

• Preferred storage is the container in which the item arrived, because it usually contains compartments for storage of contents and any descriptive information. The sturdiness of the container will determine its usefulness.

• A commercially produced replacement container is a useful option when the original one is not suitable. Library supply vendors market corrugated boxes of heavyweight fiberboard or polypropylene, plastic or vinyl albums, and hanging bags. Some containers require assembly. All three options can be free standing on shelves.

• Kits may be stored in locally made custom-built containers.

• A less physically attractive solution may be to use shipping or cardboard boxes tied with cord or string. This method is inexpensive and effective for bulkier items.

• An alternative storage method is to house parts of kits separately in various locations according to their similar formats (e.g., videos with the video collection, filmstrips with the filmstrips, books with books, etc.).

Kit Labeling: Processing the Individual Parts

All significant parts of a kit should be labeled with the same call number and/or accession number to ensure that if they are separated, they can easily be traced back to their original container. (See the section on labeling in Chapter 2 for a more complete discussion.)

Option a: Processing without labels

Using a pen with permanent ink, print the call number and the copy number and/or accession number (if used) on each individual piece. If a single barcode is used for the kit container, another option for kit pieces is to write the unique portion of the barcode number on each individual piece. A drawback to the latter option is that when a barcode is lost or damaged and a new one is used to replace it, the number would have to be changed on each kit piece as well.

Option b: Processing with labels

Print with a pen using permanent ink or type the call number and the copy number and/or accession number (if used) on a label to be placed on each individual piece. The size of the part will determine how much information will be placed on the label. Labels may be placed in areas lacking important information.

Ownership marks. Ownership marks should be placed visibly on all significant parts of the kit according to locally established guidelines. Small pieces may not be large enough for both an ownership mark and a unique identification number. A library may have to decide whether number identification for items in a container is more important than ownership marks.

Figure 9.1
Kit Container Labeling

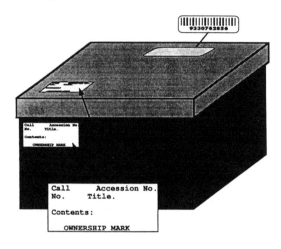

Kit Labeling: Processing the Container

Option a: Processing without labels

Using a pen with permanent ink, print the call number, accession number (if used), author, title, and physical contents of the kit on the cover of the container in a location consistent with library policy and lacking important information. A library may choose to write this information in a standard location such as the upper left corner of the front or top of the container's surface, where it may be easily read by both patron and staff. Another option is to write all the information, including the physical contents, immediately adjacent to the circulation pocket.

Option b: Processing with labels

On a label, print with a pen using permanent ink or type the call number, the accession number (if used), the author, the title, and the physical contents of the kit. This label may be placed on the upper left corner of the top of the container (see Figure 9.1) or on any prominent location that is easily visible to both patron and staff and does not cover important information.

Spine labels. The title of the kit may already be commercially printed on the spine of a commercial container. If no title appears on the spine, prepare a title label to be placed on the upper portion of the spine. Using a pen with permanent ink, print or type a call number label to be placed on the lower portion of the spine in a location consistent with library policy.

Ownership marks. Ownership marks should be placed visibly on the front or

Figure 9.2
Outside Pockets on Kit Containers

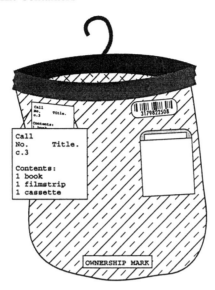

side of the container using either a preprinted label, permanent stamp, or marker with the library's name.

Pockets for Circulation

Consistency of pocket placement is important, but it will be affected by the availability of a flat surface lacking important printed information. Although the least protected place for the pocket is the exterior of the container, circulation pockets may be attached to the outside of large containers so that the pocket is visible when the box sits on the shelf or a bag hangs on a rack (see Figure 9.2). Pockets may also be attached to the inside of a kit container using glue, cement, or the hinging method with tape. The hinging method allows the user to read information printed beneath the pocket. Self-adhesive clear vinyl pockets allow the reader to view information under the pocket, although the print may not be completely legible.

Barcodes

Individual library policy will determine the number of barcodes needed for a kit as well as where they are to be placed. If the policy is to use duplicate barcodes or one-and-a-half barcodes, the complete barcode may be placed on the container and the other part(s) on prominent components. When determining the location for barcodes on items and/or their containers, consistency of placement will be important for those checking out the materials. A barcode may be attached to either the inside of the container or to the outside of the container in a location consistent with library policy. A good location for the barcode is directly adjacent to the pocket. For smaller components, OCR barcode numbers may be printed directly on kit pieces or typed on small labels and attached to various pieces. Either method links all the pieces to the whole.

For multipiece kits in one container, some libraries may prefer to use duplicate barcodes and place one on the container and the other on the individual piece. This procedure results in having more than one unique barcode on the container, one below the other. During checkout, staff can scan the barcodes on the container; but at the time of check-in, staff are required to scan the barcodes on the individual pieces to assure that each piece has been returned.

If parts of the kit can be checked out individually, a different barcode should be applied to each part because each circulating item will need to be recorded in the system. Individual barcoding of items will assure that each item is accounted for upon return. This practice results in increased costs for barcodes and staff time but may save on replacement costs for the kit. For specific suggestions about barcoding different media formats, refer to the respective chapters elsewhere in this manual.

Security Devices

Security strips or labels may be placed on the kit container providing that the disabling of such devices does not destroy information stored in the kit. Special precautions must be taken with magnetic materials such as computer software. Security devices that need to be camouflaged may be hidden behind tape or labels used for call number and title identification or the library's ownership mark. Security devices also may be hidden behind or under dividers in kit containers or under circulation pockets.

Accompanying Material

There are a variety of accompanying materials associated with kits. Follow the guidelines discussed in Chapter 2 for the general treatment of such material. When possible, all accompanying material should remain in the container with the kit. If folding is required to fit any of the accompanying material into the container, it will be necessary to weigh the damage factor resulting from folding against the possibility of loss of the item. If the kit container is a three-ring binder, it may be necessary to punch holes in the accompanying material. Larger pieces of accompanying material should receive more permanent covering. Accompanying material should always be linked to its companion container or parts. Consistent ownership marks (stamps or labels) should appear on all accompanying material. When accompanying material is stored separately and barcodes are in general use for the rest of the collection, a unique barcode should be placed on each piece of accompanying material. This practice will help the library keep track of each separate circulation.

Gift Plates

Gift plates may be attached to each significant component piece or to the kit container. For placement of gift plates on individual formats, refer to the respective chapters elsewhere in this manual. Gift plates may be attached to the inside or outside of the container's top or adjacent to the circulation pocket. If important information would be covered in these areas, a library may prefer placing the gift plate on the inside bottom of the box.

INTERACTIVE MULTIMEDIA

Definition: Media residing in one or more physical carriers (videodiscs, computer disks, computer optical discs, computer audio discs, etc.) or on computer networks. Interactive multimedia must exhibit both of these characteristics: 1) user controlled, non-linear navigation using computer technology and 2) the combination of two or more media (audio, text, graphics, images, animation and video) that the user manipulates to control the order and/or nature of the presentation. (ALCTS. CCS. CC:DA. The Interactive Multimedia Guidelines Review Task Force. *Guidelines for Bibliographic Description of Interactive Multimedia* 1994: 1)

General Information

Interactive multimedia comes to the library on one or more information carriers that appear to be physically similar to carriers of other kinds of nonprint media. These carriers may include CD-ROM discs, videodiscs, and compact discs alone or in combination with each other and/or computer disks, sound cards, color graphics cards, and user guides. They may require a microcomputer; a level III, IV, or V videodisc player; a special operating system; a color monitor; and a color printer. Another consideration is that the computer data may be stored on a hard disk in a computer, a sophisticated videodisc player, a local area network (LAN), or a floppy disk.

If there is more than one information carrier, a decision must be made regarding whether to keep the carriers together in one container, to keep them on the shelf together but in separate containers, or to house them separately according to their own material types. The first option may offer the easiest solution as far as circulation is concerned. If the second or third option is chosen, the library will have to decide how to track the individual carriers and their locations. Recommendations for processing individual nonprint formats are found elsewhere in this manual.

Libraries that promote browsing and open access to all formats will find detailed labeling of containers helpful to their patrons. System requirements labels alert the user to the make and model of the computer or video player required for running the interactive media, the amount of computer memory required, the required operating system, the software requirements, and the kind and characteristics of required or recommended peripherals. In libraries in which interactive media is not available for browsing and in which patrons depend on the catalog for choosing interactive media, library personnel may decide that detailed labeling is too labor intensive to justify its use.

Processing accompanying textual materials should follow the options discussed in Chapter 2 (in the section on accompanying material) or the library's local standard procedures for processing print materials. Interactive multimedia is frequently accompanied by manuals or other forms of documentation that provide crucial information for the use of the package. If documentation is stored separately from the interactive carrier(s), detailed informational labeling will be necessary on all items to assure that both patrons and circulation personnel are aware of the documentation's availability and separate location.

Interactive multimedia may be limited in use by special licenses, signed agreements, or hardware keys. If a signed agreement is required by the vendor who sells the interactive material, the agreement may stipulate specific limitations, such as "use on only one machine at a time" or "no network usage." Some licenses prohibit renting or lending of software, and some prohibit public performances. A hardware key requires installation on the computer parallel port and protects the library from unauthorized copying and use.

Considerations for Storage

- Interactive multimedia should be stored in a dry area with stabilized temperatures and away from direct sunlight, dust, and magnetic fields.

- Interactive multimedia should be stored upright in the original containers.

- Preferred storage is the container in which the interactive media arrives, as long as it is sturdy and houses all the components, including the user documentation.

- A commercially produced replacement container is an option when the original one is not suitable. Library supply vendors market polypropylene or vinyl albums, corrugated boxes of heavyweight fiberboard, and plastic cases.

- An alternative storage method is to house parts of an interactive multimedia package separately in various places according to their similar formats (e.g., videodiscs with the video collection, computer disks with the computer software, compact discs with the musical CDs, and CD-ROMs with other CD-ROMs).

- Laser optical discs should be kept free of dust, grease, and anything that might scratch the disc's surface.

- Magnetic computer disks should be stored away from magnetic fields such as telephones, televisions, computers, fans, and any other electric motors.

Interactive Multimedia Labeling: Processing the Individual Parts

As with kits, all significant parts of a multimedia package should be marked with the same call number or other unique number to ensure that, if separated, they can be linked back together. For more detailed information on marking compact discs, videodiscs, computer optical discs, and computer disks, see the sections on labeling in Chapters 4, 5, and 7, respectively.

Option a: Processing without labels

Avoid writing directly on the plastic coating covering metallic surfaces of laser optical discs (CD-ROMs, compact discs, and videodiscs). Latest research indicates that chemicals used in permanent marking pen ink may corrode the plastic covering and eventually damage the metallic surface. An alternative marking option is to use a pen with permanent ink to print a brief call number and/or ownership mark on the clear inner gripping ring of the compact disc or CD-ROM or on the commercial paper label of the videodisc. This practice allows discs to be identified uniquely and to be linked to a container or manual that can provide more complete information (see Figure 9.3).

Markings placed on commercial videodisc labels may raise some controversy. Some believe that using permanent marking pens on the commercial paper label in the center of the videodisc may cause chemical damage to the plastic surface beneath the label. Be sure to examine the latest available research before making final processing decisions. The preceding instructions should be considered within that context.

Care should also be taken when marking computer disks. One may write directly on the hard plastic encased disk, but writing on flexible floppy casings with anything other than a felt tip pen can cause damage to the computer data. Stamping flexible disks should also be avoided.

Ownership marks. Handwritten ownership marks or stamps can be used on the commercial paper labels attached to both videodiscs and computer disks and to the clear inner gripping ring of compact discs and CD-ROMs. Another option is to use an embossing device developed for use on the clear plastic ring of compact discs and CD-ROMs. Because of the fragile nature of laser optical discs, however, caution should be exercised when considering any devices that might place a strain on the disc's protective lacquer coating.

Option b: Processing with labels

Labels should never be attached to the plastic-coated metallic surface of compact discs, computer optical discs, or videodiscs. Distortion of data can result from the slightest weight differential (often referred to as spin wobble). For compact discs and CD-ROMs, circular center labels are available that will not affect balance. Brief call numbers or other identification numbers may be typed on them before they are placed over the clear inner gripping ring. Another option

Figure 9.3
Processing Interactive Multimedia without Labels

is to label only the jewel box container for the compact disc or computer optical disc (see Figure 9.4).

For videodisc labeling, print with a pen using permanent ink or type the call number, the disc or part number (if the disc is part of an interactive multimedia package), and the copy number and/or the accession number (if used) on a label to be placed on the commercial label, being careful not to cover any important information (see Figure 9.4).

Labels for computer disks may be placed on the commercially supplied labels. The call number, the computer disk or part number (if there are multiple parts in the interactive multimedia package), and the copy number and/or accession number (if used) may be printed or typed on small labels and applied to the commercially produced label, taking care not to cover important information (see Figure 9.4).

Ownership marks. The center label for the computer optical disccan be pre-printed with an ownership mark or stamped with a circular stamp. Type or stamp the library name on the commercial videodisc label or use a preprinted label that can be attached to the commercial label where space allows (see Figure 9.4). For computer disks, preprinted or stamped ownership labels may be placed

Figure 9.4
Processing Interactive Multimedia with Labels

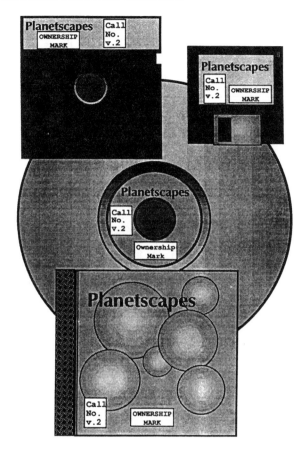

on the bottom of the commercial label or on another area on the top of the disk
that will not cause it to become stuck in the computer.

Interactive Multimedia: Processing the Container

Because interactive multimedia may consist of one or more different kinds of
physical carriers, the containers may vary considerably. If the interactive item
consists solely of a CD-ROM disc, the container may be nothing more than a
jewel box. If an accompanying manual is part of the package, it may be separate
or they both may be contained in a vinyl album or a three-ring binder. If the
interactive package consists of one or more videodiscs, one or more computer
disks, and documentation, the pieces may be housed either in separate containers
or all in one large album or box. Videodisc recordings should be kept in inner

Figure 9.5
Interactive Multimedia Container Options

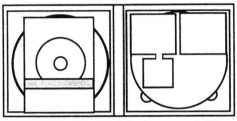

Holds one videodisc, two CDs in jewel cases, one 3.5" floppy
disk, and 8-1/2" x 11-1/2" x 1/4" literature.

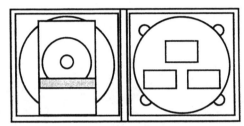

Holds one 12" videodisc, three 3.5" floppy disks, and
literature 8-1/2" x 11-1/2" x 1/4".

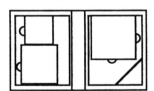

Holds two CDs or CD-ROMs in jewel cases, and
one 3.5" and literature 5-3/4" x 8-1/2" x 1/8".

sleeves to assure maximum protection. It is not necessary to label the inner sleeves, but ownership marks are a good idea to deter theft. Based on local library policies, decisions will need to be made about whether to retain the original packaging or to repackage items in a new single container. Figure 9.5 illustrates examples of various packaging options.

Option a: Processing without labels

Using a pen with permanent ink, print the call number, accession number (if used), author, title, and physical contents of the interactive multimedia on the cover of the container in a location consistent with library policy and lacking important information. A library may choose to write this information in a standard location such as the upper left corner of the front or top of the container's surface, where it may be easily read by both patron and staff. Another option is to write all the information, including the physical contents, immediately adjacent to the circulation pocket.

Ownership marks. Ownership marks should be stamped visibly or printed on the top and/or sides of the multimedia container in a position consistent with library policy.

Informational labels. It is useful to write system requirements information on the outside of the container if it is not already commercially printed there (e.g., MACINTOSH COMPUTER, 1.5 MB AVAILABLE HARD-DISK SPACE, 4 MB OF RAM, QUICK TIME 1.5, A CD-ROM DRIVE, AND A 13-IN. COLOR MONITOR).

Option b: Processing with labels

Interactive multimedia housed in its original container(s) usually features commercial labels with the author, title, publisher, and physical contents on it. If this information is missing or the multimedia has been repackaged, type an identification label with the author (if there is one), title, and physical contents of the container, call number, part number (if there is more than one container), and copy number and/or accession number (if used), and place it in a consistent location on the top of the container that is easily visible to both patrons and staff and does not cover important information.

Spine labels. The title of the interactive media may already be commercially printed on the spine. If a title is lacking on the spine, prepare a title label to be placed on the upper portion of the spine. Write or type a call number label to be placed on the lower portion of the spine in a location consistent with library policy.

Ownership marks. Ownership marks should be placed visibly on the front of the container using either a preprinted label, permanent stamp, or marker with the library's name.

Informational labels. If system requirements are not part of the commercial information on the outside of the container, it is useful to make up a system requirements label (e.g., IBM PC OR 100% COMPATIBLE 386SX OR BETTER, 8 MB RAM AND 40 MB HARD DRIVE, MOUSE, 14-IN. [MINIMUM 640 × 480] VGA COLOR MONITOR WITH 512K GRAPHICS ADAPTER CARD, AND PC-COMPATIBLE CD-ROM OPTICAL DISC PLAYER). If items are stored separately, other kinds of informational labels may be appropriate (e.g., ACCOMPANIED BY: 1 VIDEODISC, 1 VIDEODISC INDEX, 1 USER'S GUIDE, and on the individual pieces something like ACCOMPANYING VIDEODISC FOR CD-ROM). Another label which might be appropriate on a videodisc that is housed separately from the other pieces is ACCOMPANYING COMPUTER DISK(S) AVAILABLE ON LIBRARY PC; CIRCULATING DISKS ALSO AVAILABLE.

Pockets for Circulation

The least protected place for a pocket is the exterior of albums and boxes, but there are times when there is no alternative. For CD-ROM jewel boxes, a small pocket attached to the outside front or back of the box may be the only choice. If computer optical discs, videodiscs, and computer disks are housed in albums, binders, or boxes, pockets may be attached to the inside of the front cover or lids of such containers. Opaque pockets and self-adhesive clear vinyl pockets may also be attached to the inside of album cover sleeves along the back open edge. If used on the outside, clear pockets allow the user to read information beneath the pocket, although there may be some distortion. Hinging a pocket is another alternative to allow access to important information. Alternatives to pockets are the permanent pressure-sensitive date due labels that may be placed on the front cover of containers.

Barcodes

Barcodes should *never* be placed on either side of a computer optical disc's metallic surface. At present, there is still some disagreement about the effects of putting additional labels on the commercial videodisc label. One should examine the latest available research before deciding to put barcodes on the commercial videodisc label. Barcodes may be placed on the top edge of computer disks, where one holds onto the disk during insertion into the disk drive.

If the library's policy is to use duplicate barcodes or one-and-a-half barcodes, the main barcode can be attached to the container and the half or duplicate barcodes can be attached to the individual interactive pieces. Several barcode locations are possible on the outside or inside of the container depending on institutional guidelines. Some libraries prefer to place the barcode adjacent to the circulation pocket. Other libraries may prefer to locate the barcode in the upper center edge of the front or back of the container, where it is easily accessible. Another possibility is the back of the container, parallel to the spine on the upper right corner of the back of the container to allow for easy access during inventory. One other option is on the inside of the front cover of an interactive multimedia container. For multipiece interactive multimedia in one container, some libraries may prefer to use duplicate barcodes, placing one on the container and the other on the individual piece. This procedure results in having more than one unique barcode on the container, one below the other. During checkout, staff can scan the barcodes on the container; but at the time of check-in, staff are required to scan the barcodes on the individual pieces to assure that each piece has been returned.

Security Devices

Option a: Securing individual items

Librarians may wish to check with security vendors before applying any security device directly to computer optical discs, laser videodiscs, or computer disks. For a more detailed discussion of this topic, see the section on security in Chapter 1 and the sections on videodisc security in Chapter 5 and computer disk and computer laser optical disc security in Chapter 7. Librarians are cautioned to review the latest literature and check with their security vendors to determine the long-range safety of using any security devices directly on interactive multimedia.

Option b: Securing the container

Security strips or labels may be attached to the multimedia container. If a jewel box container is used, one location for the security strip or radio label is the paper cover under the molded plastic holder which secures the computer optical disc. Strips may also be placed in the spine of the container, making sure that they are not visible. Almost any place on the outside of jewel boxes, albums, and other multimedia containers is a good location for security labels and covered strips. Strips may be applied to any location where they are inconspicuous and can be covered with a long label or opaque strip of tape. Security labels are embedded in several varieties of labels: blank labels, date due slips, ownership labels, or other specially printed messages. Whichever is chosen, its placement should follow library guidelines for consistent location.

Accompanying Material

Treatment of accompanying documentation for interactive multimedia should follow the guidelines discussed in Chapter 2. When possible, all accompanying material should remain in the interactive multimedia container. Accompanying material should always be labeled with its appropriate call number and enough other information to make sure that wherever it is stored, it will be easily identifiable. The call number should be visible on the outside and the inside of accompanying material. Larger pieces of accompanying material, such as user manuals, texts with barcoded pictures, computer disks, and sound boards, will require more permanent handling. If such items cannot be housed in the main multimedia container, either provide substitute packaging to accommodate everything or provide extensive labeling for the other parts which are housed elsewhere. Ownership designations (stamps or labels) should also be placed in consistent locations on all parts according to established local guidelines. When accompanying material is stored separately and barcodes are in general use for the rest of the collection, a unique barcode should be placed on each piece of accompanying material. This practice will help the library keep track of each separate circulation.

Gift Plates

A gift plate may be applied to the container which stores the interactive multimedia. It may be glued or cemented to an outside surface or to the inside of a front cover if space is available. The hinge method of attachment may be necessary so that useful information is not covered. A gift plate may be cut to size and applied to an area void of important information, or a plate may be inserted into the circulation pocket. Another option is to use a small pressure-sensitive label and type GIFT OF followed by the donor's name (if used). This may be applied to the container or to the outside or inside of the circulation pocket, depending on the availability of space.

REFERENCES

Anglo-American Cataloguing Rules, Second Edition, 1978, ed. by Michael Gorman and Paul W. Winkler. Chicago: American Library Association.

Anglo-American Cataloguing Rules, Second Edition, 1988 Revision, ed. by Michael Gorman and Paul W. Winkler for the Joint Steering Committee for Revision of AACR. Chicago: American Library Association.

Association for Library Collections and Technical Services. Cataloging and Classification: Description and Access. The Interactive Multimedia Guidelines Review Task Force, 1994. *Guidelines for Bibliographic Description of Interactive Multimedia.* Chicago: American Library Association.

Ullmer, Eldon J. 1990. *Interactive Technology.* Lister Hill Monograph, LHNCBC 9 90-2. Bethesda, MD: U.S. Dept of Health and Human Services, Public Health Service, National Institutes of Health, National Library of Medicine.

Appendix: Processing
Suppliers and Products

SUPPLIERS	PRODUCTS
AUDIO BOOK CONNECTION 1865 Ranch Circle Dr. Estes Park, Colo. 80517 800-222-5613 FAX 800-222-5614	Vinyl audiobook cassette albums of various styles and sizes and Norelco cassette boxes
AVERY DENNISON Consumer Division 20955 Pathfinder Road Diamond Bar, Calif. 91765 800-336-6476	Specialty labels of all types including Destrux labels for nonremovable applications and day-glo colors for special warning messages
BRODART 1608 Memorial Ave. Williamsport, Penn. 17705 717-326-2461; 800-233-8959 FAX 800-283-6087	General library and audiovisual supplies, equipment, furniture; storage cabinets, AV equipment, globes, and office/computer products
BROWSER DISPLAY SYSTEMS Chicago One Stop, Inc. 401 West Superior Chicago, Ill. 60610 312-822-0822; 800-822-4410 FAX 312-642-7880	Patented video, CD & laserdisc Browser Paks and a variety of multimedia display fixtures
CABCO PRODUCTS E. 4th Ave. Columbus, Ohio 43201 614-267-8468; 614-263-0284	Sound recording supplies
CHECKPOINT 550 Grove Road Thorofare, N.J. 08086 609-848-1800; 800-257-5540 FAX 609-848-0937	Radio frequency security systems for print and nonprint materials and electromagnetic compatible products
DEMCO 4810 Forest Run Road Box 7488 Madison, Wis. 53707 608-241-1201; 800-356-1200 FAX 608-241-1799	General library and archival supplies, furniture, storage cabinets, audiovisual and computer products including the KWIK-CASE security container and the Code-A-Disc security system for CDs

SUPPLIERS	PRODUCTS
FRANKLIN DISTRIBUTORS PO Box 320 Denville, N.J. 07834 201-267-2710 FAX 201-663-1643	Archival storage materials for slides, prints, & negatives
GAYLORD PO Box 4901 Syracuse, N.Y. 13090 315-457-5070; 800-448-6160 FAX 800-272-3412	General library supplies including a copyright warning label for software and a warning label for videos; equipment, furniture, and a full line of archival products
GRESSCO 328 Moravian Valley Road PO Box 339 Waunakee, Wis. 53597 608-849-6300; 800-345-3480 FAX 608-849-6304	Supplier of storage and displays for all types of media including Kwik-case for security protection of CDs, videos, and sound cassettes
HIGHSMITH W 5527 Highway 106 PO Box 800 Fort Atkinson, Wis. 53538 414-563-9571; 800-558-2110 FAX 800-835-2329	General library supplies for schools & libraries including furniture, supplies, and equipment
JANWAY 11 Academy Road Cogan Station, Penn. 17728 717-494-1239; 800-877-5342 FAX 717-494-1350	Supplier of bags for transportation and storage of library materials
KAPCO 930 Overholt Road PO Box 626 Kent, Ohio 44240-0011 216-678-1626; 800-843-5368 FAX 800-451-3724	Acid-free self-adhesive library products for providing protection to paper and fiberboard containers
KNOGO NORTH AMERICA 350 Wireless Boulevard Hauppauge, Long Island, N.Y. 11788-3907 516-232-2100; 800-645-4224 Telex: 716852166	Electronic security system using Electro Thred targets

SUPPLIERS	PRODUCTS
LIFT DISPLAY 115 River Road Suite 105 Edgewater, N.J. 07020 201-945-8700 FAX 201-945-9548	Space-saving metal fixtures for CDs, cassettes, & video formats for floor display or specially designed storage cabinets
LIGHT IMPRESSIONS 439 Monroe Ave. PO Box 940 Rochester, N.Y. 14607-3717 Customer Service: 800-828-9859 To order: 800-828-6216 FAX 800-828-5539	Archival library supplies and image conservation products
MONACO Box 40 Bethel, Conn. 06801 203-744-3398; 800-448-4877 FAX 203-744-3228	Clear plastic HangUp bags to store and circulate audiovisual materials and racks to display the bags
PLASTIC REEL CORPORATION Brisbin Ave. Lyndhurst, N.J. 07071 201-933-5100; 800-772-4748 FAX 201-933-9468	Manufacturer and supplier of plastic shipping and storage cases for video cassettes and reels, archival film, video and audio flame-retardant canisters
POLYLINE CORPORATION 1233 Rand Road Des Plaines, Ill. 60016 708-390-6464 FAX 708-827-6851	Supplier of audio, video, and computer packaging, corrugated shippers, albums, and boxes
POLYQUICK 1243 Rand Road Des Plaines, Ill. 60016 708-390-7744 FAX 708-390-9886	Supplier of audio recording and duplicating supplies including storage sleeves, jewel boxes, and pockets to store CDs
PROFESSIONAL MEDIA SERVICE CORP 19122 S. Vermont Ave. Gardena, Calif. 902248 310-532-9024; 800-223-7672 FAX 310-532-0131	Library supplier for sound recordings and videorecordings, with or without full MARC cataloging and/or full processing. Also supplies containers for audio and video products.

SUPPLIERS	PRODUCTS
RELIANCE PLASTICS & PACKAGING 217 Brook Ave. Passaic, N.J. 07055 201-473-7200 FAX 201-473-1023	Manufacturer and supplier of vinyl albums for sound cassettes, videocassettes, CDs, optical discs, and other electronic media
SHAMROCK SCIENTIFIC SPECIALTY SYSTEMS PO Box 143 Bellwood, Ill. 60104 3112-992-1187; 800-323-0249	Specializes in custom labels, e.g., specialty photography labels, computer labels
SUNRISE PACKAGING, INC 9937 Goodhue St., NE Blaine, Minn. 55449-4433 612-785-2505; 800-634-8160 FAX 612-785-2210	Manufacturer and supplier of storage products for sound cassettes, videocassettes, software diskettes, CDs, laser discs, and loose-leaf materials
TEK MEDIA SUPPLY CO 4700 W. Chase Lincolnwood, Ill. 60646 708-667-3000; 800-323-7520 FAX 708-677-1311	Supplies & equipment for video, film, and AV materials
3M 3M Center Bldg. 225-4N-14 St. Paul, Minn. 55144-1000 800-328-0067 FAX 612-733-3294	Electronic security systems using Tattle-Tape security strips and labels
UNITED AD LABEL CO, INC 700 Columbia St. PO Box 2345 Brea, Calif. 92622-2345 800-998-7700 FAX 800-998-7701	Label supplies including FBI Warning labels, custom and pin-fed products for VHS, Betacam, Betamax videocassettes, u-matic and mini u-matic, laser discs, Hi8 and 8-mm formats, sound recordings including DAT cassettes, and computer disks
UNIVERSITY PRODUCTS, INC 517 Main St. PO Box 101 Holyoke, Mass. 01041-0101 413-532-9281; 800-628-1912 FAX 413-532-9281	Archival materials for conservation and preservation as well as library and media center supplies, equipment, and furnishings

SUPPLIERS	PRODUCTS
VERNON LIBRARY SUPPLIES 6901 Peachtree Industrial Blvd. Suite A Norcross, Ga. 30092-3666 404-446-1128; 800-878-0253 FAX 404-447-0165	Manufacturer and supplier of library supplies including a variety of labels and label printing software
VINYLWELD 2011 W. Hastings St. Chicago, Ill. 60608 312-242-0606; 800-444-4020 FAX 312-942-0693	Manufacturer and supplier of vinyl vacuum-formed packaging for multimedia and software, including 3-ring binders and casemade binders & slipcases
Ztek Company PO Box 1055 Louisville, Ky. 40201-1055 800-247-1603	Supplies for sound recordings and videorecordings including containers for videodiscs

Selected Bibliography

Alonzo, Patricia. 1975. "Conservation and Circulation in Map Libraries." In *Map Librarianship: Readings,* compiled by Roman Drazniowsky. Metuchen, NJ: Scarecrow Press. (First published in Special Libraries Association, Geography and Map Division. *Bulletin* 74: 15–18. New York: The Division. 1968.)

Anderson, Lou, Sandra Brug, Barbara L. Burke, and Holly R. Lange. 1990. "Handling Printed Materials with Accompanying Computer Disks." *Computers in Libraries* 10, no. 4 (April): 23–25.

Anglo-American Cataloguing Rules, Second Edition, 1988 Revision. 1988. Ed. by Michael Gorman and Paul W. Winkler for the Joint Steering Committee for Revision of AACR. Chicago: American Library Association.

Association for Library Collections and Technical Services. Cataloging and Classification Section. Cataloging and Classification: Description and Access. The Interactive Multimedia Guidelines Review Task Force, 1994. *Guidelines for Bibliographic Description of Interactive Multimedia.* Chicago: American Library Association.

Association for Library Collections & Technical Services. Preservation Section, Library/Vendors Task Force. 1990. "Glossary of Selected Preservation Terms." *ALCTS Newsletter* 1, no. 2: 14–15.

Bahn, Catherine I. 1975. "Map Libraries—Space and Equipment." In *Map Librarianship: Readings,* compiled by Roman Drazniowsky. Metuchen, NJ: Scarecrow Press. (First published in Special Libraries Association, Geography and Map Division. *Bulletin* 46: 3–17. New York: The Division. 1961.)

Baker, Sylvia. 1985. "Organizing the Collection." In *Museum Librarianship,* ed. by John Larsen. Hamden, CT: Library Professional Publications.

Berglund, Patricia. 1986. "School Library Technology." *Wilson Library Bulletin* 60, no. 6 (February): 39–40.

Bierbaum, Esther Green. 1985. "The Third Dimension: Dealing with Objects in Public Library Collections." *Public Library Quarterly* 6 (Fall): 33–48.

Colby, Edward E. 1969. "Preservation and Storage of Materials Other Than Paper. Part 1, Phono-discs, Phono-Tapes: Preservation of the Human Heritage Through Sound Recordings and Motion Pictures." *World Conference on Records and Genealogical Seminar,* Salt Lake City, Utah, August 5–8, 1969. Salt Lake City: Genealogical Society of the Church of Jesus Christ of Latter-Day Saints, Inc.

Dewey, Melville. 1906. "Library Pictures." *Public Libraries* 11: 10–11.

Dick, Jeff T. 1990. "Laserdisc Redux." *Library Journal* (November 15): 37–39.

Dictionary of Computing. 1990. 3rd ed. Oxford: Oxford University Press.

Dudley, Dorothy H., Irma Bezold Wilkinson, and others. 1979. *Museum Registration Methods.* Washington, DC: American Association of Museums.

Dunlap, Kent. Letter to Eric Childress, Special Materials Cataloger, Elon College, North Carolina, January 6, 1992.

Dunn, Walter S., Jr. 1969. "Preservation and Storage of Materials Other Than Paper. Part II, Paintings, Portraits, Pictures." *World Conference on Records and Genealogical Seminar,* Salt Lake City, Utah, August 5–8, 1969. Salt Lake City: Genealogical Society of the Church of Jesus Christ of Latter-Day Saints, Inc.

Eaton, Nancy L., Linda Brew-MacDonald, and Mara R. Saule. 1989. *CD-ROM and Other Optical Information Systems: Implementation Issues for Libraries.* Phoenix: Oryx Press.

Ellison, John W., ed. 1985. *Media Librarianship.* New York: Neal Schuman Publishers, Inc.

———, ed. 1987. *Nonbook Media: Collection Management and User Services.* Chicago: American Library Association.

Evans, Hillary. 1981. *Picture Librarianship.* New York: K. G. Saur.

Frost, Carolyn O. 1989. *Media Access and Organization.* Englewood, CO: Libraries Unlimited, Inc.

Gorman, Michael. 1990. *Technical Services Today and Tomorrow.* Englewood, CO: Libraries Unlimited.

Hahn, Harvey. 1987. *Technical Services in the Small Library.* Chicago: Library Administration and Management Association, American Library Association.

Harrison, Helen P. 1973. *Film Library Techniques: Principles of Administration.* New York: Hastings House.

———, ed. 1981. *Picture Librarianship.* Phoenix: Oryx Press.

Hart, Thomas L. 1973. *Conceptualizing a Model for Access to Multi-media Materials in Elementary and Secondary Schools: A Study of Cataloging and Processing by Commercial, Centralized and Local Processing Units,* Ph.D. dissertation, Case Western Reserve University.

Hoffman, Frank W. 1979. *The Development of Library Collections of Sound Recordings.* New York: Marcel Dekker.

Intner, Sheila S., and Richard Smiraglia, eds. 1987. *Policy and Practice in Bibliographic Control of Nonbook Media.* Chicago: American Library Association.

Irvine, Betty Jo, and P. Eileen Fry. 1979. *Slide Libraries; a Guide for Academic Institutions, Museums and Special Collections.* 2nd ed. Littleton, CO: Libraries Unlimited.

Johnson, Jean Thornton, Marietta Griffin Franklin, Margaret Palmer McCotter, and Veronica Britt Warner. 1973. *AV Cataloging and Processing Simplified.* Raleigh, NC: Audiovisual Catalogers, Inc.

Kogon, Marilyn. 1980. *Organizing the School Library: Canadian Handbook.* Toronto and New York: McGraw-Hill Ryerson.

Larsen, Dean A. 1984. "Preservation and Materials Processing." In *Library Technical Services: Operations and Management,* ed. by Irene P. Godden. Orlando, FL: Academic Press.

Larsgaard, Mary Lynette. 1987. *Map Librarianship: An Introduction.* 2nd ed. Littleton, CO: Libraries Unlimited.

Library of Congress. Geography and Map Division. 1991. *Map Cataloging Manual.* Washington, DC: Cataloging Distribution Service, Library of Congress.

Light, Richard B., D. Andrew Roberts, and Jennifer D. Stewart, eds. 1986. *Museum Documentation Systems: Developments and Applications.* London: Butterworths.

Locatis, Craig. 1992. *An Interactive Multimedia Technology Primer.* Lister Hill National Center for Biomedical Communications, National Library of Medicine, Bethesda, Maryland. Prepared for the Online Audiovisual Catalogers Conference, Bethesda, Maryland, October 1–3, 1992.

Marshall, Mary E. 1991. "Compact Disc's 'Indestructibility': Myth and Maybe." *OCLC Micro* 7 (February): 20–23.

McLuhan, Marshall. 1964. *Understanding Media: The Extensions of Man.* New York: McGraw-Hill.

McQueen, Judy, and Richard W. Boss. 1986. *Videodisc and Optical Digital Disk Technologies and Their Applications in Libraries.* Chicago: American Library Association.

McWilliams, Jerry. 1979. *The Preservation and Restoration of Sound Recordings.* Nashville, TN: American Association for State and Local History.

Miller, Shirley. 1979. *The Vertical File and Its Satellites; a Handbook of Acquisitions, Processing and Organization.* 2nd ed. Littleton, CO: Libraries Unlimited.

Naisbitt, John. 1982. *Megatrends: Ten New Directions Transforming Our Lives.* New York: Warner Books.

Nichols, Harold. 1982. *Map Librarianship.* 2nd ed. London: Clive Bingley.

Nickel, Mildred L. 1984. *Steps to Service: A Handbook of Procedures for the School Library Media Center.* Rev. ed. Chicago: American Library Association.

Olson, Nancy B. 1988. *Audiovisual Material Glossary.* Dublin, OH: OCLC Online Computer Library Center.

———. 1992. *Cataloging of Audiovisual Materials: Manual Based on AACR 2.* 3rd ed. DeKalb, IL: Minnesota Scholarly Press.

Pickett Andrew G., and M. M. Lemcoe. 1959. *Preservation and Storage of Sound Recordings.* Washington, DC: Library of Congress.

Prostano, Emanuel T. 1987. *The School Library Media Center.* 4th ed. Littleton, CO: Libraries Unlimited.

Racine, Drew, ed. 1991. *Managing Technical Services in the 90's.* New York: Haworth Press.

Redfern, Brian L. 1978. *Organizing Music in Libraries.* Vol. 1, *Arrangement and Classification.* 2nd ed., rev. Hamden, CT: Linnet Books.

Reibel, Daniel B. 1978. *Registration Methods for the Small Museum: A Guide for*

Historical Collections. Nashville, TN: American Association for State and Local History.

Ristow, Walter W. 1980. *The Emergence of Maps in Libraries.* Hamden, CT: Linnet Books.

Shaw, Renata V. 1972. "Picture Organization: Practice & Procedures." *Special Libraries* 63, pt. 1–2 (October–November): 448–456, 502–506.

Shera, Jesse Hank. 1970. *Sociological Foundations of Librarianship.* New York: Asia Publishing House.

Shores, Louis. 1973. *Audiovisual Librarianship: The Crusade for Media Unity (1946–1969).* Littleton, CO: Libraries Unlimited.

Smisek, Thomas. 1985. "Circulating Software: A Practical Approach." *Library Journal* 10, no. 8: 108–109.

Sullivan, Peggy. 1990. "Preservation and Judgment." *School Library Journal* 36, no. 7: 16–19.

Talob, Rosemary. 1987. "Back-ups: A Controversial But Necessary Part of Software Collections." *Small Computers in Libraries* 7, no. 3 (March): 36–37.

Ward, Alan. 1990. *A Manual of Sound Archive Administration.* Brookfield, VT: Gower Publishing Co.

Weihs, Jean. 1991. *The Integrated Library: Encouraging Access to Multimedia Materials.* Phoenix: Oryx Press.

Wisconsin Library Association. 1981. *Cataloging, Processing, Administering AV Materials: A Model for Wisconsin Schools.* 3rd rev. ed. Ed. by Margaret Hohenstein, Kjun J. Chung, Olive Collins, Jo Davidson, Irma Harder, and Rose Holmes. Madison, WI: Wisconsin Library Association.

Index

tion, 46–48; security devices, 47; stor-
age considerations, 44
"Glossary of Selected Preservation
Terms," 12
Goals, 4–6
Gramophone disc. *See* Sound disc: Ana-
log
Graphic materials, 123–152; definition,
123, general information, 123
*Guidelines for Bibliographic Description
of Interactive Multimedia*, 213

Hart, Thomas L., 22
Horizontal map storage, 50
Housing. *See* Containers
Hypermedia, 208. *See also* Interactive
multimedia

Identification labeling, 28–32; location,
30. *See also* Labeling *under individual
material types*
Informational labeling, 9, 14, 28, 32–34.
See also Labeling *under individual material types*
Informational content label, 25–26
Inner sleeve. *See* Sleeves, inner
Integrated collection, 9–11
Intellectual contents label, 29, 32–33,
161, 163, 170
Interactive multimedia, 207–208, 213–
222; accession number, 216, 218–219;
accompanying material, 221; barcodes,
220; container labeling, 217–219; definition, xiv, 213; general information,
213–214; gift plates, 221–222;
individual parts labeling, 215–217; informational labels, 219; ownership
marks, 215–216, 219; pockets for circulation, 219–220; security devices,
220–221; spine label, 219; storage
considerations, 214–215
Intershelving nonprint materials, xxii, 6,
9–10, 21, 155, 174

Jacket. *See* Album jacket
Jewel box or Jewel case, 21, 79, 82,
174–175, 178, 216–217, 219, 221
Jeweler's tag, 195

Kits, 207–213; accession number, 209–
210; accompanying material, 212–213;
barcodes, 211–212; container labeling,
210–211; definition, 208; general information, 208; gift plates, 213; individual
parts labeling, 209; ownership marks,
209–211; pockets for circulation, 211;
security devices, 212; storage considerations, 209

Labeling, 5, 9, 19, 25–26, 28–34. *See
also under individual material types*
Label-printing software programs, 30
Labels, 5, 8, 12, 18, 20, 23, 26–34, 36.
See also Labeling *under individual ma-
terial types*; Security labels
Labels, magnetic, 14
Lacquers and other protective coverings,
34. *See also* Varnish
Lamination, 12, 19, 22
Larsen, Dean A., 18
Laser disc, 110, 115
Laser disk, 173. *See also* Computer laser
optical disc; Laser disc
Laser optical disc. *See* Computer laser
optical disc
Laser optical videodisc. *See* Videodisc
Letterbox format, 106, 113
Library management, 3
Library manager, xxii, 3, 6, 11, 15
Library of Congress, *Cataloging Service
Bulletin*, 154, 173
Library of Congress, *Rule Interpretations*,
154
Library philosophy, 4–6
Library users, xxi–xxiii, 4–5, 7–15, 17–
18, 22, 24, 29, 32–33, 37–38
Licenses, 154–155, 214
Local processing manual, 30, 38

Magnetic disk. *See* Computer disk
Magnetic security system, 14, 24, 103,
117, 155. *See also* Security devices
Mailers, 23
Management factors, 3–8
Management policies, xxii
Map cases, 49
Map cylinder, 49

About the Authors

KAREN C. DRIESSEN is a Professor, Media Librarian, and Acting Director of the Mansfield Library Instructional Media Services at the University of Montana. She has taught courses in technical processing and audiovisual communication, has conducted workshops in media cataloging and processing, has authored media reviews, and is immediate past President of Online Audiovisual Catalogers, Inc.

SHEILA A. SMYTH is a Professor, Associate Director, and Director of Technical Services at the Lorette Wilmot Library at Nazareth College of Rochester. She is Chair of the Association of Library Collections and Technical Services Audiovisual Committee, and a former President of Online Audiovisual Catalogers, Inc. She has also written various book reviews and articles, and has made several presentations on media cataloging and local systems.